Sacred Angkor

SACRED ANGKOR

The Carved Reliefs of Angkor Wat

Vittorio Roveda
Photography by Jaro Poncar

First published and distributed in
the USA and Canada by
Weatherhill, Inc.
41 Monroe Turnpike
Trumbull, CT 06611

Acknowledgments

I would like to acknowledge my appreciation for the influential role of Dr. Tania Tribe and Elizabeth Moore from S.O.A.S. London, in the conception of this book. I am in great debt to Don Downwiddie who spent a considerable amount of time in reading the manuscript and suggesting innumerable improvements. My gratitude goes also to Narisa Chakrabongse for her support and recommendations. Finally, for their contribution towards my fieldwork, I would like to thank the Apsara Authority of Siem Reap and UNESCO of Phnom Penh, Dr. T. Teneishvili, and of Paris, Anne-Marie Le Maitre.

A River Books Production.
Copyright © collective work: River Books
Copyright © text: Vittorio Roveda
Copyright © photographs: Jaro Poncar,
except where otherwise indicated.

British Library Cataloguing-in Publication Data.
A catalogue record for this book is available from
the British Library.

Editor: Narisa Chakrabongse
Designer: Holgar Jacobs
Production supervision: Paisarn Piemmattawat

ISBN 0 8348 0524 3

Printed and bound in Thailand by
Amarin Printing and Publishing Co., Ltd. (Public)

Cover: Sita's svayamvara, detail, NW corner pavilion.
Back cover: King Suryavarman II parading with his troops. SW gallery, 3rd enclosure.
Previous page: Krishna on Garuda, SW corner pavilion.
Opposite: Rama and Valin, detail, NW corner pavilion.
Opposite Preface: Heavens and Hells, detail, LP. 3.

Contents

Chapter 5: Reliefs from other Sites

Chapter 6: Interpretation of the Reliefs

Chapter 7: Conclusions

Appendices

Preface

Angkor Wat, the greatest of Khmer temples, is a text in itself. The hundreds of reliefs sculpted on its stones narrate the events from the Hindu Epics and the *Puranas,* and symbolically communicate the fundamental religious, philosophical, ethical and political principles of the Khmers at the time of Suryavarman II. The objective of this book is to expose and clarify such concepts, and show how they collectively contributed to a sacred discourse focused on Vishnu.

Central to this decoding are the beautiful narrative reliefs of the gallery of the 3rd enclosure, the so-called Large Panels, extending for an extraordinary length of about 520 metres, and the less-known reliefs of the two western corner pavilions of the same enclosure, adding 48 more metres of visual story-telling. Their variety of themes and richness of meaning contribute to the definition of Angkor Wat's sacredness. This is further emphasised by the meaning of narrative reliefs from other sites of the temple which include those from readable pediments, half pediments, lintels and pillars, as well as the characteristic 'tapestry' reliefs.

The reliefs have a level of meaning underlying that revealed by iconography. Every society gives life to signs in which the production of the sign bears only half its meaning, the sign's reception representing the other half. So, in the case of Angkor Wat, at one level the narrative reliefs concern Vishnu and episodes from the lives of his avatars, Krishna and Rama, and at another level they are symbolic of Suryavarman II's devotion to Vishnu and perhaps, more importantly, of his temporal power affirming his right to rule the Khmer in intimate association with the divine. Moreover, they were used for creating the image of a sacred universal meaning, a visual representation of Khmer metaphysics.

The myths depicted in the reliefs play a dominant part in this book. "Myths are always true (or else no true myths)" (Coomaraswamy 1997: ix). They can be perceived from different points of view: from the philosophical or psychological standpoint as the expression of fundamental human emotions and the dramatisation of conflicts. From a symbolic approach myths are the metaphorical translation of natural phenomena (e.g. meteorological, astronomical) which are difficult to explain. From the sociological point of view, myths reflect the structure of society and offer, ideally, a solution to problems that cannot be resolved in reality. Myths served to understand cosmology, how the Universe came into being.

Myths are about so many things – about life and art and the universe and the imagination. In a single myth several perhaps contradictory messages may simultaneously exist. In this lies the dilemma of Angkor Wat's reliefs. As Wendy Doniger O'Flaherty (1980: 10) rightly says: "...when a single theory is used to extract a single meaning from a broad corpus of myths, the result is a thread of truth that may be illuminating when woven into a wider fabric of understanding but is pitifully only one part of the story." This book endeavours instead for a looser collation of theories and therefore, hopefully, for more than simply one thread of the truth.

In the first chapter, a general picture of the historical figure of Suryavarman II is presented, together with the form of Vaishnava beliefs in vogue at that time. One should not fail to note that, despite abundant epigraphic records, very little is known about this king and the temple he built. A review is then presented on the way previous authors have considered Angkor Wat, the symbolism of the reliefs and how they fit within the overall architectural symbolism.

The description and analytical comments on the reliefs that follow in Chapters 2, 3, 4, 5, and 6 highlight the complexity and richness of the symbolic meaning of the reliefs individually and in association, with their thematic choice and emplacement in specific sites of the temple. Critical comments are then presented (Chapter 7) examining in detail the meaning of figures and elements of the various narrative reliefs, their multiple symbolism, and their impact on the construction of an overwhelming sense of sacredness which is reaffirmed in the conclusion presented in Chapter 8.

Chapter 1

Introduction

Suryavarman II

Angkor Wat is 'the' temple of Suryavarman II who reigned from 1113 to about 1150 AD. Little is, unfortunately, known of this king, and that which can be known has been gleaned from the inscriptions of Preah Vihear, Phnom Rung, Phnom Sandak and Ban That.[1] What can be established is that Suryavarman II, although probably a vassal prince from the Mun valley (in present-day northeastern Thailand) and certainly a maternal grandson of a sister of Jayavarman VI (r.1080-1107), was not in direct line of succession to the Khmer throne. His great uncle Dharanindravarman (r.1107-1113) had legitimately inherited the throne from his elder brother Jayavarman VI. According to inscriptions, young Suryavarman challenged the aged Dharanindravarman in a battle which "lasted only for one day" and that he "jumped on the enemy king's elephant and killed him, stripping the defenceless royalty from Dharanindravarman". The Ban That inscription confirms that he fought the battle when still "in his early youth, at the end of his studies".

Suryavarman's usurpation of the throne marks the consolidation of the Mahidharapura dynasty, which was to prove one of the most brilliant in Khmer history, providing such great kings as Suryavarman himself and Jayavarman VII (r. 181-c.1215). Suryavarman was very much a warrior king and launched repeated expeditions against Dai Viet (Vietnam) and Champa (in the centre of present-day Vietnam). With the Chams he is also known to have formed alliances against the Dai Viêt. Most of these campaigns ended in defeat, although his expansion to the West met with better success, and Khmer forces managed to occupy Thai territory, and in particular the town of Lavo (Lopburi, present-day Thailand). Suryavarman seems to have died during a maritime expedition against the Champa and Dai Viêt between 1148 and 1150.

One of the greatest mysteries of Suryavarman II's reign is why Angkor Wat, the largest Khmer temple built up to that time, and one of the largest in the world, is dedicated to Vishnu. Although the Pancharatra sect of Vaishnavism had enjoyed a certain degree of popularity in Cambodia since early times, we know from inscriptions that Shaivism remained the dominant form of Hinduism within the kingdom. On the whole, the Khmer kings had been largely Shaivite in their beliefs. It is even possible that Suryavarman II was himself primarily a devotee of Shiva. Given the absence of any historical records treating this subject, one can only speculate whether Suryavarman II's departure from the strict Shaivism of his Angkorean predecessors was part of an increased syncretism, allowing the contemporaneous veneration of two sectarian beliefs, or whether it in fact reflected a personal preference of Suryavarman II for the Pancharatra sect. There had been an illustrious precedent in King Suryavarman I (r.1002-1050) who, although a Shaivite, permitted, and possibly encouraged, Buddhism. One could hypothesise that the new king through his own name may have believed himself to be connected with Surya, the old Vedic god of the solar dynasty who had been gradually replaced by a far more powerful god of the same dynasty, Vishnu. Or it may be that as a usurper, Suryavarman II identified himself with Krishna who in the original texts was seen rightfully to usurp the worship of Indra. Thus Angkor Wat's relief depicting the story of Krishna fighting the Indra cult (S.12), and instructing the cowherds to abandon the old ritual and to worship him, could symbolise Suryavarman's replacement of the older cult of Shiva with a new spirit of Vaishnavism. Other possible reasons for this switch

FIG. 1 View of the central tower from the NW. (V. Roveda)　　　　　　11

of royal cults may be that Suryavarman was looking for a deity more 'helpful' as a protector against the internal and external strife that attended his accession to the throne. After all, a god like Vishnu had incarnated in order to redeem man, and he also promised a final release from the endless cycle of reincarnations.

Besides building Angkor Wat, Suryavarman II also completed the construction of the Shaivite Vat Phu temple that had been initiated during the last year of the reign of Jayavarman VI, and many images were erected in it by royal ordinance between 1118 and 1139. Suryavarman made no attempt to remove the celebrated Bhadreshvara *linga* of Shiva of this temple from its position as the national divinity of the Khmer nation. He also restored the Shaivite temple of Ishvarapura (Banteay Srei), and completed the Phimai complex in northeastern Thailand, which was dedicated to both Shiva and Vishnu. All of this would seem to indicate that the devotion and patronage of Suryavarman II was syncretic towards the two great Hindu sects.

Angkor Wat

Although there is no evidence identifying the architects of the temple, it is likely that Divakarapandita, the brahmin in Suryavarman's service, contributed to its conception and planning. Divakarapandita was from a long line of illustrious brahmins, and he must have been quite old by Suryavarman's accession, having served the previous two kings Jayavarman VI and Dharanindravarman I.[2] The building of the temple commenced upon Suryavarman taking the throne and continued for approximately the next thirty years.

A variety of Indian myths and legends from Hindu texts are skilfully illustrated at Angkor Wat in the reliefs of the 3rd enclosure: in the two western corner pavilions and along the galleries where they are displayed in extraordinarily long panels. Called here Large Panels, they have a height that remains constantly in the region of 240 centimetres; the length of each of the eight reliefs varies from 48 to almost 94 metres. It is important to mention here that out of the eight Large Panels, only six were sculpted in the XII century. Indeed, the relief of the

Churning of the Ocean of Milk was abandoned before completion, despite being so important for symbolising the concept of creation essential to the Pancharatra cult. The wall surfaces of the northeastern quadrant were not sculpted until the XVI cetury, as their inscriptions indicate.[3] Nevertheless, they were possibly done on the basis of drawings stencilled in ink in the XII century on the walls of the galleries (Roveda, 1991).

Each of the western corner pavilions is sculpted with 12 exquisite panels which are of fundamental significance within the symbolic framework of the temple. Furthermore, they are almost surely contemporaneous to the enclosure's Large Panels (excluding the ones of the northeastern quadrant) since they are sculpted in the same style, they all are completed, and no inscriptions prove the contrary. In contrast, the two eastern corner pavilions of the same enclosure were left bare of reliefs; again, emphasis is on the western part of the temple in accordance with being dedicated to the lord of the West, Vishnu.

Vaishnavism in XII century Angkor

From at least the early centuries of the Christian era, the Khmers were familiar with Hinduism as well as Buddhism. By Angkorean times, Hindu religious belief was focused on the concept of the Trinity of Brahma, Vishnu and Shiva who fulfilled the three cosmic functions of creation, conservation and dissolution. Hinduism was also concerned with the monistic tendency of both Shaivism and Vaishnavism, which emphasised the transcendence and immanence of one god. In Vaishnavism, greater importance was laid on the devotional aspect, or *bhakti* – the trusting abandonment of the self to the god, which alone is the source of salvation.

By the end of the X century the worship of Vishnu was divided between three different schools: Pancharatra, Bhagavata and Satvata. By far the most popular of these was the Pancharatra,[4] a doctrine requiring the worship of Vasudeva (Vishnu) as the highest (para-Vasudeva) central source from whom four forms (*vyuha*) successively emanate. The first to be manifested from him is Vishnu-Vasudeva, followed by his brother Samkarshana (Balarama), his son Pradyumna and his grandson Aniruddha. This takes place in a sequence where each emanation originates from the anterior one "like a flame proceeding from another flame". In other terms, the *vyuha* are distinct manifestations of the undifferentiated central reality of para-Vasudeva, and each has its own characteristics called *guna* (glorious attributes). In addition to the *vyuha*, the Pancharatra texts outline the other manifestations, somehow at a lower level, in which para-Vasudeva 'descends' (incarnate) in this mundane world. These are detailed in a variety of *avataras*, the best known of which are the *deshavataras*, or ten incarnations of Vishnu. These manifestations are understood as a hierarchical cosmic diagram (mandala) with para-Vasudeva at the centre of ever-expanding permutations of his power, like ripples in a pond (Atherton Packert 1985: 211).[5]

In Cambodia, the earliest mention of the sect is in the inscription of Prince Gunavarman of Funan (V century), followed by the Stele of Baset (VII century) which mentions the five daily rites required of the faithful. The inscriptions of Kuk Sla Ket (XI century; K.522) and of Thvar Kdei (K.165), both contain the concepts of the Four Emanations. By the IX and X centuries, the Pancharatra had become a significant force in Khmer society and underwent some divergence from the Indian orthodoxy. In the inscriptions of Pre Rup (961 AD) and Prasat Kok Po (X-XI century) the Khmers inter-preted Vishnu's emanations as having the qualities of Nature *(gunas)*, while standard Pancha-ratra doctrine considered them 'supernatural'.[6] Khmer Pancharatra, however, still retained its quietism, a passive devotional contemplation, with withdrawal from all things of the senses.[7]

With regards to the visual representation of Pancharatra concepts at Angkor Wat, it has to be noted that although reliefs narrating stories of Vishnu's *avataras* are very common, there are no images of Vishnu, Samkarshana, Aniruddha and Pradyumna as *vyuha*. There are, though, illustrations of earthly events of Aniruddha as the prisoner of Bana (pediment of the southern gallery of the 3rd enclosure), and of Pradyumna in the battle of Krishna against Bana to free Aniruddha (in the Large Panel LP. 6). However, Pradyumna and Aniruddha are perceived as *avatara* and not as *vyuha*;

they derive from Puranic myths and not from the early Pancharatra texts.

One of the basic themes of the Pancharatra doctrine, that of the creation-dissolution cycle, has a prevalent position at Angkor Wat's main entrance. Over the central door of the Western *Gopura*, one can see a lintel (Plate 16) elaborately sculpted with Vishnu immersed in sleep on the snake Ananta who himself rests in the Ocean of Eternity. Vishnu is ready to activate his power at each new period, starting thus a new cycle of creation. This myth is reproduced also in the Cruciform Pavilion and in the northwestern corner pavilion. Since the myth of the Churning of the Ocean of Milk is considered here to be associated with the Pancharatra's concept of creation, it is not surprising to find it depicted in several reliefs throughout the temple (LP. 4, S. 1 and on various doorjambs).

The concept of the *avatara* is also essential to the Pancharatra. The prefix *ava* means 'down' and the Sanskrit verb 'tri' translates into 'cross over'; *avatara,* therefore, means the coming down of the deity. Western dictionaries' translation is that of 'incarnation', a more materialistic, carnal term than one that would explain the transfer of an infinitesimal part of Vishnu (a hair in the above myth) from high in the sky down to earth into the form of one of his *avataras*. It is interesting to note that, amongst the Hindu pantheon, the *avatara* doctrine refers essentially to Vishnu. Shiva takes the human form only once, that of an enchanting mendicant in the episode of the Pine Forest (*see relief S. 4 in the southwestern corner pavilion*). In modern belief, an *avatara* has the function of allowing the divinity to become the object of the devotee's worship and meditation. It is to Vishnu alone that the *avatara's* doctrine refers and he appears in ten different manifestations: as a fish (Matsya), a tortoise (Kurma), a boar (Varaha), a man-lion (Narasimha), a dwarf (Vamana), and in manly semblance as Parashurama (Rama with an axe), Rama, Krishna, Buddha (disputed) and Kalki (the *avatara* still to come).

The texts illustrated

The entire temple is richly decorated with splendid reliefs, mainly of the narrative type[8] which are visual retellings of episodes from the two Sanskrit Epics the *Mahabharata* and the *Ramayana,* and the *Puranas,* and as such, they can be considered a narrative genre in their own right. The proliferation of narrative reliefs in Cambodia since Angkorean times suggests that they had become a popular device for communicating religious beliefs and historic events through the medium of 'stone writing'. Although images in reliefs endure in time and space, they or their content have to be reactivated each time by the viewer for narrative completion.

Khmer narrative reliefs are not accompanied by a text giving the name of the story or of the personage depicted, or written clues that allow the identification of the text, as in mural paintings and sculptural reliefs from India and other parts of Southeast Asia. The short inscriptions exceptionally found on the Large Panels of the Historic Procession and of the Heavens and Hells at Angkor Wat (LP. 2 and LP. 3) only give the names of the main personages and the names of the punishments without revealing to what text or circumstances the reliefs refer.

Nevertheless, Angkor Wat's narrative reliefs clearly refer to popular events from the Epics and the *Puranas,* visually narrated in a way which is generally faithful to the original Sanskrit texts in terms of the plot – even down to the last detail. The reliefs reproduce and continue the emotional values of the original texts without altering them, and in strict obedience to the orthodoxy imposed by the brahmins and elite. The constant concern of the Khmers to adhere closely to the Indian texts applies also to other reliefs of the Angkorean period (IX through XIII centuries) from different locations and centuries, implying that their creators must have relied either on written texts or on a faithfully maintained oral tradition. One is tempted to assume that, as in India, *Ramayana* manuscripts written on palm leaf could have been common amongst the elite.[9] Another reason for such faithfulness to the original texts could be that the sculptors adhered fanatically to a set of *shilpashastras* (sculpting manuals). In particular, such manuals would have offered only a limited choice of subject matter, and thus excluded the possibility of any idiosyncratic choices. Unfortunately, for the moment, there is no answer to all these assumptions, since no written text predating the XVII century has been found in Southeast Asia.

Remaining faithful to the original texts may not have been easily achieved, considering the possible existence of different 'tellings' of the *Ramayana,* various Puranic versions of the same story, and popular local folkloric legends. The complexity of this relationship is further increased by the inevitable problems inherent in any translation of literary texts into visual images, between the meaning of words and the meaning of images. When looking at the reliefs under consideration, we face the process of production and exchange of meanings. The Khmers have encoded the messages (the reliefs) with particular meanings on the basis of the significance that Indian texts had within the culture of their time. It seems that if the *Puranas, Harivamsa* and *Mahabharata* were addressing general metaphysical, religious and political principles, the *Ramayana* emphasised personal values in the figure of the protagonist, Rama the hero, who could be easily identified with the figure of the king, explaining thus his great popularity. *Mahabharata* stories are known at Angkor Wat primarily from a Large Panel of the 3rd Enclosure (LP. 1), where the only event chosen is that of the greatest conflict of Indian mythology, the battle of Kurukshetra. It may be that the Khmers could not see in the *Mahabharata* the heroic figure of the god/king they needed, since even Arjuna – the most popular personage – was considered too dependent on Krishna for choosing the path of action.

The Ramayana

This story of Rama is the most widely diffused tale in South and Southeast Asia. The date of Valmiki's compilation of the Sanskrit poem of the *Ramayana* remains obscure.[10] Its core may not date to later than the middle of the VI century BC,[11] while the first and last books are probably later additions. The collation of a definitive version took place between the II century BC and the III century AD.

The basic story, like those in many different Asian oral and literary traditions, has branched out in a variety of plot developments, with different beginnings and endings. It has various forms of narrative, numerous incidents, different kinds of characters, and remarkable details woven into an intricately interconnected series of events. Several of these events may have been introduced according to the taste and fancy of a long lineage of narrators around

FIG. 2 Girls presenting gifts, Heavens and Hells. (V. Roveda)

central or subsidiary ideas, heroes or villains. In northern India, the story of Rama is mentioned in the *Mahabharata* (about 800 BC), and the Tamil version contains verses referring to Valmiki's epic. This posits the existence of Rama's story well before its literary versions. It is likely that these, or similar oral traditions, circulated in Southeast Asia with the arrival of Indian traders.

The Thai and Cambodian written versions of the story of Rama, respectively the *Ramakien* and the *Ramaker* (The Glory of Rama) are XVII to XIX century compilations of previous tellings, and are too late to have been used for the reliefs of Angkor Wat. They diverge from other Asian versions insofar as they do not emphasise Rama's heroism, or his victory, but instead the 'glory' of his spiritual order. It has to be noticed that both the *Ramakien* and the *Ramaker* are composite names revealing a Sanskrit linguistic construction (Rama-glory or *Ramakirti*), the reverse of the normal Thai or Khmer construction. Therefore, these texts may refer to the title of an old Indian work, now lost, or a local sanskritised name of an Indian version, not of local origin. The term *Ramaker* is often replaced by *Ramkier, Reamker* or by the Sanskrit *Ramakerti* (Bizot 1989: 28).

In the Cambodia of the Angkorean period, it seems that the *Ramayana* in use pertained to Valmiki's tradition. The stele of Veal Kantel of the VII century[12] mentions that the *Ramayana* (and therefore possibly Valmiki's version, and not a local version such as the *Ramaker*) had to be recited daily, without interruptions, as were the *Harivamsa* and the *Puranas*. Exceptionally, however, there is at Angkor Wat a divergence from Indian texts with regard to the iconography and details of a few scenes. This problem was stressed by some scholars who advanced the theory of the existence of an 'elusive' version of the *Ramayana* not only in Cambodia but also in other countries of Southeast Asia.[13]

Scholars started to speculate that probably this 'elusive' local version might be reflected in the text of the *Ramaker*, arguing that there are some elements foreign to the *Ramayana* which are common in the *Ramaker*. Many singularities apparent in the *Ramaker*, however, lose their uniqueness when compared with the texts of the rich Puranic literature or the *Mahabharata*, or even with other sectarian Bengali, Tamil, Jaina and most of all, Malay legends of Rama.[14]

At this point, one can assume that the Khmers must have been familiar with an oral and/or written version of the *Ramayana* that was very close to Valmiki's telling but that excluded the first and seventh books of the Valmiki version. Some local colour had also been added in such details as the presence of a monkey in the scene of the Churning, the strange moving target with a bird which Rama has to hit at Sita's *svayamvara*, the belief that Rama and his friends returned to Ayodhya by boat and not on the Pushpaka chariot (Phimai, Thailand), and the sea animals which attempt to destroy the causeway to Lanka (Phimai; see Boeles 1969: 163). Furthermore, there are some iconographic anomalies in the representations of the *rakshasas* Viradha and Kabandha. Some of these variations of the 'elusive' Khmer version were incorporated into the *Ramaker* and *Ramakien* in their written form of the XVI and XVII century. Could it be called 'Proto-Ramaker'?

The Puranas

The *Puranas* are Sanskrit verse texts of a non-Vedic origin containing mythological accounts of the events in the lives of Hindu gods. They were all composed between 500 and 1500 AD, but are based on much earlier material. Of the two categories – the *Mahapurana* (or 'great', 'major') and the *Upapurana* ('minor') – the former includes the texts illustrated in Khmer reliefs, the most popular being the *Bhagavata Purana* (made around 950), the *Shiva Purana* (730-1350), the *Vishnu Purana* (made around 450) and the *Brahma Purana* (900-1300). The *Puranas* stress *bhakti* and miraculous manifestations of divine grace, and remain the dominant texts of Hinduism's religiosity. They also reflect the theoretical cosmogony of the two epics, the *Mahabharata* and the *Ramayana*, expanding and systematising their chronology. They are the more exact and better worked-out versions of the subcontinent's mythology and historical traditions. Most *Puranas* have a strong sectarian bias, so that the same myths appear in very different versions in different *Puranas*.

The *Bhagavata Purana* is the Puranic text that has exercised the most direct and powerful influence on the opinions and feelings of the Indian and Khmer people. Dedicated to Vishnu, or Bhagavata, it consists of 18,000 verses grouped in 332 chapters and divided into 12 books (*skandha*). Its tenth book, narrating in detail the stories of Krishna's life, has been the most frequently consulted for the study of the reliefs of Angkor Wat; its stories are also the most popular in Indian folklore.

The Mahabharata and the Harivamsa

The *Mahabharata* comprises 100,000 verses divided into 18 books, supplemented by a nineteenth, the *Harivamsa* which deals more with events concerning Krishna's life. Like the *Ramayana* and the *Puranas*, it grew into its present form over a long period of time, from about 400 BC to 400 AD.

The epic narrates the events before, during and after the great battle for kingship fought at Kurukshetra between the Pandavas and the Kauravas, two families descended from the great hero king, Bharata. Central to the *Mahabharata* is the decline of *dharma*, the cosmic law and order, at the onset of the Kali Yuga age of history (the present era). To the sixth book of the *Mahabharata* belongs the *Bhaghavad Gita*, the fundamental Hindu text. In it the emphasis is on Krishna's (an ally of the Pandavas) transformation of the battle of Kurukshetra from a mythic one between *devas* (Pandavas) and *asuras* (Kauravas) into a cosmic event during which Krishna re-establishes the *dharma*. The battle is also referred to as the *dharmakshetra* (field of *dharma*) because during it, the *dharma* met its ultimate test. At the most critical moment of the fight, Krishna – as advisor of the Pandava prince Arjuna – transcends the action and evokes a compa-rable transcendence in those who attend him, making his discourse to Arjuna, the Gita, itself the locus of *bhakti*.

The *Harivamsa*, probably composed around 400 AD, is generally considered as an appendix of the *Mahabharata*, although some scholars believe it is a Puranic compilation, probably of southern Indian origin. Of its three parts, the first is introductory and gives details of the creation and of the patriarchal and regal dynasties; the second contains the life and adventures of Krishna; the third deals with the future worlds and the corruption of the Kali age. The second part is the most relevant here, since it has inspired the reliefs at Angkor Wat depicting events in the life of the god.

The life of Krishna can be divided into three main parts, of which the third conteins the events in the *Mahabharata*. The first part of his life, his infancy through his adolescence, concerns several miraculous deeds that gradually reveal his divinity. However, during this first period, Krishna is also involved in fights against the demons sent to kill him by his evil cousin Kamsa. These events are amply illustrated both at Angkor Wat, and in many other Khmer temples. As Krishna's adult life was chronicled in the *Mahabharata*, the *Harivamsa* was needed to relate the story of his birth and childhood. The *Harivamsa* subtly captures Krishna's dual character as epic hero and religious teacher; it is both a tale of adventures and a way to express religious truths.

The second stage of his life starts with the slaying of Kamsa, which brought him into conflict with Jarasandha and his supporters and many others whose atrocities were afflicting the world. As an adult, Krishna has to face hard social and political realities, and his slaying of Jarasandha is a very significant event in his life because with it he liquidates his political enemies. During this period, he is also involved in epic events such as his abduction of the beautiful Rukmini, the imbroglio of the recovery of Satrajit's jewel, the combat with Indra for the possession of the Parijata tree, the fight against the *asura* Bana to rescue his son Pradyumna, and the uprooting of Mount Maniparvata. These episodes, as well as violent battle scenes, are common in late Indian iconography.

The function of the reliefs

The reasons for the creation and execution of the reliefs have been debated at length by numerous Western scholars. What was the scope for their existence? This analysis is important because the function of the reliefs may determine their meaning. Were the stories narrated in the reliefs addressed only to a select few? Were they instead meant to educate and illuminate the pilgrims or visitors to the temple – ordinary people, or were they meant to be simply part of the sculptural decoration of the temple, having purely an aesthetic appeal? Was the decoration of temples with reliefs an element of the mechanism of merit-gaining on the part of the king? One aspect of the problem was approached by George Coedès [15] in his theory of the magic function of the reliefs. Thus, in Khmer monuments the role of the decorations (statues and reliefs with scenes and personages) was not aesthetic, because the Khmers did not have the concept of 'art for art's sake'. For them the reliefs had an 'evocative' function, that of bringing life to the temple. Coedès believed that the images of the gods had a 'magic' power that would transform the temple into a real divine world. The representation of *apsaras* and *devatas*, celestial dancers and courtesans, all over the walls of the temples would transform a terrestrial stony residence into a heavenly palace. At Angkor Wat, the celestial palaces as seen in the relief of the Heavens and Hells (LP. 3), are in the shape of pavilions flying in the sky supported by garuda and lions. At the royal terraces of Angkor Thom, robust caryatids/atlases have the task of transforming symbolically the monument into a flying palace.[16]

It follows that this celestial transformation is enacted also by reliefs representing legendary events of gods and mythological heroes, which would give life to the temple with their real presence. In this sense the reliefs were not made to edify visitors, but to contribute to the materialisation on earth of the divine world. The reliefs of Angkor Wat narrating the stories of Suryavarman II, and the ones of Bayon dealing with Jayavarman VII, had the objective of animating the temples with the actual presence of these kings. This is why – Coedès believed – it is essential for the images to be exact, correct in every detail, otherwise they would fail the objective, like a magic ceremony in which the essential rite was omitted or wrongly performed. This resulted in the simplification and, at the same time, complication of the iconography's task. If the sculptors knew the specific texts or were following a particular tradition, they could control all the details of the image and the iconographic interpretation would be simple. If not, the identification of the scenes would be doubtful or incomplete, if not impossible. It was essential to make clear which text the reliefs referred to, or by which version the sculptor was inspired, otherwise the scenes could not be totally explained and so could not be claimed to fulfil their function.

In the same publication, Coedès expressed his other theory that Angkor Wat had a funerary function. This was based on the discovery of some sort of sarcophagi in various Khmer temples, Coedès being unconcerned that these 'sarcophagi' may not have been contemporaneous with the construction of the temple, or that they may have been moved by tomb robbers. For him, in general, royal temples were funerary buildings, private rather than public temples. Palace-like, they were the eternal dwellings of the Khmer kings, where their mortal remains would rest, and where a statue representing the monarch with the traits of a god was erected.

The concept that the main function of the reliefs was the glorification of the king formed the key element of Bosch's theory.[17] For him, the apotheosis of the king was well expressed in the sequence and meaning of Angkor Wat's Large Panels of the 3rd enclosure, which would reveal an analogy between the cycle of the sun and the life of Vishnu. Vishnu's qualities as the Vedic god of solar light, energy and expansion, were embodied in the king's person and activities. All the Large Panels follow a 'gradation' sequence in which the sun moving in the sky is equated to events in the life of Vishnu, the sun-king, the king who is a solar god. Since Angkor Wat was dedicated to Vishnu, the creators of the reliefs glorified the Khmer king by identifying him with Vishnu, and at the same time attempted to make eternal his terrestrial events through their interpretation according to Vishnu's own legends.

Hinting at the religious function of the reliefs was the theory of Maurice Glaize.[18] This author was of the opinion that Khmer temples were personal monuments of kings or aristocrats, pious foundations aiming at obtaining 'merits' for those who contributed to its building. Furthermores, the reliefs of the galleries of the 3rd enclosure, as any other narrative reliefs, would visually exemplify religious precepts and acquire a religious function. Glaize added that the Khmer faithful could walk in procession around the sanctuary in the ceremonial direction of the *pradakshina*, by keeping to the right, or in the opposite *prasavya* direction, reserved for funerary processions. If all the reliefs were accessible to the faithful it is not mentioned in any Khmer inscriptions nor we have proof. It is now believed that public access may have been possible only during festivities or special occasions, and under the guidance of brahmins, as in modern practice. It is likely, however, that the pilgrims were not allowed to go beyond the 3rd enclosure. In the past, in India the devotee was not permitted to enter the shrine, nor did he need to do so. When the priest invoked a deity in the image that stood inside the *garbhagrha* ('sanctum sanctorum'),the layman stood at the threshold to witness the god's presence and experience the divine.

Jean Filliozat[19] was the first to perceive that the reliefs' function could be part of broader astronomical and numerological concepts embedded in Khmer architecture. He exposed his theories in the study on the Bakheng, the temple-mountain (*see p. 11*) built in strict accordance with Indian planetary cosmology at the centre of the first town of Angkor founded by Yashovarman at the end of the IX century. In its totality, the temple (with its decorations) was conceived as a model on which the Khmer microcosm was constructed.[20]

In 1976, a group of American scholars, R. Stencel, F. Gifford and E. Moron, published a paper revealing a cosmic symbolism created by the relationship between structures and meaning in the design of Angkor Wat. The theme was considerably expanded by Eleanor Mannikka[21] in her controversial book of 1996. On the basis of the study of a very large number of measurements of architectural elements at Angkor Wat, she established that the temple's dimensions were encoded with the meanings of Indian cosmology and numerology. She also noticed that some alignments of the monument's structures are closely related to astronomical events. The temple's architecture is a sort of religious and astronomical text, a text that could be read by knowledgeable people walking along its main pathways. For example, as the sun progresses on its annual round, it illuminates in a specific way the great continuous series of reliefs of the 3rd gallery, revealing a most intriguing relationship between the passage of the sun and the content of the reliefs. In the first part of the year, it illuminates the main protagonists of the creation act ('Churning of the Ocean of Milk'). During the autumn equinox, on the side of the setting sun, the highlighted reliefs depict the terrible battle of Kurukshetra. During the dry season, the north gallery loses the sun, while the reliefs on the south gallery, lit up by the sun, take as their theme the kingdom of death (LP. 3).

In conclusion, the views of the previous authors contain, to a greater or lesser extent, elements of truth and provide the scholar with a better understanding of Khmer religious symbolism of the transformation of an earthly site into a celestial palace, introducing the possibility of a metaphysical vision of Angkor Wat. Bosch and Mannikka's theories have the virtue of stressing the importance of astronomy and cosmology, of which the Khmer seem to have had great knowledge. On the other hand, the deco-rative and religious functions were especially rele-vant to the reliefs of the 3rd Enclosure's western corner pavilions. It is clear that the king would acquire further merit if his temple were ornamented with decorative and narrative reliefs, the symbolism of which enhanced and evidenced a religious belief. It was also making concrete his extraordinary power as a king. The sculptural low reliefs transformed a terrestrial building into a godly palace on a mytholo-gical mountain, and each of the narrative reliefs further contributed to the building-up of a sacred discourse permeating the entire temple of Angkor Wat.

Architectural symbolism

In ancient Cambodia, as in India, the highest religious authority, the brahmins, formulated the sacred concepts on which the temple was based, and the main architect, who was also a religious teacher, carried out its construction. The importance of the role of the architect/s is attested by an Indian legend in which a divine genealogy was provided for the chief architect and his three assistants.[22] They were believed to descend from the four sons, by daughters of the gods, of the faces of Brahma. The myth itself absorbed spiritual power from all directions of space, and endowed it upon the builders involved in the enterprise of erecting a temple. The ceremonial nature of temple-building became a minor religion in its own right, complete with a set of deities, a mythology and a system of rituals unique to the science of sacred architecture (*vastu-vidyah*).

The Khmer temple was conceived according to the Indian tradition of a temple-mountain, of being the image of the mountain where the gods lived, Mount Meru. This mountain was located north of the Himalayas, surrounded by the four water extensions (seas or rivers) which separate the four continents. Mount Meru floats over the primordial ocean, symbolically represented by moats or the *barays* surrounding the temple (or the city as in the case of Angkor Wat). Since this mountain had four peaks with a higher fifth at the centre, the central sanctuary of Angkor Wat had to have a similar configuration.[23] Moreover, since Mount Meru was the centre of the universe in Indian cosmology, Angkor Wat too had to be the centre of the cosmos. This centre of the world was 'the centre' by defini-tion, the infinitesimal point through which the cosmic axis passes; it did not represent a profane geometrical space, but a place charged with sacred meaning. It was the idealised 'centre' of the Khmer empire and the residence of the god with whom the king had an intimate affinity.

The ritual definition of a 'centre' imposed the accurate orientation of the temple. Through the application of the formulas in place at that time (cosmological, astrological, geomantic, numerologi-cal, architectural, iconographic and so on), a space was charged with meaning and physically given form, like a mandala. The rite of deciphering or decoding, this pattern-space by walking around the temple, either by the *pradakshina* or the *prasavya* way, would have brought the visitor to discover certain truths and his/her own 'centre'. This trip, as an act of initia-tion, may be compared to the Tantric trip from an external mandala into an interiorised mandala. The ascent to the terraces of the mountain-temple as an ecstatic journey to the centre of the perfect Hindu universe, must be seen as ultimately symbolic of the perfection of the Hindu world over which Suryavar-man II ruled with the blessing of his god, Vishnu.

Besides being at the centre of a town and the capital of the kingdom, Angkor Wat may have been the goal of a pilgrimage from other parts of the Khmer kingdom. The focus of the pilgrimage would have been its shrine in which was condensed the element of hope which justifies all pilgrimages. However, since there are no inscriptions giving light on the time of Suryavarman II, this aspect of the Khmer faith and tradition also remains unre-solved.

The orientation of temples has always been an essential feature of Indian architecture. The brah-mins believed that the whole earth, once floating and mobile, became stable when fixed by the cardinal points. The main points, or corners, of earth are those where heaven and the earth meet, where

the sun rises and sets, the east and west. The other cardinal points complete the square and each of them has its own regent. According to Sanskrit trea-tises on religious architecture, the northeast is also the place where the principle of Shiva is positioned, while the position of Surya is in the east, that of Vishnu to the west, that of Yama to the South and of Brahma at the centre. The general Indian rule that the temple's orientation must face east was adopt-ed by the Khmer. There were only a few exceptions of orientation to the west, the better known being that of Angkor Wat because its was dedicated to Vishnu.

That the western orientation of the temple had an intense meaning for Angkor Wat's planners and builders is demonstrated by the main architectural elements being located on the western side of the temple: an imposing causeway, entrance pavilions, cruciform cloister, libraries, main shrine opening to the west, etc. Furthermore, the decorative elements (including the narrative reliefs) were completed first in the western gallery of the 3rd Enclosure and its two corner pavilions.

The site on which the temple was constructed was a landscape space, chosen for its uniqueness and for some specific quality, such as its having had significance for the ancestors, or being the only large piece of land available within the precincts of the old town of Yashodharapura (founded in the X century), which included pre-existing ancient foundations. It may have been chosen for its proxi mity, on the northeast, to the old site on which the city of Kapilapura (?X century) was built. The temple's architecture transformed this natural space into a religious and political realm by means of the symbolic mediation of its shrines' pinnacles, the *gopuras*, the statues of the god and the reliefs. Those who produced this space, the brahmins and the kings, also managed it; they were the religious-political forces that occupied this space and controlled it.

Techniques of visual representation

It is evident that in order to visually narrate myths and stories, the Khmer sculptors made great use of the most common pictorial device, the ground line, or base line, on which the figures appear to stand in

Fig. 3 Aerial view of Angkor Wat from the southeast.

the relief. This was probably in order to supplement a weak concept of picture space and the lack of a systematic perspective system. The ground line evolves into a supporting surface, a sort of narrow platform on which images rest and from which they spring. It anchors the figures and objects and links them together on the picture plane, giving them a rudimentary but definite spatial orientation. The use of ground lines leads to a horizontal arrangement of the elements of the relief, and this in turn leads to another important characteristic of Khmer reliefs, the use of registers. A register is in effect a strip existing between two parallel ground lines. It is used as a means to organise a complex narrative. One of the best examples can be seen in the panel of 'Heavens and Hells' (LP. 3).

Within the registers, the personages are organised in groups of figures each performing some characteristic action, so that we read them sequentially like a strip cartoon. But Khmer artists used registers with some freedom and we have principal figures breaking through the ground line and occupying two or more registers (cf. Yama in the 'Heavens and Hells' relief). The term pseudo-register is used when the ground lines are not sculpted as such, and the scenes are simply overlaid one on top of another without any indication of a break. In some panels of the western corner pavilions, the stories of Krishna are told in six pseudo-registers (Krishna bringing back Mount Maniparvata [N. 2], Sita's *svayamvara* [N. 10]) or even eight pseudo-registers (Sita meeting Hanuman).

Chapter 2

The Large Panels of the 3rd Enclosure

Introduction

The large relief panels of the galleries of the 3rd enclosure are the first narrative reliefs that one encounters when entering the temple. They surprised the first explorers and still astonish the modern visitor. Due to their great beauty and rich narrative content, they made Angkor Wat famous. The Large Panels, are sculpted in the long galleries forming the rectangular perimeter of the temple proper, and on entering the enclosure they immediately engage the eye, drawing the visitor along the galleries. The panels' dimensions are enormous, ranging from 48.35 to 93.60 metres in length and of over 2.40 metres in height. Like most of the murals in the temple complex, they are sculpted in low relief and it has been conjectured that originally they were painted or lacquered. However, the traces of colour and black lacquer visible at present are more likely the remains of restoration and embellishment from the centuries following the temple's creation. As mentioned before, the relief of 'The Churning of the Ocean of Milk' was left unfinished at the time of the construction of the monument, and the two panels of the northeastern quadrant (LP. 5, 'Victory of Vishnu over the *Asuras*' and LP. 6, 'Victory of Krishna over the *Asura* Bana') were sculpted in the XVI century.

Unquestionably, the Large Panels are, together with the reliefs from the western corner pavilions, an outstanding contribution to the sacredness of Angkor Wat. Because of their impact on any visitor, they have been described in detail by early scholars like F. Garnier (1869-83), L. Delaporte (1880), J. Moura (1883), A. Bastian (1886), and E. Aymonier

(1901-4). In 1911, George Coedès summarised the knowledge of the time about the stories depicted in the panels. Later, from 1929 to 1932, together with Louis Finot and Henri Parmentier, he published the monograph on *Le temple d'Angkor Vat* in seven volumes, with a total of 608 large duotone photographic reproductions.[1] These 'introductory chapters' were due to be followed by a major text; unfortunately this was never completed or published. After this major work, a long series of books and guidebooks with beautiful photographs but scant descriptions continued to embellish the literature on Angkor Wat. It was mainly the French scholars, however, who made known data and opinions relevant to the temple in specialised publications, regrettably out of reach of the layman. For example, a full chapter on the two late reliefs of the northeastern quadrant is included in Madeleine Giteau's monograph on the iconography of post-Angkorean Cambodia (1975: 93-123).

In 1995, the extraordinary photographs of Jaroslav Poncar and his team formed the basis for a book with the text by Albert Le Bonheur, the latter being a revision of Coedès's paper of 1911. Regrettably the book's format and economic considerations did not do justice to the photographic documentation. Recently, Eleanor Mannikka (1996) examined the Large Panels in the context of astronomical and cosmological meaning. Further descriptions and interpretations based on Hindu texts are to be found in the present author's book on Khmer mythology (1997).

It is an accepted practice that the Large Panels

FIG. 4 Vishnu or Indra at the top of Mount Mandara, Churning of the Ocean of Milk. (V. Roveda)

23

Fig. 5 The Pandava army moving to the battlefield.

are to be visited in a counter-clockwise (*prasavaya*) direction because that follows the direction in which the action unfolds in each of these narrative reliefs. Entering the gallery of the 3rd enclosure from the direction of the main entrance, one is compelled to proceed to the right, following the compositional flow in the Battle of Kurukshetra. Turning left into the enclosure would mean reading the narrative of the adjacent Battle of Lanka against what seems to be the compositional flow. After the Battle of Kuruk-shetra, one encounters the relief of the Historic Procession followed by that of Heavens and Hells, both of which consistently lead the eye to the right, and this compositional direction continues until one

reaches once again the western portal and the end of the relief of the Battle of Lanka.

Many authors have interpreted the counter-clockwise progression as being indicative of the funerary function of the temple. Eleanor Mannikka (1996: 129), instead suggests that Khmer astronomers believed the sun to travel in a counter-clockwise arc after the spring equinox, and this, therefore, motivated a counter-clockwise narrative progression. At the present state of our knowledge on the customs and traditions of the XII century Khmers, any 'logical' order of visiting would be hypothetical. The visiting order proposed in this volume is purely one of convention.

Description of the Reliefs

LP. 1 - The Battle of Kurukshetra

Sculpted in a single panel 48.35 metres in length along the southern wing of the western gallery, this relief has been divided in two symmetric halves: on the side nearest the western entrance of the 3rd enclosure is grouped the Kaurava army (Fig. 6), while on the other, southern side, are the Pandavas (Fig. 5). They engage battle at the exact centre of the panel, while the northern and southern extremities depicting the respective armies marching to battle are relatively calm. The event is further divided laterally into pseudo-registers, with the infantry at the base surmounted by two much more vaguely defined pseudo-registers where the leaders of the two armies are highlighted by their slightly larger size against a background of fighting soldiers.

Nevertheless, in the fury of the battle scene it is difficult to distinguish and count the leaders. On the side of the Kauravas there appear to be 43 or 44 large figures, while the Pandavas seem to have only 27 leaders on chariots, in addition to two mounted on elephants and three or five on horses. With the exceptions of Bhishma, Drona, Krishna and Arjuna, these leaders are sculpted without specific features that would allow their individual identification.

The two similarly-equipped armies closely resemble the Khmer army depicted in the following panel of the Historic Procession. Their chiefs, mounted on chariots or elephants, have the conical *mukuta* identified with royalty and/or divinity; their rank is further expressed by the number of parasols, banners and other attributes surrounding them. Some of the soldiers marching past in the lower register have breastplates and others carry a curved shield on their chests. Most striking is the image of Bhishma, the general-in-chief of the Kaurava army, wounded by hundreds of arrows shot by Arjuna heading a group of the Pandava army. He is so skewered with arrows that his body does not touch the ground (Fig. 9) and to provide him with a head support, a 'warrior's cushion', as he calls it, Arjuna

shoots three arrows into the ground. Remarkably, Bhishma survives until after the battle, choosing the auspicious time for his death.

Aymonier (1904: 246) suggested, without much evidence, that the royal personage standing on an elephant, not far to the right of Bhishma, may be the blind king of the Kauravas, Dhritarashtra, with his charioteer Samjaya. Further to the right is Drona (Fig. 7) who, beside being a brahmin, was the military teacher of both the Pandava and Kaurava.

Towards the middle part of the panel, Arjuna is represented in his war chariot, definitely identifiable by the presence of the four-armed Krishna serving as his charioteer, and having the unique headgear of a flared cylindrical *mukuta* (Fig. 8). The relief depicts several episodes from the *Mahabharata's* famous battle of Kurukshetra (I: 184-92).

FIG. 6 Leaders of the Kaurava.

The story begins in the Ganges Valley, in the heart of Northern India, where Bhishma, son of King Santanu, having taken the vow of celibacy, consults with his step-mother Satyavati on how heirs to the throne could be obtained. To this purpose he invites two girls to unite with the sage Vyasa, the son that Satyavati had miracu-lously procreated before marrying Santanu. One child, born blind, becomes the great king Dhritarashtra, father or the Kauravas; the other child, born very pale, becomes Pandu, later the father of the five Pandava brothers, of whom by far the most renowned is Arjuna.

Dhritarashtra, unhappy at occupying a place unsui-table to his infirmity, allows his sons, grouped around the eldest, Duryodhana the Nasty, free rein and they proceed to bully their cousins, the five sons of Pandu. Given their virtue, the old king would like to leave the kingdom to the Pandavas, but his sons oppose this. By treachery, they first obtain the exile of their rivals, and then deny them even the smallest rights. Inevitably, war breaks out between them.

The battle lasts for many days and nights, with end-less acts of bravery and heroism. At the end of the ienth day, Bhishma (on the Kauravas' side) lies mortally wounded on a bed of Arjuna's arrows. Of semi-divine origin and able to choose the time of his death, the great lord decides not to die till the sun has moved into the northern hemisphere. On the evening of the eighteenth day, Arjuna and his charioteer Krishna engage in the discourse that became the sacred text of the Bhagavad Gita. *When Arjuna refuses to fight for a kingdom for which he has to kill his own people, Krishna pronounces the philosophy of karma for him, saying the battle of Kurukshetra was essential for the re-establishment of universal harmony, of the dharma.*

So spurred on, the Kaurava army is soon afterwards totally defeated, and the Kurukshetra battle finally comes to an end. The eldest Pandava, Yudhishthira, is crowned king and rules for many years until he abdicates. Then, together with his four brothers and their common wife Draupadi, he migrates to Mount Meru in the Himalayan Mountains, where they enter the realm of the gods.

The representation of this pivotal episode of the *Mahabharata* – and with it the *Bhagavad Gita* – is placed within the position of great prestige flanking the western entrance, and thereby linked to the direction sacred to Vishnu. This western entrance of the 3rd enclosure is in many ways the second main gateway to the temple (the first being the western *gopura* giving access to the core of the temple through the Cruciform Pavilion. The main reasons for having this panel in such a prominent position may lie in the need to highlight the event during which Krishna spoke his words of deep religious and moral significance, reciting the 'The Song of the Lord' narrated in the *Bhagavad Gita*.[2] Triggered by Arjuna's crisis of conscience at the carnage of his friends and kindred, Krishna, while acting as his charioteer, tells him that it is his dharma as a warrior to fight. If he does not do so, he will loose his status, renouncing his duty and honour, and that a war justly fought opens the door to heaven. Towards the end of section 18 (*sloka* 17), Krishna comforts Arjuna by saying: "He whose mind is free from any ill-will, even if he kills all these warriors, he kills them not and he is free".

Krishna then points Arjuna to the path of knowledge, action with detachment and devotion to God. In this context, the term yoga may serve to indicate the union of the three paths, respectively Light, Life and Love. Arjuna must be a warrior and kill desire, the powerful enemy of the soul and he must kill with the sword of wisdom the doubt born of ignorance that lies in one's heart. Only deeds done without attachment to consequences and through devotion (*bhakti*) to God and trust in his grace can lead to the realisation of Brahman, the Supreme all pervading Spirit, the Impersonal Absolute God. Krishna concludes by exhorting Arjuna to leave everything behind, and join him for his salvation because he will make Arjuna free from the bondage of sins. "I am the soul which dwells in the heart of all things. I am the beginning, the middle and the end of all that lives". Moreover, Krishna points out that he is the god of love and emotion, and that this love not only flows from the god to the devotee but also from the devotee to the god. This love of God for his worshippers is emphasised in the *Gita* for the first time in Hindu theology.

The *Bhagavad Gita* is the essence of the symbol-ic meaning of the battle of Kurukshetra as a conflict between the sons of Darkness (the Kauravas) and the sons of Light (the Pandavas). In the verses of section 10, Krishna claims to have all the powers elsewhere attributed to the Impersonal Absolute God (Brah-man) or to Vishnu. "I am the seed of all things that are; not a being, standing or moving, can exist with-out me". The human hero taking part in the

FIG. 7 Drona, teacher of the military arts.

FIG. 8 Arjuna and Krishna, his charioteer.

FIG. 9 Bhishma on a bed of arrows.

battle is becoming a god, and the god has taken a human form. He is the divine Krishna, supreme lord, *avatara* of Vishnu himself. He presents a vision of God in all things and of all things in God. The great battle of Kurukshetra is thus transformed from a conflict for an earthly kingdom to one for the kingdom of heaven – the kingdom of the soul, Arjuna being the soul of men and Krishna the charioteer of the soul.

In terms of ideology of sacrifice, this requires both the action and its results to be offered to God. In contrast to Vedic/Brahmanical beliefs where the results accrue to the agent, here the results accrue to God. Thus the real agent with regard to any action, is God. God is the only true actor and humans are merely the instruments of his action. In reality, God has already destroyed Arjuna's enemies; Arjuna is only an instrument bringing about what has already happened.

On a profane level, the final event of the Battle of Kurukshetra with Krishna as charioteer of Arjuna, may have symbolically alluded to Suryavarman being guided by Krishna to fight the enemies of the Khmers, and that it was the Khmer king's destiny to bring an end to the political and civil disorders afflicting the empire. As in the Epic, with the defeat of the 'forces of Darkness' in the civil war, Suryavarman II accomplished the task of restoring the *dharma* and initiated a period of prosperity for his people.

Around the corner from the Kurukshetra relief, this panel extends for 93.60 metres along the western wing of the southern gallery. It is not clear whether it was intended to represent a standard parade of Suryavarman II's forces, or a particular ceremony. The small inscription near the king's image identifying him (as well as helping to signal the image as a non-mythical subject) can, however, be interpreted in many ways. It can either read as "His Lordship Paramavishnuloka on Mount Shivapada receiving homage from his troops", or as "Paramavishnuloka bestowing Shiva's power from above upon the troops." Yet another reading would be "Paramavishnuloka who makes his troops descend Mount Shivapada" and it is this last interpretation that is adopted for this discussion. Besides being depicted in audience with his ministers, King Suryavarman II is represented again as the main participant in the military procession, standing on his elephant. As Eleanor Mannikka noticed (1996: 125), this is the first time that images of "a real king, living or dead, and his men of rank were sculpted onto temple walls traditionally reserved only for the gods and their main manifestations." This image, therefore, sets the precedent for the suite of historical reliefs of the outer gallery of Bayon, sculpted 75 to 80 years later.

George Coedès observed that the event displayed in this relief has a religious character because of the representation of the Sacred Fire (*vrah vlen*) in the centre of the composition. This is further supported by the fact that only the king and the priests wear jewellery, as prescribed by the edict of Yashovarman (r. 889-900) (CC 367 of Coedès, *Inscriptions Sanscrite,* 1937-66). Moreover, the presence of this relief amongst the large mythological panels of the same enclosure suggests it must have depicted something particularly important and meaningful in the king's reign.

In the relief, the first representation of Suryavarman II (Fig. 10) shows him seated at ease on a low throne covered with rugs, with his right elbow resting on a pillow, and his right hand holding a small elongated object, probably a piece of jewellery in the shape of a lotus (G. Groslier, 1921: 82, fig. 51). He wears a finely sculpted conical *mukuta*, and has heavy earrings. A large necklace and two thin crossbands decorate his torso; he also wears armlets, bracelets, large anklets and carries a small dagger tucked in his beautiful belt. His left arm is raised and extended towards his ministers; the hand also holds a small object.

Amongst the brahmins (or pandits as they are referred to in the inscription) surrounding the king in the first scene, is – from the far left – a small group of what look like *rishis* characterised by a cylindrical chignon tied by a cloth. They simply wear a thin loincloth, and one of them seems to be dressed in bark. At their centre stands the *rishi*

FIG. 10 The king gives orders to his ministers.

who presents the offerings to the king. The other group, placed closer to the king, has the traditional hairstyle of the brahmins with the hair in a bun at the top of the head and tied up by a knotted string or ribbon. They have pointed beards and wear short *sampots*; some wear small earrings on their elongated earlobes.

To the viewer's right, the king is shown extending his left arm towards four important ministers, whose rank is marked by their slightly larger representation and by the inscriptions below. Each kneels with his right arm raised to the heart, a typical pose of loyalty and obedience seen throughout the reliefs. Further to the right, at the same level, are three or four royal officers without ornaments or weapons, as well as six army chiefs wearing helmets, armour and carrying shields; they salute the king before departing to join the parade.

Below this scene, the relief illustrates a procession of female figures en route to join the rear of the royal parade; they perhaps represent queens, princesses or ladies of the court. Amongst the highest-ranking, six are carried in hammocks, and five on palanquins covered with a canopy, attended by female and male servants, including dwarves. These ladies, elegantly dressed in the fashion of most of the *devatas* sculpted on the walls of the temple, seem to be attending to their hair and appearance. At the head of the procession a lone woman is depicted presenting scrolls to a standing male figure with a stylus, as if he were going to mark them. The procession takes place in a dense forest replete with monkeys, deer, and birds on tree branches – in other words, at the foot of Mount Shivapada.

Proceeding to the right, at about one third of the way along the panel, the soldiers are depicted descending from the mountain (Fig. 12) and thus the formal parade begins. The infantry is marching in order, escorting the generals and high dignitaries mounted on elephants. Suryavarman II himself and his 19 ministers (or generals and governors) are identified by a short inscription recording the name and rank of each, the latter being confirmed by the number of parasols, fans, flywhisks and banners. The king, surrounded by several servants, is protected by 14 parasols, five large fans on long handles, two peacock fans and four flywhisks (Fig. 13). The king and his ministers each carry a spear, sometimes

the characteristic *phkak* and hold leather shields for protection. Like the infantry, they have their lower body clothed in a *sampot* whose long tails hang down from the belt to gather on the side; the upper part of the body is covered by a light cuirass that contains two knives. None of the 19 personages is wearing a crown or helmet. The generals are depicted on their elephants in three different attitudes: the 'parade attitude' when standing with one foot on the back of the elephant and the other in the howdah, the 'resting attitude' when sitting in the howdah with one leg hanging out, and the 'battle attitude' when standing with both legs splayed (Jacq-Hergoualc'h 1979: 97). The mahouts, sitting on the elephants' neck, are splendidly accoutred and always of smaller size than the lord. The howdahs, on which the dignitaries sit or stand, are of two varieties: ones with the sides designed in an undulating arch, often with convolutions, and ones with rectangular sides. The first variety is the most common, used by dignitaries and generals.

Each platoon of soldiers wears helmets with a different small animal head as their insignia to distinguish them from other troops. They are armed with long bows or spears and carry round shields. They march in good order, sometimes accelerating the step.

The parade also includes various groups of brahmins, with high chignons and ringing small bells; the *rajahotar* (royal chaplain) is carried in a hammock and seems to be holding a sort of pointed instrument, as if in the act of writing. Ahead of him is the ark with the Sacred Fire (Fig. 11) that always accompanied the Khmer army; the fire – the primary symbol of the state – sanctified the battles and attracted the benevolent attention of the gods. The ark has the shape of a miniature pavilion with the poles of the canopy as well as the roof having finials in the shape of *naga* heads.

Trumpets, drums, conch players, and an enormous gong beaten with a large mallet by a brawny musician precede the ark's numerous porters. Two dancing clowns are also depicted, as well as some banner-carriers humorously balancing their long banners on the nose or chin. The play of the legs of the marching infantry (ahead of the Sacred Fire) seem to follow a rhythm which subtly varies in speed from the soldier at the front to the ones at the back.

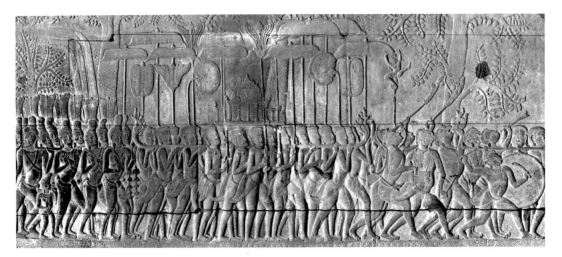

FIG. 11 Soldiers carrying the Sacred Ark.

FIG. 12 Soldiers descending from Mount Shivapada.

FIG. 13 The king on his royal elephant.

FIG. 14 The leader of the 'Syam kuk' and his troops.

At the very head of the procession, a group of unusual people appears, with extravagant costumes, long vests with pendants, bizarre, long and braided hair with three or four plumes and five rows of superimposed beads (Fig. 14). They hold spears with spikes. Their leader, standing in parade attitude on his elephant, is covered with bracelets and necklaces and many other decorative elements; like his mahout, he has a sort of apron at the back of the *sampot*. The inscriptions sculpted below them indicate that the soldiers are 'Syam kuk' and that their leader represents King Peman, who is otherwise unknown to us. Much has been written about the meaning of 'Syam kuk'; it seems that 'syam' refers to dark-skinned people and not to Siamese (Thai), as some historians would like to interpret. Therefore, they probably are Khmer allies or mercenaries from some nearby Asian country but not necessarily from the region of Thailand.

To better understand this relief it is imperative to read the small Sanskrit inscriptions that are engraved near the various personages, collectively known as Inscription K.268. For convenience they have been numbered from left to right (west to east). They were translated firstly by E. Aymonier in 1904 and then revised by George Coedès in 1911. From the list it is confirmed that the king is represented twice, as are two of his ministers and the *rajahotar*. There are six *Vrah kamraten an* (VKA: His Grace or His Lordship), two *Kamraten an* (KA: Lord and master) and eleven *Anak sanjak* (AS: in charge of the close protection of the king), making a total of 19 dignitaries. There is also another VKA, but he is from the outlying town of Lavo, which refers to Louvo or Lopburi, the town in present-day Thailand. Other 'foreign elements' include the 'Syam kuk' soldiers with their general on an elephant and their prince Jen Jhala riding a horse.

1. 'Tanvay kamraten an pandita' ('The presents from the honourable pandits'). This inscription is engraved under the arm of the chief of the brahmins; it is the order given by the chief of the hermits to his fellows to bring a plate of fruits to the king seated nearby. They presumably belong to the group of *rishis* who lived on Mount Shivapada where the ceremony takes place.

2. 'Samtac Vrah pada kamraten an Paravishnuloka na stac nau vnam Shivapada pi pancuh vala'. 'His Majesty Paramavishnuloka, at the moment when he is on Mt. Shivapada to make the army descend' (*see comment above*). This inscription is traced under the royal parasols.

3. 'VKA Shri Virasinhavarman'. This minister is depicted in profile, kneeling in front of the king, without any body decoration; even the elongated earlobes do not have earrings.

The inscription 3 Bis (written together with the inscription number 3) reads: 'KA ta mula Shri Varddha'. The figure related to this title is the first minister, depicted frontally but with his head turned towards the king, wearing as decoration only a simple necklace. His right arm rests on his chest as a sign of loyalty and obedience.

4. 'KA Dhananjaya'. This minister squats with one arm on the chest and the other on his left thigh. Like Virasinhavarman, both Dhananjaya and Varddha are being depicted at the centre of the ministerial group and sitting slightly higher than the others on thick decorated rugs or plinths. Despite their importance, however, they have not been given the title of -*varman*. They also don't have the term *vrah* (saint), perhaps because they were not brahmins or did not previously occupy a religious position.

5. 'VKA granadosha ta pvana' (un-named). He is the minister 'in charge of inspections of the qualities and faults' (i.e. of criminal justice). Also depicted with his hand on his heart, this unnamed minister is leaning slightly forward supported by one hand on the ground. He occupies the fourth ministerial position, the two most important being those of the ministers Varddha and Dhananjaya.

6. 'VKA Shri Jayendravarman Ldau'. His Grace 'from the land of Ldau' (a plant) is depicted in parade attitude on his elephant, holding a lance and a shield, in front of the insignia of his rank – six parasols and two long banners on flexible poles. In addition, he is preceded by four horsemen.

7. 'VKA Shri Virendradhipativarman Chok Vakula'. His Grace 'from the land of Chok Vakula' (a tree with small fragrant flowers) is shown standing in parade attitude on an elephant, armed with a

phkak on his right shoulder and using his left hand to hold on to the howdah. His signs of rank are only nine parasols. In front of him are three horsemen. Coedès has identified him with the person that in 1108, under the rule of Dharanindravarman I, had the image of the Buddhist deity Trailokayavijaya consecrated in the temple of Phimai (Vimaya) in northeastern Thailand. According to Coedès, at the time when he was depicted at Angkor Wat he was still a KA.

8. 'AS Kancas Pryak ti hau VKA Shri Virayudhavarman'. He is depicted standing on his elephant in battle attitude, holding bow and arrows. His insignia are six parasols, two fans and a standard with the statuette of Garuda.

9. 'AS Mat Gnan ti hau VKA Shri Jayayudhavarman'. He stands in parade attitude on his elephant, holding the *phkak* and a shield, surrounded by eight *varddha*, parasols and a standard with a statuette of Hanuman; his soldiers have helmet crests in the shape of deer heads.

10. 'VKA Shri Mahipatindravarman Canlattai.' His Grace 'from Canlattai', (a type of cactus) is shown armed as the previous lord, standing in parade attitude, surrounded by the signs of his rank: six parasols, two elongated fans, and a standard with a statuette of Hanuman holding the mace.

11. 'AS Vidyashrama ti hau VKA Shri Ranaviravarman'. This lord is depicted standing in parade attitude – slightly off balance – armed with a pike and a large knife at the belt (Fig. 15). He has the standard of Garuda and six parasols and two fans. Two groups of three horsemen precede him, each protected by a parasol.

12. 'AS Virajaya ti hau VKA Shri Rajasinhavarman.' This lord is represented in a resting attitude, half-seated on the howdah with his head turned back towards Mount Shivapada. He is armed with a *phkak* and three small daggers, one of which hangs at the centre of his chest. He is protected by thirteen parasols, and preceded by two groups of horsemen with five parasols and two long banners.

FIG. 15 Lord Ranaviravarman.

13. 'AS Aso Vnya Chlan to hau VKA Virendhadhipativarman'. This lord 'by the name of ? White flower called Virendhadhipativarman' is illustrated in parade attitude, holding the *phkak* in his right hand and the howdah's bridles in the other. His signs of rank are nine parasols and two banners carried by the horsemen who precede him and who are themselves protected by five parasols.

14. 'AS Anak Cih ti hau VKR Narapatindravarman'. The *sanjak* 'by the name of Cih, called saint lord and master Narapatindravarman' stands in battle attitude, with bow and arrows, covered with a light armour. He merits 10 parasols and 2 banners. His mahout makes the animal twist his head towards the spectator.

15. 'AS Vni Satra ti hau VKA Shuradhipativarman'. The *sanjak* 'by the name of Vni Satra called Saint Lord and Master Shuradhipativarman' stands on his elephant in battle attitude, with both legs splayed. He holds his javelin as if about to throw it. Eight parasols, three banners and a standard with a statuette of the leaping Hanuman highlight his rank.

In front, two horsemen brandish their swords and are protected by three parasols.

16. 'KA Dhananjaya'. (The lower part of the inscription between the legs of this lord is very damaged). The name is an epithet of Arjuna, the hero of the *Mahabharata*, meaning 'the conqueror of richness'. This lord is the same already shown squatting in audience on Mount Shivapada. Being the king's first minister and, as such, a very important personage, it is surprising that his title does not have the honorific particle '*Srî*' (see inscription 4). His high rank is indicated by ten parasols, three banners and a standard with Hanuman. He stands in parade attitude on his elephant, holding the *phkak* with his right hand and the bridles with his left. His dress differs from that of other lords by having, in addition to the large flapping loincloth, other bands of cloth loose at the sides of the legs. He is depicted riding behind Suryavarman II, although this may be intended to indicate being on the king's left. His howdah is of the type with straight, rectangular borders.

17. 'Vrah pada kamraten Paramavishnuloka', which translates as 'The holy feet of his Grace Paramavishnuloka.' King Suryavarman II is repre-sented standing on the royal elephant in parade attitude, with his head facing back in a three-quarter turn but with his body towards the viewer. His right hand holds the *phkak* leaning on his shoulder, attesting the high esteem in which this weapon was held. The crown, the jewelled belt, the earrings, the armlets, bracelets and anklets reveal his royal status, as does his elaborate *sampot*. His elephant wears a very large and richly decorated crown, making it unique amongst the elephants. The howdah is of the rectangular type, like those of his two flanking ministers. He is accompanied by 15 parasols, five fans of two different shapes, six flywhisks of two different types, four banners and a standard with the statuette of Vishnu on the shoulders of Garuda. The image appears at the centre of the panel, and is the largest of all the parading figures. In front of him are five horsemen bran dishing their spears under seven parasols.

18. 'AS Trailokyapura'. This poorly preserved inscription was only deciphered by Coedès in 1938. The unnamed *anak sanjak* from Trailokyapura must have been a powerful minister of the king since he rides ahead of him (or to his right, Fig. 16). He stands in parade attitude on his elephant with one hand on the dagger in his belt, and the other grabbing the bridles of the howdah of the rectangular type. He has eight parasols, one fan, five banners and a standard with Hanuman holding a club. The locality of Trailokyapura does not appear anywhere else in Khmer epigraphy.

19. 'KA ta mula Shri Varddha'. This lord has already been seen attending the audience on Mount Shivapada, being another minister of the king (*see inscription 3 bis*). He stands in parade attitude on his elephant holding a javelin and a long shield, one end of which is supported by his knee. His signs of rank are 12 parasols, two banners and a standard with Hanuman holding a club. He is preceded by four horsemen in two groups, with six parasols and two banners.

20. 'AS Aso Lngis to hau VKA Shri Rajendravarman'. 'The White *sanjak* called Rajendravarman' seems to be in resting attitude, in part sitting in his howdah, with the head turned to look back and the torso twisted towards the viewer. The chair is of the rectangular type. In his right hand he holds a heavy sword (or mace) with a richly-decorated hilt. He is surrounded by eight parasols, three banners, and a standard with the statuette of a leaping Hanuman, and is preceded by four horsemen protected by six parasols.

21. 'Rajahotar'. The royal chaplain and his acolytes interrupt the parade of warriors and noble lords. He is carried in a simple hammock by brahmins with the usual hairstyles of the first group seen on Mount Shivapada (*see inscription 1*). Coedès (1911: 201) suggested that they may be same as the Shaivite ascetics or *tapasvin* observed by Zhou Daguan at the end of the XIII century. In the reliefs, the *rishis* are illustrated wearing a double-belt on the chest and a small loincloth. They all have elongated earlobes, and some wear large earrings. One of the Rajahotar's porters moves from his sore shoulder the post of the hammock, making a comic but natural grimace to the spectator. The royal chaplain's cortege carries 13 fans and three banners; towards

the head of the group some brahmins are ringing small bells.

22. 'Vrah Vlen' ('The Sacred Fire'). It is carried in an ark on a sort of palanquin by a distinctive group of attendants with short hair, elongated ear lobes and each wearing a single, simple necklace. They wear loincloths with tails and are surrounded by ten parasols, seven fans of three different kinds, and a standard with the leaping Hanuman. An orchestra precedes them, composed of players of drums, conches and an enormous gong. A small group of jugglers playing with banners is at the head of this peculiar element of the procession.

23. 'AS Travan svay ti hau VKA Shri Prthivina-rendra'. The *sanjak* 'from the marsh of mangoes called Prthivinarendra' is adorned with a thick cuirass, holds a javelin and is surrounded by six parasols as a sign of his rank. Standing in parade attitude on his elephant, he is preceded by three horsemen with swords and six parasols.

24. 'AS Kavishvara ti hau VKA mahasenapati Shri Virendravarman'. The personal name of Kavishvara means 'Prince of the poets'; the personage is a great general *(mahasenapati)* and the signs of his rank are seven parasols, one fan and two banners. He is depicted standing in parade attitude on his elephant, holding with his right hand a large dagger inserted in his belt, while the other holds the bridles of the howdah. His bow and quiver are fixed vertically in front of the howdah, and he is preceded by three horsemen with five parasols.

25. 'VKA Shri Sinhaviravarman (the name is barely readable due to damage). This lord stands on his elephant in war attitude, protected by a shield, and ready to throw a javelin. From his simple necklace hangs a large pear-shaped pendant. Seven parasols, two banners and a standard with Hanuman's statuette mark his rank. Preceding him are three horsemen with an unusual braided hairstyle, and behind them are five parasols.

26. 'VKA Shri Jayasinhavarman kamlun vrai nam vala Lvo'. 'Jayasinhavarman in the forest, leading the troops of Lavo' is shown standing on his elephant

in war attitude, the *phkak* on the shoulder and a shield in the left arm, wearing a light cuirass. He wears a necklace with three pendants. He must be a powerful lord, considering that his 17 parasols outnumber by two those of the processing Suryavarman II. He does not have a military standard, but has a long fan, two banners, and two other banners carried by the two pairs of horsemen that precede him.

27. 'Neh Syam kuk.' This inscription has recently been vandalised and the gap filled with cement. This disorderly group of soldiers or mercenaries is lead by an unnamed commander standing in parade attitude on his elephant, one leg leaning against an elaborate howdah, holding bow and arrow, ready to shoot (Fig. 14). They all wear unusual clothing and ornaments and have braided hair gathered at the top of the head with a tuft of plumes. The unnamed commander is depicted with a necklace and bracelets with strings of beads; from the belt a multitude of bead strings and other ornaments hang midway down his long skirt. The soldiers – who are unusually dressed and also wear plumed hats – carry pikes and javelins decorated with plumes; other soldiers have long shields. Some of them seem to have tattoos on the cheeks, their faces revealing a foreign ethnicity

28. 'Anak rajakaryyabhaga Paman Jen Jhala ta nam Syam kuk' which translates as 'Jen Jhala is the vassal prince representing King Paman (?).' The terms of this inscription are difficult to translate and Coedès's interpretation, presented here, is still tentative. This personage is the *anak rajakaryyabhaga* ('participant in the royal service') and a commander of the 'Syam kuk'. He is the only horseman honoured with an inscription. Depicted immediately behind a group of his foot soldiers, he is brandishing a lance with hooks and has a knife hanging on his chest. His helmet terminates in the shape of a bird, like that of the soldiers; three parasols are the sign of his rank.

Concerning these inscriptions, one has to notice that *Paramavishnuloka* ('He who has reached the realm of the Supreme Vishnu') is the posthumous title of Suryavarman II, and therefore would only be used after his death. The inscription making

FIG. 16 The minister from Trailokyapura.

this ceremony or celebration. It must have been a very important one considering that Suryavarman's ministers and feudal princes (or governors) representing the strength of the country are all formally united on Mount Shivapada. The presence of the female royalty and the deployment of troops give a historic character to the reunion, but that of the brahmins, the royal chaplain, and the sacred fire, also connote a religious observance.

The image of Suryavarman II seated in state depicts his left arm raised in a horizontal gesture towards the five dignitaries. This could be a gesture of command, but his hand holds another unspecified object, thus obscuring the gesture's possible meaning. The king's throne is a raised chair, its height being a signifier of power, and its presence indicating that Suryavarman is firmly installed as a king. The throne and the obligation for others to kneel in front of it demonstrate the king's total control. The scene represents the ideology of paternal power and/or kingship, of the dominant male person concerned with maintaining his power and right to rule.

This relief contains perhaps the greatest number of elephants of any at Angkor (more than in the panels depicting the Victory of Vishnu over the *Asuras*, LP. 5). The king and his two most important ministers Dhananjaya and Trailokyapura, who ride at his sides, have the simpler howdah, with horizontal rails supported by colonettes. Rajendravarman who occupies the important position in the procession between the King and the *rajahotar* uses a similar chair, but more robustly formed. The arms and the armour carried by the parading soldiers have been treated elsewhere in the work of Jacq Hergoualc'h (1979) and will not therefore be discussed in any depth in the present volume.

Concerning the layout of the relief, it should be noticed that the representation of Suryavarman on his elephant at the centre of the panel acts as the axis of the composition. In the corresponding panel in the north gallery depicting the 'Battle of the *Devas* and *Asuras*' (LP. 7), the figure of Indra occupies an identical position. If the Historic Procession were juxtaposed with the latter, the two monarchs would face each other, respectively symbolising secular and divine leadership (Mannikka 1996: 152).

reference to the sacred Mountain Shivapada ('Shiva Footprints') rather than the usual symbolic Mount Meru may be due to its engravers ignoring Suryavarman II's preference for Vaishnavism and enforcing the traditional Shaivite cult prevailing after his death. The implication is that this inscription, like the others listed above, were engraved at a later date than the sculpting of the relief. Furthermore, the style of the very low-engraved inscriptions inserted in the free space between personages is different from that of other inscriptions contemporaneous with Angkor Wat's construction. They are, instead, very close to those of the period of Jayavarman VII (r.1181–c.1220) (C. Jacques in Le Bonheur 1989: 169). However, Jacques is of the opinion that the inscriptions were added only a short time after the death of Suryavarman II, around 1150.

This relief attracted the interest of many scholars including Aymonier (1904, III: 247) and Coedès (1911: 185), who both described it in some detail, as did Le Bonheur (1995: 18). One of their mutual objectives was to define the character of

FIG. 17 The fork in the road which leads to either the Heavens or the Hells.

FIG. 18 Noble figures are carried to the Heavens.

Following the 'Historic Procession' is a panel stretching for 66.05 metres in the eastern wing of the same gallery.[3] Divided laterally in three registers, the inscriptions leave no doubts that the upper two registers represent the heavens and the lower one depicts the hells. Starting from the panel's western end and proceeding towards the right, the two upper registers (Fig. 17) depict a long procession towards the heavens of the great Khmer nobility who are carried on palanquins by their slaves (Fig. 18), followed by ladies and noblemen of lesser rank, while the commoners walk along quietly, some with their children. The group of 19 men carried on palanquins in the top registers may represent the ministers and generals seen in the Historic Procession. At a certain point, all three registers are interrupted by a large figure of Yama[4] (Fig. 32) surrounded by his army. The God of Time and Eternal Death brandishes clubs in his many arms, and is seated on his mount, the buffalo. Further on are his two assistants seated in the middle register and beyond them in the upper two registers begins a frieze of Garudas and Atlases supporting 37 heavenly palaces. Each of these is composed of three chambers, the central of which is occupied by a happy soul – alternatively a king (Fig. 22) or queen (Fig. 19) sitting on a throne. In the other two rooms are retinues of beautiful courtesans, fanning their lord or lady, and presenting them children for paternal or maternal caresses. Others offer fruits and flowers, or bring a mirror to the ladies. Several of the blessed hold a small object in one hand, probably a jewelled sachet with perfumes (as the one held by Suryavarman II in the previous relief). *Apsaras* dance above the palaces.

In the bottom register on either side of the figure of Yama are the sinners converging towards him. Of his two assistants Dharma – who is another form of Yama – pronounces the sentences that are recorded by Citragupta (Fig. 21), rewarding the good and punishing the bad by throwing them into the different hells. Inscriptions revealing the victims' sins also record their appropriate torture and the name of the hells where the tortures will take place.

Although only a small number of punishments are depicted in the relief, the elaborate list of sins

certainly paints a colourful picture of Angkorean society. 12 different hells are reserved just for the thieves: those who steal land, residences, elephants, horses, vehicles, shoes or sandals, parasols, rice, strong liquors, the goods of priests, the goods of the poor, and the wives of others or the wife of a friend or of their guru. A particular hell is reserved for those who steal flowers from Shiva's garden. Other hells are destined for those who burn villages, or towns and parks dedicated to Shiva's bull; those who urinate or defecate in temples; those who cut down trees not designated to be cut, or from sacred areas, and those who otherwise defile sacred areas. Other punishments await those who denigrate gods, the sacred fire, the object of sacrifice, the gurus, the brahmins, the learned ones and the teacher of Shiva's devotees, their mothers, their fathers, their friends. Murderers have a hell all for themselves, as do those who vandalise wells and gardens, are charlatans or liars, who desire somebody's death or misfortune, and those who cause abortions. Other categories of hell exist for the insane, those who abuse a confidence, and those who are gluttons, debtors, arsonists, or are avaricious.

The representation of heavens and hells has attracted the interest of several scholars but it is again thanks to the works of Aymonier (1904, III: 265) and Coedès (1911: 204) that a complete understanding of the inscriptions explaining the hells' punishments is possible. In a poor state of preservation, the inscriptions – in an ungrammatical Sanskrit – were engraved on the narrow line at the top of the register. Nonetheless, they do provide a complete nomenclature of Khmer hells. Unfortunately, most of the 36 inscriptions that Coedès was able to decipher were lost when the gallery collapsed in 1947, causing great damage. Here the hells are listed and numbered from left to right (west to east) as one progresses along the gallery.[5]

1. 'These, the two higher (ways), are the route to the heavens (*svargga*)'. This first inscription is engraved between the parasols of the figures ascending the 'middle path' represented by the middle register (Fig. 17). Knights, lords and several ladies protected

Fig. 19 A princess in her heavenly palace.

Fig. 20 The Kriminkaya hell.

by parasols, occupy the two ways leading towards the skies, conversing among themselves, and waiting for the palanquins that will transport them. The ladies savour the fruits that servants are offering on trays. This privileged queue terminates where it meets the waiting empty palanquins with their porters kneeling on the ground. A few of the figures are shown mounting the palanquins, and proceeding towards their heavenly destination.

2. 'This is the lower (way) to the hells (*naraka*)'. This inscription is engraved on a band defining the base of the middle register, just above the first tree depicted in the hells. Below it, the emaciated damned are chained, seized by their jaw or hair or by ropes through their noses by terrifying demons wearing helmets with a large crest (Fig. 24). The condemned are also pierced by the horns of deer, bitten by dogs, torn to pieces by lions and stamped on by elephants and rhinoceros (Fig. 25). Glancing in despair towards the blessed above, all these miserable and terrified men and women – the latter depicted with pendulous breasts – proceed towards Yama and his two assistants, their implacable judges.

3. 'Vrah Yama.' Sovereign of the Underworld, he is depicted in his terrible aspect with multiple arms and hands holding maces, wearing a tall crown, and seated on a low throne over his buffalo (Fig. 32). Many parasols, flywhisks and fans of different types surround him. His large size extends across the upper two registers interrupting the procession.

4. 'Vrah Dharmma Vrah Citragupta.' The name of the first deity Vrah Dharma, ('Saint Justice') is, in fact, another name of Yama, who is therefore present in two aspects in the relief. As Vrah Dharma, he is depicted as a relatively modest deity sitting on the ground, wearing a crown, several necklaces, bracelets, and other royal jewellery. He seems to be holding a small object in his left hand (Fig. 21). The deity to his left is Citragupta, whose image has been defaced. Citragupta is the scribe, the clerk of Yama, the one who reads out the bad deeds of mortals. He is depicted like a crowned *rakshas*a, seated on a plinth, pointing with a club in the direction of the damned being brought forward by demons.

5. 'Avici. Those who [live] in abundance and still live [?] only in sin'. The damned of this first hell – the hell 'without rest' – are thrown on a stake or spiky tree. To the left, one sinner, lying on a table, is flayed alive with a scraper (Fig. 23).

6. 'Kriminikaya. Those who despise the gods, the sacred fire, the gurus, the brahmins, the knowledge-able persons, the teachers of the dharma, the Shaivite, their mother, father and friends'. These damned are thrown into a 'mass of worms' and beaten with clubs (Fig. 21).

FIG. 21 Citragupta pronouncing the sentences.

FIG. 22 A royal figure in his heavenly palace.

FIG. 23 The Avici hell.

7. 'Vaitarani nadi. The people who … Those who despise the science … the thieves, the deceivers, those who steal the *rasa*'. The sinners, kept in a foetid river, have their tongues extracted with pincers and their mouths impaled.

8. 'Kutashalmali. Those who … the false witnesses'. This inscription is very poorly preserved. In this hell, the sinners are thrown on spiky trees, after having their tongues extracted with long tongs and their bones broken.

9. 'Yugmaparvata. Those who wish to murder… who wish bad things on others, to harm other living beings [?]'. Pairs of sinners are squashed against rocks in the hell of the 'oppressing mountains'(Fig. 28).

10. 'Nirucchvasa. The insane, the violent, those who abuse the confidence of others, those who kill women and children'. In this suffocating hell, the damned are thrown on a pyre or are tied up with ropes and made to roll on thorny branches (Fig. 27).

11. 'Ucchvasa. The people who live in debauchery, those who … [?] the sins of others, those who eat unconsecrated meat'. In this 'hell of weeping' amongst the sinners being chained and beaten with great clubs, are some women, as always in the hells, with pendulous breasts.

12. 'Dravattrapu. The people who …; those who steal the land, the house, the residence of others'. They are immersed in basins of 'molten lead'.

13. 'Taptalakshamaya. Those who set fire to houses of others and to forests, those who poison others'. These damned are tied against spiky trees or thrown onto braziers (Fig. 26).

14. 'Asthibhanga. The people who degrade gardens, houses, ponds, … , wells, shelters, or other types of residence. Those who damage the *tirtha* of others, and who act against the laws'. This is the hell of 'broken bones' where the sinners have their bones smashed to pieces and clubs stuffed in their mouths.

15. 'Krakaccheda. The greedy'. Men and women are crushed with heavy maces, or have their jaws smashed with vices.

16. 'Puyapurnahrada. Those who steal strong liquors, the woman of another, or approach the wife of their guru'. In this hell, birds of prey tear the damned to pieces; the latter are then thrown in the 'lake of liquid sticky pus'.

17. 'Asrikpurnahrada. Those who steal meat, the wives of others, take the wife of their guru ….' First horribly beaten, these sinners are then thrown into 'the lake full of blood.'

FIG. 24 Sinners pulled by ropes through their noses.

FIG. 25 The damned are attacked by a rhinoceros and lions.

FIG. 26 The Taptalakshamay a hell.

FIG. 27 The Nirucchvasa hell.

FIG. 28 The Yugmaparvata hell.

FIG. 29 The Kshuradharaparvata hell.

18. 'Medhoharada. The greedy, those who indulge into concupiscence'. Those condemned to this hell, mainly women with pendulous breasts, are grabbed by their hair and thrown into the lake of 'marrow and serum'.

19. 'Tikshnayastunda. The people who take the offering [?] not meant for them, those who steal rice'. These damned are shown with enormous stomachs and are being beaten with clubs.

20. 'Angaricaraya. The arsonists of villages, towns, the parks of the sacred cows. Those who urinate or leave excrement in the places consecrated to the gods'. They are thrown on 'heaps of (glowing) embers'.

21. 'Amvarisa. Those who cause the wives of others to abort, and who approach the wife of a friend'. In this hell of the 'frying pan', the damned are tortured in couples, tied down, hacked with knives and then thrown into nets.

22. 'Kumbhipaka. The persons charged of a mission by a king … who steal the wealth of a guru, live in baseness, steal the goods of the poor, of the … knowledgeable brahmins.' They are thrown, head first, into cauldrons.

23. 'Talavrksavana. The people who cut trees which are not designated [?] to be cut, those who cut the trees of places consecrated to the gods, and defile these

FIG. 30 The Shita hell.

FIG. 31 The Maharaurava hell.

places'. In this hell of the 'forest of palm trees' some of the sinners are condemned to have a thick vice around the neck; others to be bound by ropes and suspended head-down.

24. 'Kshuradharaparvata. The people who steal elephants, horses, vehicles, the sandals …, despise the pandits, the objects of rituals'. These are crucified on trees amongst bonfires, or are ground up in mortars (Fig. 29).

25. 'Santapana [?]. Those who harm others, despise others, steal parasols, the sandals …'. These dammed are thrown onto braziers. Like the following one, this inscription is very damaged.

26. 'Sucimukha. The people who do …'. As the inscription is incomplete, it is impossible to decipher the sin. In this hell, the damned are suspended by ropes, and then thrown to the ground and beaten.

27. 'Kalasutra. Those who sow discord between the kings [?], and are greedy of wealth'. These sinners are impaled and then thrown onto braziers.

28. 'Mahapadma. Those who pick flowers, …'. The damned in this hell of the 'Grand Lotus' are thrown onto braziers, torn by birds of prey, made to hang from thorny trees and shot full of arrows.

29. 'Padma. Those who steal flowers, pick flowers from Shiva's gardens'. Some of the damned in this 'Hell of Lotus' are tied to trees and have nails beaten into their heads with a heavy hammer. Others are devoured by wild dogs and birds of prey.

30. 'Sanjivana. All the great criminals'. The sinners, their legs attached to two trees, are suspended upside-down over a pyre. Others are hung by the neck, while crowds of birds devour them.

31. Unreadable; un-named hell. The damned are picked up by tongs and a pole is inserted in their mouth.

32. Unreadable; un-named hell. The damned have their tongues wrenched out by pincers.

33. 'Shita. Those who steal…are all cold'. In this frozen hell, the damned shiver in cold waters, their arms held together tight to their chest (Fig. 30).

34. 'Sandratamah. The people who steal torches [?]; the impure, the layers'. In this hell of 'thick darkness', the eyes of some of the sinners are put out with awls, while others, pierced with nails, are suspended by the waist and pulled by heavy weights attached to their head, hands, and feet. They are then hacked to pieces with knives. Others are shown waiting in terror for their turn.

35. 'Maharaurava ….' In this indeterminate hell, the sinners are suspended by their hands on pulleys and pulled down by weights attached to their feet, while thick nails are transfixed all over the sides of their body (Fig. 31).

36. 'Raurava. The dispossessed ones, who live in exile [?]… who do not pay their debts'. This is the 'hell of the sobbing' where the damned are tied up, and stacked over braziers heated by long flames.

The Vedic hymns tell of endless happiness to be found in the heavens in the company of gods, and of a 'deep pit' where certain sinners are thrown (Dange 1984: 125). In the Vedic period (first millennium BC), the concept of hell was not yet developed. It took form in the *Purana*, where it was initially associated with the underworld darkness and Yama, the God of the Dead. His sovereignty had already been mentioned in the *Mahabharata* when the God of Gods (Vishnu) had to take the place of Yama during the terrible times of the *Krita Yuga*. In the *Bhagavata Purana* (V, 26, 7), Yama has the authority to punish sinners. He decides on the punishments, according to which a sinner is sent to one of the 28 different types of hells. The chapter terminates with a note on the existence of one thousand one hundred more hells for sins not mentioned in the text, foreseeing the possibility of new sins in new circumstances.

No texts are known about Khmer beliefs on heavens and hells. Nevertheless, on the basis of the scenes depicted in this relief, it seems that the Khmer conception of hell was based on Mahayana Buddhist cosmology. The latter must have been described in some old texts not dissimilar to those used at a much later date (mid XIV century) by Sukhothai's king Luthai to compile the *Trai Phum* (The Three Worlds).[6] 32 hells are delineated in the *Trai Phum*, each with their own name (Roeske 1914: 587), of which only 12 are named in the relief under consideration.

The number of hells – 32 – is a number often found in the Khmer imprecatory formulae revealing a Buddhist influence. In fact, the Buddhists count the hells by 4, 8, 16 or 32, compared with the Hindu's 7, 21 and 28. The hells illustrated in this panel, however, have a typically Brahmanic character; no punishments are reserved for the offenders of Buddhist doctrine. Noticeable is the mention of several punishments for crimes against the Shaivite religion, the brahmins and their rituals. This may reflect the extent to which Khmer belief was rooted in Shaivism, as well as the syncretism between Vaishnava and Shaivite doctrines at the time. Alternatively, the inscriptions may be of later date, when Shaivism was once again the royal cult, after the death of Jayavarman VII.

From the above considerations one can see that, as observed for other reliefs, the Khmers must have had available texts of which no traces have survived. In the specific case of Angkor Wat, the references to Buddhist texts are not surprising because Buddhism has always been practised by the Khmers, having been introduced together with Hinduism – if not earlier – since the first centuries of the first millennium. The religion endured alternating fortunes under the Angkorean kings until the rule of Jayavarman VII who made it the official religion.

At a glance it is easy to see several points in common between the functions of Yama in this relief and those of Suryavarman II from the preceding one. As a god of the first rank, sovereign of the infernal regions, Yama is the embodiment of righteousness (*dharma*) and the King of Justice (*dharma-raja*).

As noticed earlier, the *Mahabharata* (109.32, 35) mentions that Yama's place was taken over by Vishnu during the terrible times of the *Krita Yuga*. Not only did Vishnu have to rule over the earth but also over the underworld, establishing thus a connection between the actions of people in life and their existence in hell. On these grounds,

with Suryavarman II being identified with Vishnu, he could be seen not only as the ruler of his people in their lifetime, but also after their death in the kingdom of darkness. He takes the place of the king of the dead, becoming the Khmer Yama.[7]

In Hindu belief, the concept of hell is essentially based on that of deprivation and loss. Punishment, however, is not everlasting; it is temporary and succeeded by rebirth. Hell is not the condemnation of the soul, but of its sins. Suffering in hell is thus a necessary process of purification, after which the sinner can be reborn, unstained. The idea of suffering in hell is parallel to that which is to be expected on earth and of expiatory rites to be performed by sinners. Both aim at the purification of the soul and its release from sin. The punishments in hell vary according to the punishment in society. The punishments of hells have the function of the Christian Purgatory, where the length of terrible expiation is counted in thousands of years. Nevertheless, it seems the whole concept of hell rests ultimately on the laws of social behaviour and within the system of caste.

As demonstrated by the lively variety of the relief's bottom register, human imagination is without limits when it comes to the representation of the dark and miserable. Perhaps the punishments are not purely imaginary, but were based on actual Khmer practices. On the contrary, there is little variety when it comes to imagining perfect happiness. The heavens are seen as a boundless serene space, where nothing seems to happen; a life of contemplation suspended in grace. The *Padma Purana* (Book 2, chapter 96) defines those who deserve heaven: those who live a life according to the moral and religious precepts of the scriptures, paying tribute to their ancestors. Did the Khmers, who were such great builders of irrigation systems and water reservoirs, know that 'those who construct reservoirs of water' (ibidem, sloka 39) merited entrance to the heavens? Perhaps this was a further motivation for the Khmer kings – besides the probable improvement to irrigation – to build those enormous *barays* that characterise the Angkor area.

FIG. 32 Yama on his buffalo.

FIG. 33 Vishnu directing the Churning of the Ocean of Milk.

This relief, perhaps the most famous of the 3rd enclosure, is sculpted in the southern wing of the eastern gallery, extending 48.45 metres along its wall. At the centre of the panel is the unfinished figure of Vishnu in front of Mount Mandara which serves as the churning pole, supported by his *avatara*, the tortoise Kurma, who wears a small crown (Fig. 33). Vishnu has four arms; his upper two brandish the discus and the club, while with his lower two he holds the serpent Vasuki. The small figure depicted flying above Mount Mandara, and who seems to be leaning on it with his two hands is problematic: he may either be Indra or another form of Vishnu.

Vishnu directs the churning efforts of the *devas* and *asuras*, who pull the great Vasuki acting as the rope around the post. The *asuras* are depicted identically to the *devas*: only their crested helmets distinguish them from the *devas* wearing conical crowns. Each group is led by three gigantic figures, at the front, middle and end. On the side of the *asuras*, the one holding Vasuki's head is probably Bali or Kalanemi (Fig. 35), or considering the *Ramayana*'s influence in this relief, possibly Ravana; the other two figures remain unidentified (Fig. 34). On the side of the *devas*, the figure in the front, closest to Vishnu, has the *rakshasa* hairstyle and is therefore problematic. He could be Vibhishana (renegade brother of Ravana), although Coedès (1911: 116) preferred to interpret him as Shiva or Rahu (Fig. 36). The middle figure with five faces (Fig. 37) may be Brahma (Coedès 1911: 117) but Le Bonheur believed it might be Shiva with an unusual headdress (1995: 45). The last one, holding the tail of Vasuki (Fig. 38), is a mighty crowned monkey, and possibly represents either Sugriva or Hanuman. The slow churning rhythm of the *devas* and *asuras* with one of the heroic-sized figures interspersed regularly among their ranks is an admirable example of rhythmic layout.

Along the top is a register teeming with *apsaras* in graceful flight, while at the bottom is a register depicting marine life – those creatures closest to the churning vortex being cut to pieces. Within the main register, to the right and the left of the lively action, are the reserve armies of the *devas* and of the *asuras*. They consist of infantry (bottom two pseudo-registers) and horse-drawn chariots and elephants bearing howdahs (upper two pseudo-registers). For Mannikka (1996: 161) these armies are a crowd of Khmer onlookers who would have gathered at the coronation (*Indrabhisheka*) of the king, to watch the enactment of the scene of the churning.

The textual sources for this episode can be found in the *Mahabharata* (I, chapters 15-17), the *Ramayana* (Book I, chapter 45) and the *Bhagavata Purana*. They differ in the description of the products of the churning, the order in which they appear, and the people attending the event. It is believed here that the Puranic version (Book VIII, chapter 7) adapts best to the sculptural representation. It is summarised below.

*At the beginning of the world, the gods (*devas*) and demons (*asuras*) were engaged in a thousand year battle to secure* amrita, *an elixir that would render them immortal and incorruptible. After some time, when they became tired and still had not achieved their goal, they asked the help of Vishnu. He appeared and ordered them to work together, not against each other. Working together, they then commenced the churning of the Ocean of Milk by using Mount Mandara as the pivot and the five-headed* naga *Vasuki as the rope. However, the mountain suddenly began to sink. Vishnu incarnated as the tortoise Kurma to support the pivoting mountain on his back. Many gods also assisted, including Indra, by keeping the pivot in position. The spinning of Mount Mandara created such a violent whirlpool that the creatures and fish around it were torn to pieces. The Ocean of Milk was churned for another thousand years before producing the much-desired elixir and other treasures, amongst which are the goddess Lakshmi (Sri Devi), the elephant Airavata, the horse Ucchaihshravas, a wishing tree (Parijata) and the* apsaras. *The* naga *Vasuki vomited floods of black venom due to his mishandling by the* devas *and* asuras *during the churning. This would have been enough to poison everybody had it not been for Shiva, who drank it all; as a result, his mouth remaining stained forever with a black line.*

A bitter fight then broke out between the devas *and the* asuras *for possession of the* amrita. *Vishnu intervenes again, this time as the beautiful girl Mohini, and regains possession of the* amrita *which he keeps safe from harmful use. Once peace is established, Indra is reinstalled as the king of the gods.*

This narrative and that of the *Ramayana*, contrary to the *Mahabharata*,[8] have Vishnu in very active role. He appears in the form of the tortoise Kurma to support the rotating Mount Mandara, and also as the stabiliser of the mountain. He appears simultaneously pulling the snake amongst the *devas* and amongst the *asuras*. He participates also in a gigantic form invisible to all. Furthermore, Vishnu infuses Vasuki with strength, and in his original form, invigorates the *devas* with power. He appears again later, after the churning was completed, assuming the body of a charming woman (Mohini) to regain

the *amrita* stolen by the Daityas. But Vishnu's involvement does not end here: once more he had to join battle in the final defeat of the *asuras*.

A peculiarity of this representation of the Churning is the influence of the *Ramayana* on the choice of two of the leading figures on the side of the *devas*. One has the fangs and typical hairstyle of the *rakshasas* in the relief of the Battle of Lanka (LP. 8), and is possibly meant to be Rama's *rakshasa* ally Vibhishana. The other figure of a monkey king is more likely to be Sugriva than Hanuman, since this depiction has the same physical features of the powerful monkey fighting Valin in the relief of the latter's murder in the southwestern corner pavilion (S. 8). The attendance of Vibhishana and Sugriva at the Churning is not mentioned in the Puranic text, but their inclusion, presumably, was popular

Fig. 34 An unidentified *asura* king.

FIG. 35 The *asura* Bali or Kalanemi.

FIG. 36 Vibhishana (or Shiva?).

FIG. 37 Brahma (or Shiva?).

at that time in the local version of the *Ramayana*. For this reason, it may be that one of the multi-headed and multi-armed heroic figures sculpted on the side of the *asuras* may be Ravana. A similar Ramayanic influence appears in the relief of the same myth sculpted in the northwestern inner gallery of Bayon.

Different identifications of the leaders of both factions have been proposed by Mannikka (1996: 162) on the basis of the type and amount of sunrays the personages receive during the winter and summer solstices. The middle *asura* leader to the left and the middle *deva* leader to the right she interprets as two of the many forms taken by Vishnu to assist in the Churning, in this case his 'asura form' and 'deva form'. Mannikka also suggests that the *rakshasa* leader on the *devas* side is Rahu, the demon who infiltrated the *devas* their ranks to drink some of the *amrita*.

Of the small figure in the air over the pole, leaning on or touching it with his two hands, he is believed to be another of Vishnu's manifestations contributing to the churning activity – in this case the stabilisation of Mount Mandara. Finot (1912: 190) believed this to be demonstrated by a passage of the *Bhagavata Purana* (Book 8, chapter 7- sloka 12) in which it is said Vishnu was on Mount. Mandara 'holding it with his hands, cherished by the rain of flowers of the gods' (Brahma, Indra, Shiva and others). This, however, may refer also to the large central figure of Vishnu, sculpted half-way up Mount Mandara. Alternatively, this elusive personage could be the god Indra, who we know was watching the churning – and therefore not involved in the action, ready to take for himself, as they were created, the elephant Airavata and the horse Ucchaihshravas. Unfortunately the relief is unfinished and the products of the Churning have not been sculpted; the space where they usually appear is blank. In fact, in other reliefs of the Churning (Angkor Wat southwestern corner pavilion S. 1, Banteay Samré), Lakshmi is depicted to the left at the base of the pole and over the tortoise, and Ucchaihshravas to the right. Here, instead, on the right is sketched a dragon cut in two, mirroring the fully sculpted animal on the left which occupies the space that should be reserved for Lakshmi. Even more surprising is the discovery of two outlined figures of a small horse and a tiny elephant over Vishnu's discus. Could it

be that the sculptors did these iconographic alterations due to some controversy over the ranking of the various products of the churning? The possibility that they were later additions cannot be ruled out.

Coedès (1911: 175) noticed that two snakes are depicted in this relief: one at the bottom of the ocean and the other acting as the rope for the churning. He deduced that the sculptors wanted to represent the moment before the Churning when Vasuki was resting at the bottom of the ocean before being pulled out by the *devas* and *asuras* and used as the churning rope. At the centre of the relief Vishnu is also represented twice: first as Kurma supporting Mount Mandara and then as Vishnu *Caturbhuja* (with four arms) in the act of assisting the churning and – at the same time – attempting to balance Mount Mandara. He seems to be suspended in the air in front of Mount Mandara. His left leg is not fully sculpted and below it is a blank area where the products of the churning were to be sculpted, including probably the jar of the *amrita*.

The tortoise is an important figure in Hindu mythology as it is the embodiment of creative power. In Agnicayana rituals the tortoise is placed in the lowest of the altar's five layers (Dange 1997: 246). In general, it is a common feature of Hindu temples where sometimes it is represented simply as a hexagonal figure. It is placed at the centre of the building, or in front of the main shrine of the god, to remind the faithful of its pivotal position in the Churning. In some Balinese temples the whole structure rests on the design of a tortoise, from which the head, four legs and a small tail appear to be poking out. It is a well known fact that in Cambodia, small tortoises cast in metal are often found in the foundation stone of the temple, amongst other objects constituting the 'treasure', and placed in a well dug at the centre of the temple's foundations (Pottier 1997: 17).

The parallelism between the myth of the Churning of the Ocean of Milk and that of the 'Birth of Brahma' from Vishnu's umbilicus while he rests on Ananta has been pointed out by several authors and summarised by Kamaleswar Bhattacharya (1957: VI, 1957: 211). In the Churning, Vishnu as Kurma supporting Mount Mandara corresponds to Vishnu reclining on Ananta in the Cosmic Ocean sustaining Brahma on the lotus. Mount Mandara as the churn-

Fig. 38 Hanuman or Sugriva.

ing pole can be correlated with the lotus stem arising from Vishnu's navel to support Brahma. Since both Mandara/Meru and the lotus are symbolic of the centre of the Universe, in both cases we are dealing with the quintessence of the myth of Creation.

Helene Legendre-De Koninck (1992: 47), has stressed that in the present relief of the Churning, the 92 *asuras* have a numerical advantage over the 88 *deva*, and that the general pulling movement seems to be in favour of the *asuras*. This imbalance between the two factions seems to indicate that the *asuras* are on the verge of gaining possession of the *amrita*, threatening to worsen the universal crisis already in place. This requires a new restoration of the order, and the sacrificial incarnation of a god, in a continuous process of creation. Thus the reading of the relief in the context of a sacrificial process is introduced. The panel's three registers are equivalent to three visual layers, of which the lower, filled with animals and vegetal elements, would function as the substitute of the victim. The main, middle register, with the Churning,

has Vishnu at its centre as the officiant, sacrificer and sacrificed (he had to incarnate on earth). Vasuki is the evident sacrificial victim. The highest register depicts the newly created *apsaras* rejoicing in an ideal new order. Mount Meru/Mandara, the cosmic mountain, is the sacrificial post, uniting the three worlds. Kurma, who has provided stability to the process of creation, is placed at the base of the sacrificial site, as in Hindu altars.

Finally, Mannikka (1996: 43) has called attention to commentaries by authors who maintain that the Churning of the Ocean of Milk was symbolically enacted by the Khmer as a tug-of-war exploit during special ceremonies such as the coronation of a king. The latter was symbolic of the reinstallation of Indra as Lord of the Heavens and King of the Gods afterhaving lost this status by killing Vritra who was regarded as a brahmin. To expiate his murder he had to undergo a long period of penance which called for his participation in the Churning. He was eventually re-instated after the battle for the possession of the *amrita*.

FIG. 39 A *deva* on his elephant.

FIG. 40 An *asura* on his chariot, pulled by a mythological animal.

Following on from the Churning of the Ocean of Milk is the relief of a mythic battle extending 51.45 metres along the northern wing of the eastern gallery. All the participants of this conflict have a demonic aspect, ride animals and wear the same helmet with the crest characteristic of the *asuras* or the *davanas* (giants who made war against the gods). They are displayed symmetrically around the central figure of Vishnu on Garuda, whom they are obviously attacking, in three and four pseudo-registers.

There are 15 generals riding elephants (Fig. 39) surrounded by a variety of parasols, banners and flywhisks. The generals are slightly larger than their soldiers, but do not have sufficient iconographic characteristics to allow for individual identification (Fig. 40). The howdahs are different from those seen in the relief of the Historic Procession, having a more slender structure. Also the chariots of the leaders of lower rank (28 in total) have wheels with fewer, but thicker spikes. These chariots are pulled mainly by horses although strange lions (or chimera?) are not infrequent; in one case, it is a deer-like creature with very long antlers. Out of the 15 elephants depicted in the relief, five have lost their passengers and mahouts. The pachyderms are shown converging at the centre of the panel at a marching pace or at a run. Some are falling wounded on the ground, others thrusting their heads back or having been manhandled by Garuda. One of these beasts is holding a soldier with his tusk (as in a relief in the central tower of Phnom Rung, Thailand). A curious detail is provided by four soldiers each riding a large running bird that seems to be a cross between a goose and an ostrich (Fig. 42). Altogether, the army seems to be well organised, calmly determined to eliminate the heroes. The little action that is depicted takes place at the very centre of the panel, around the figures of Vishnu/Krishna and Garuda.

Vishnu/Krishna is depicted standing on the shoulders of Garuda, fighting alone against these hordes of *asuras* that are attacking him from both sides (Fig. 41). He appears in the four-armed *Caturbhuja* form of Vishnu, the upper hands holding the discus and the conch, while the two in front hold bows and arrows, the arms of the warrior of high rank. While Vishnu/Krishna's face is turned to his right, Garuda looks to his left, each keeping an eye on one half of the attacking army. Garuda holds one elephant by the tail and grabs another by the rear leg; with his talons he has crushed the lions of a chariot and the horses of another. Thanks to his strength in disposing of the elephants of the *asuras'* generals, and to Vishnu's courage, the god's victory is assured.

Around the image of Vishnu/Krishna are four *danavas* generals thrown down from their elephants and killed. They may be the ones mentioned in the extract below of the *Harivamsa* (CXXII) whom Krishna overcomes before storming the city of Pragjyotisha, namely Muru, Nisunda, Hayagriva and Pancanada.

The asura *king Naraka is hiding in the city of Pragjyotisha after having stolen Aditi's* [9] *earrings produced by the Churning of the Ocean of Milk, and given to her by Indra. The city was protected by nooses with razor-sharp edges installed by the great demon Mura. On hearing Krishna's army approaching, Mura arises from the waters and rushes towards Krishna but he is killed by the god's chakra. The same divine tool is used by Krishna to decapitate Naraka. Thereafter, the god enters Naraka's personal apartments and releases 16,001 ladies who had been imprisoned by Naraka. Krishna marries all of them, uproots with his arms Mount Maniparvata where they are kept, places it on Garuda and returns to Dvaraka. Following this, Krishna goes to heaven with the famous earrings and gives them back to Aditi.*

Several other possible battles could explain the one sculpted here, particularly that which Vishnu has to engage in to recover the *amrita* stolen by the *asuras* after the Churning, narrated in the *Matsya Purana* as well as in the *Ramayana* (Book I, 45).

The emergence of the *amrita* amongst the products of the Churning of the Ocean of Milk caused great disarray since the sons of Aditi fought with those of Diti for its possession, and the *asuras* allied themselves with the *rakshasas* causing terror in the Three Worlds. Vishnu had to intervene and take, by the magic of Maya, the semblance of a graceful girl, Mohini, who used her charm and sensuality to trick the *asuras* and quickly recovered the *amrita*. It was through deception and not war that Vishnu concluded the event.

Both interpretations of the relief – as a depiction of the battle for recovering Aditi's earrings or the stolen *amrita* – are a logical sequel to the one of the Churning of the previous panel. In the case of the Churning, this relief would represent a generic battle that the gods, under the leadership of Vishnu, had to sustain against the *asuras* furious for not having been given any *amrita*. It is possible that the Khmers avoided representing Vishnu in the final act of recovery of the elixir, when he took the appearance of a charming beautiful woman; furthermore they may have preferred not to allude to Vishnu regaining the *amrita* not through a battle, but an act of deception and trickery.

The date of the reliefs of the northeast quadrant

Stylistically, this relief is the most 'crudely' sculpted of those of the 3rd enclosure galleries. Some of the large personages look like flat silhouettes stuck on the wall. In many instances groups of soldiers of identical shape, size and attitude are displayed marching close together, replicated coarsely overlapping each other, as if the sculptors wanted to save time and labour. At the base of this relief and of the succeeding one (LP. 6), there are small Sanskrit inscriptions engraved in a writing style very different from that of the small inscriptions elsewhere in this system of reliefs (*see LP. 2 and LP. 3*). They are closer to those sculpted on the pillars of the cruciform cloister and of the main shrine. Aymonier attempted to translate them in 1904 without great success. However, in 1962, Coedès was able to decipher them on the basis of new 'rubbings' he had taken of them:

1 – The inscription on the relief of Krishna's victory over the *asura* Bana, (LP. 6) reads approximately: 'His Majesty Mahavishnuloka did not have two panels completed; when His Majesty Brah Rajaonkara Paramarajadhiraja Ramadhipati Pramacakravartiraja became king, he gave the order to Brah Mahidhara of the royal artisans, to sculpt on the panels a story, in the *shaka* year of the 8th [decade], year of the Horse, Wednesday, full moon of Bhadapada'.

2 – The second inscription, written along the base of the relief under consideration (LP. 5), is in an even worse state of preservation. Coedès, though, was able to decipher the following: 'His Majesty Mahavishnuloka did not have two panels completed; when His Majesty Brah Rajaonkara Paramarajadhiraja Paramapavitra became king, he had a story sculpted. An effort was made to complete in 1485 *shaka*, the year of the Pig, full moon of Phalguna, Sunday. The two galleries and balusters were completed as in the past'.

The first inscription contains a date (not including the year) when the order was given to initiate the works of these two reliefs, while the second inscription gives the year when the panels were finished. The latter corresponds to Sunday 27th February 1564 AD and – as a consequence – the first inscription's complete date was determined to be Wednesday 8th September 1546. The time span thus indicated falls within the reign of King Ang Chan who ruled over Cambodia from 1516 to 1566. Although Ang Chan's capital was at Lovek,

FIG. 41 Garuda carrying Vishnu on his shoulders.

FIG. 42 Soldiers riding strange birds.

it seems that, in 1540, Ang Chan was in the region of the former capital of Angkor to fight a Siamese invasion. Once having repelled them, he (and his son Paramaraja?) decided to engage in major restoration works at Angkor Wat, considered at the time as a national sanctuary. The main objective was the sculpting of the panels in the galleries of the northeastern quadrant that had been left uncarved but probably were covered with the original sketches. The works started in 1546 were completed after 18 years, in 1564.

Some scholars[10] have suggested that the sculptors might have executed them by following these original XII century drawings, and recently discovered ink sketches on the walls of the 2nd enclosure's northwestern pavilion support this hypothesis (Roveda, 2001). In this case, the choice of subjects for and the general composition of the reliefs would have been XII century choices, and thereby these two reliefs can be seen as being within the original narrative programme of the monument's creators. However, the XVI century sculptors may have introduced some iconographical modifications and possibly increased the number of elephants to be depicted in the relief, reflecting the practice of warfare at that time.

FIG. 43 Krishna depicted as Vishnu on Garuda, flanked by Pradyumna and Balarama.

Around the corner, in the enclosure's northern gallery is the second of the XVI-century reliefs, which extends 66.03 metres in length. The story is divided in three and four pseudo-registers rhythmically interrupted by gigantic figures of the protagonists, sometimes extending the full height of the relief at each stage of their action. All four registers depict the infantry and the commanders of the armies of Krishna and Bana marching towards each other, from the east and from the west, respectively. However, the lowest pseudo-register also contains a great quantity of the fallen, and perhaps the largest number of severed heads ever represented in any relief. This exceptional number of severed heads could be related to an exaggeration of the efficiency and magic powers of Krishna's discus, the 'Sudarshana' that Vishvakarma made with fragments of the sun's rays. In the text Krishna uses it to overpower Bana by cutting off his arms. Perhaps the sculptors imagined that it was used also against the army of *asuras*, resulting in a massive decapitation.

The army of the *devas*, Krishna's friends and allies, is depicted moving from left to right, in the same direction as his image. Scattered throughout, riding harnessed horses, are the generals sculpted the same size as the soldiers, and like them they are generic in nature, presenting no further traits that would aid a more specific identification. The army of the *asura* Bana marching in the opposite direction, has several commanders riding in war chariots or on mythical animals such as lions with dragon/*makara*'s heads (?chimera), gigantic tigers and *nagas* (similar to those depicted in the previous relief). There are only seven elephants in the army, and they are comparatively small in scale; their howdahs are quite elaborate and of different design to those seen in the previous panel. The war chariots have wheels with many spikes, but are undecorated. In total contrast with the previous relief, here the signs of rank such as parasols, fans and banners are restricted to Krishna, including the new design of treble parasols with fringes.

The *asura* Bana, with 1,000 arms, is depicted standing on a large chariot pulled by two colossal lion-dragons, and in which two personages seem to be squatting (Fig. 44). Only their heads, of recognisable Chinese cast, are visible. One seems to hold a lotus flower. Another interesting element of this relief is the presence of several military orchestras with players of suspended gongs, trumpets, double drums, cymbals, conches and the Khmer circular sets of gongs (*khong*).

The relief begins at the eastern end with the first image of Garuda carrying Krishna on his shoulders (Fig. 43) amidst the great army of *devas*, identifiable as such by their conical *mukuta*. They march in battle array, led by musicians. Krishna is here depicted as Vishnu with many arms and holding the following attributes: arrow, javelin, discus (*chakra*), conch, club, thunderbolt, bow and shield. It is impossible to count the number of his faces, but they probably total 15, although the texts say there 1,000 are. His brother Balarama and possibly his son Pradyumna, both standing on the wings of Garuda, accompany him. Krishna does not appear again on Garuda until he finds himself face-to-face with Bana.

The next large image is of Garuda (Fig. 45) confronting the wall of flames created by Agni. On the other side of the flames, Agni is represented as a giant with six heads and four arms riding his traditional Khmer mount, the rhinoceros (Fig. 46). The ensuing furious melee related in the text is well illustrated by the soldiers locked together in hand-to-hand combat. The conclusion of the story is represented at the western end of the relief with the meeting of Krishna and Shiva and their conversation about Bana (Fig. 53). Shiva has a distinct Chinese aspect, squatting on a high pedestal (probably symbolic of his superiority to Krishna) and receiving the respects of Krishna, winner of the battle against Bana, kneeling in front of him, on a lower pedestal, his hands joined at his chest.

The battle between Bana and Krishna is related in several texts, namely the *Harivamsa* (CLXXV), *Vishnu Purana* (V, 33), *Bhagavata Purana* (X, 63) and *Shiva Purana* (*Rudrasamhita*, Section 5, 53-55). According to the latter:

When Usha, the daughter of Bana, falls in love with Aniruddha [son of Pradyumna and grandson of Krishna] she has him brought to her by magic arts. Bana [called also Kumbhanda] was a demon with 1,000 arms, the eldest son of Bali, friend of Shiva and enemy of Vishnu. Bana discovers his daughter's dalliance and, while trying to escape, Aniruddha is captured by Bana's magic arrows which transform themselves into snakes (nagapada), binding him prisoner. On hearing that Bana holds Aniruddha captive, Krishna organises a great army and, mounted on Garuda, marches towards Bana's capital Shonitapura (chapter 54). With him are his brother Balarama, his sons Pradyumna [from Rukmini], Bhadra and Samba [perhaps sons of Krishna and Jambavati]. The allies include Nanda [the cowherd who raised Krishna], Upananda [Nanda's brother], Yuyudhama [or Satyaki, Krishna's kinsman and charioteer] and many others. On Bana's side are Shiva [Rudra] and his son Karttikeya [Skanda] and the Pramathas [demi-gods or demons of Shiva], all riding the bull Nandin.

When Krishna and his army arrive at Shonitapura's doors, they are halted by a wall of fire. However, according to the Harivamsa, Garuda extinguishes it with water taken from the Ganges which he transforms into rain. A fierce and horrifying battle follows, during which many of the heroes are wounded. Brahma and the gods, the sages and the apsaras witness the event from the sky. The fight continues, with Agni, Yama, Varuna, Karttikeya and other divine and semi-divine personages distinguishing themselves by their heroism.

Initially, Bana's army is scattered and he has to use special, powerful arrows to counter-attack Krishna. The latter approaches Shiva to explain why he has come to Shonitapura, to cut off the hands of Bana. Shiva understands Krishna's mission and allows him to pursue his task on the condition, however, that he [Shiva] be made numb by a magic arrow of Krishna so as not to see the latter mutilating Bana. Krishna confronts Bana in a terrible exchange of 'missiles', but he has to resort to his chakra to overpower Bana and cut off several of his arms, leaving him with only four. When Krishna is on the verge of also cutting off his head, Shiva intervenes claiming he had granted Bana the boon that he 'will be cured of his haughtiness' after his arms had been cut off. Shiva orders Bana to leave the battlefield and go back to his people. The victorious Krishna returns jubilant to Dvaraka with Aniruddha and Usha.

The composition's complexity requires careful analysis of all elements, not least because it was sculpted in the XVI century to a XII century design. There follows a list of some unusual elements:

Fig. 44 The asura Bana.

Fig. 45 Garuda confronting Agni's fire.

Fig. 46 Agni on his rhinoceros.

Fig. 47 The fourth appearance of Krishna on Garuda.

Fig. 48 The fifth appearance of Krishna on Garuda.

Fig 49 The second appearance of Krishna on Garuda.

Fig. 50 The sixth appearance of Krishna on Garuda.

Fig. 51 The third appearance of Krishna on Garuda.

FIG. 52 Balarama fighting on the ground.

1. Krishna appears seven times in this long panel; six times standing on Garuda and once kneeling in front of Shiva (Figs. 43, 47, 48, 49, 50, 51). He is depicted with eight arms and 15 visible heads, except in his third image from the left, where he is shown having four arms and a single head. We do not know what these differences signified to the Khmers. In five of his depictions mounted on Garuda, Krishna is accompanied by Balarama and Pradyumna on Garuda's wings. The iconography of his image kneeling in front of Shiva is quite extraordinary. Two of his hands are joined in the praying *anjali mudra*; one of his right hands holds a bow and the other two a sword; three of his left hands hold a small branch. The meaning of these attributes and of their arrangement is unknown. Madeleine Giteau has observed that no similar aspects of Krishna are described in any text, even in some late Thai texts (*Tamra Deva Rupa*). The repetition of the figure of Krishna on Garuda may serve to create a visual rhythm that facilitates the reading of this chaotic composition.

2. Garuda's human half is confined to his torso and arms, the latter attached to the wings. His lower body and the head are those of a bird, but he does have almost human ears. The tiara and the rich jewellery he is wearing show the influence of post-Angkorean design, perhaps Siamese.

3. Agni is represented on a rhinoceros, and with six faces arranged on two levels, which is meant to suggest eight faces if the deity were to be seen in the round. His attributes are, to the right, the sword and the bow, and to the left a toothed disc and an arrow. In Hindu iconography, Agni is usually depicted with two heads and sometimes four arms riding a goat. According to the *Agni Purana*, his attributes are 'the rosary, a jar of water, the javelin, and what looks like a garland of flames'. As Francois Martini has noticed (1950), the depiction of Agni riding his rhinoceros and having up to eight heads is unique to Khmer art. As a god of fire, in this relief he functions as the protector of Bana's city.

4. In the five instances in which Balarama and Pradyumna flank Krishna on Garuda's wings, it is impossible to distinguish who is who. The one to the left of the viewer is sometimes holding a bow and arrow, sometimes a sword or a javelin. The one to the right usually holds javelins/spears or swords; on one occasion (the 6th from the right) this figure carries a *phkak*. As persons related to Krishna, they both are of royal status, as confirmed by the crown they wear. There is little evidence to support Coedès' identification of Balarama fighting alone (1932: 408; Fig. 52) to the right of the second depiction of Krishna on Garuda.

FIG. 53 Krishna paying respect to Shiva.

5. Bana. This terrible *asura* is depicted with 24 arms and one head (Fig. 44), although as a descendant of Bali, he should have multiple heads. In each hand he holds a magical spear or javelin; the lions pulling his war chariot conform to traditional Khmer iconography. Bana's father was the infamous Bali who dared to challenge Vishnu who had to manifest as the Dwarf in order to take over with three steps Bali's three worlds: the earth, the sky and the lower regions.

6. At the end of the relief, three figures are displayed seated between Krishna and Shiva (Fig. 53). One is Ganesha holding the *ankusha* (the crook used to give commands to elephants); the identification of the others is more tentative. The one close to Shiva seems to have multiple faces and holds a parasol. He could be Brahma with his four heads. The figure close to Krishna holds an instrument like an axe with a long handle. Since he is sitting on the same throne with Ganesha, he could be his brother Karttikeya (Skanda). Alternatively he may be the ubiquitous Vishvakarma, the divine architect of the gods, always depicted holding an axe.

7. Shiva is represented as an ascetic sitting on Mount Kailasa (Fig. 53). He has a plump body and a round face with a sparse beard in the Chinese fashion.

Dressed in soft drapery, covered by scarves and jewellery, only his hairstyle in the manner of a *rishi* attests to his ascetic state. The halo around his head reveals a Siamese influence. In his right hand, he holds a *trisula* (trident) with much more tapering points than the ones of the XII century. His left hand seems to caress his long beard. Such a depiction of Shiva has no precedent in Khmer sculpture, and seems heavily influenced by Chinese imagery. To the right of Shiva are nine crowned female (or possibly male) figures in the act of adoration, kneeling on the same pedestal.

8. Further to the right of Shiva are eight or nine female figures with diadems, probably palace women, possibly headed by Parvati – the Mahakshatriyani – carrying royal objects. Amongst these, Madeleine Giteau (1975: 93) has recognised the oldest representations of a betel set in Southeast Asia, with a container for the lime, three boxes, and, vertically placed in a small vase, the leaves of the presumed betel.

9. The setting of Mount Kailasa is depicted by curved imbrications replacing the lozenges symbolising rocky mountains of the XII century. The sacred mountain is full of caves inhabited by meditating and conversing hermits, and where also some *kinnaris* live – popular celestial creatures of the XVI

century. Indeed the overall XVI century conception of Mount Kailasa is radically different from that of the XII century (*see S. 7 and S. 11*).

Because this relief was sculpted in the XVI century, it raises questions on the style of representation. The most intriguing concerns the so-called Chinese influence. In this relief, as in the previous one, the execution of the figures is, besides being stylistically different, of inferior quality to the rest of the reliefs in the enclosure. Goloubew (1924: 513) went so far as to attribute the sculpting to Chinese artisans on the basis of the presence of some iconographic elements he believed to be inspired from Chinese art, and in particular the Chinese appearance of Shiva and some of his ascetics. Moreover the form of the small clouds is reminiscent of Chinese images of clouds, and the fire of Agni, is also outside the Khmer tradition.

Jean Boisselier (1962: 244) was of the opinion that, rather than being a direct Chinese influence, it instead came from the art of Siamese Ayutthaya of the XV century, which in turn had been influenced by Chinese art. In support of this would be the way horses are harnessed; the circular set of gongs appearing in the orchestra; the *mukuta* with side-wings; men depicted with trousers under the *sampot*, and belts with diverging curved tails. Women have scarves obliquely drapped across their chests. Even more convincing are the presence, in the relief narrating the story of Krishna and Bana, of typically Siamese *kinnaris*, and of parasols with fringes. Boisselier also believed that – on stylistic grounds – almost all the upper part of the preceding relief of the 'Victory of Vishnu over the *Asuras*', had been completed in the XII century, with merely details added in the XVI century. Moreover, the sculpting of Garuda in LP. 5 was in the best of the Angkor Wat tradition. Boisselier attributed the persistence of Hindu iconography at Angkor in the XVI century, to the use of manuals of the type of the Thai *Tamra Deva Rupa* depicting Hindu divinities. However, the presumed use of these manuals does not explain the realisation of large compositions that required a general visual scheme. Despite some differences, concluded Boisselier, the reliefs of the XVI century remained very close to those of the XII in their iconography, composition and sense of movement. He believed it was possible they defined a new style, and went so far as to call it the 'style of Ang Chan'. This style would also be manifested in the statuary and some reliefs from Angkor Thom and the province.

In 1975, Madeleine Giteau compared the stylistic and iconographic variations and discrepancies of these two late reliefs with the reliefs of the XII century. In her opinion, the third image of Krishna in the Victory of Krishna over the *asura* Bana is in the best tradition of the Angkor Wat style, and the figure of Agni must have been sculpted following drawings of the XII century. In agreement with Boisselier, she concluded that: "if the images are in the strict iconographic tradition of the XII and XIII centuries, it is perhaps because the artists worked on a canvas sketched in the XII century, canvas which already gave to the images the essential lines of their contours."

LP. 7 - The Battle between the *Devas* and the *Asuras*

The western wing of the northern gallery is given over to a great battle between the *devas* and *asuras*, extending for 93.60 metres. In the upper part of the composition are 21 of the greatest deities of the Hindu pantheon, shown in heroic posture and size, riding their mounts. As they are depicted in battle, however, they do not all have their usual attributes which would allow for their individual identification. They are all armed with bows and arrows or javelins, and the symbols of their status are indicated by a variety of parasols, fans and banners, as in the Historic Procession (LP. 2, Fig. 54). The standards carried by the soldiers of the *devas* are the statuettes of Hanuman, Garuda and Vishnu, while Indra displays Airavata. As standards, the *asuras* have the statuette of a small *rakshasa* with splayed running legs. Each member of the *devas'* infantry is involved

in a ferocious attack, mostly hand-to-hand combat, with an *asura* from whom he differs only by the shape of the helmet. A military orchestra (to the left, below the image of Varuna) plays drums and a large gong. Close to Kalanemi, two *asuras* carry a very large and dec rated bell.

Although there are many occasions when the *devas* battle with *asuras*, it is possible that this relief refers to the confrontation narrated in chapter 9 of the *Vamana Purana*.

When the asura *Prahlada, a devotee of Vishnu, refuses to govern the kingdom of the* asuras, *the task is then given to the* asura *Andhaka who is considered blind despite his 2,000 eyes in his 1,000 heads. The gods disapprove of this and a fierce battle follows between them and the* asuras: *Indra confronts Andhaka, Yama confronts*

FIG. 54 *Devas* and *asuras* in the midst of battle.

Prahlada, Varuna confronts Virochana, Agni confronts Maya, Kubera confronts Jambha and Vayu confronts the demon Suchara.

Another story, also taken from the *Vamana Purana* (47-48; in Dimmitt & Van Buitenen 1978: 299), presents a different version of this battle.

Bali, originally a virtuous Daitya king, had acquired such tremendous power through devotion and penance that he dared to challenge the gods. He was the son of the powerful demon king Virochana and grandson of Hiranyakasipu. When he is told that the gods have annihilated his family, he decides to go to war against them. The ferocious demon general Maya heads the troops, while Bali marches in their midst with Bana, and the terrible demon Kalanemi brings up the rear. Vama is on the left flank and Taraka the right. The army of millions of asuras *(both* Danavas *and* Daityas*) attacks the gods and after a gruelling fight win the battle. Indra and the other gods flee to Brahmaloka. With his sons, brother and relatives, Bali becomes the ruler of heaven. He takes on the role of Indra (Sakra), Bana that of Yama, Maya that of Varuna, Rahu that of Soma, Prahlada that of Fire, Svarbhanu that of Surya, and the other* asuras *those of the various other* deva. *To restore order in the Three Worlds, Vishnu incarnates as the dwarf (Vamana) and restrains Bali with the trick of the three steps (Vishnu Trivikrama).*

The first version of the story emphasises the supremacy of Vaishnavism because Prahlada, a devotee of Vishnu, refuses to govern the kingdom of the devilish *asuras*. Andhaka who does so in his place, is punished by Vishnu. In the second version, the apparent defeat of Vishnu's army exemplifies the fact that the gods do not always have the upper hand and often are subjected to humiliation. However, an important theme of Hindu mythology is that only when the powers of evil are allowed to dominate the powers of good, and chaos is imminent, can the value of the good be realised.

Of the twelve *deva* in the upper register, the following list contains possible identifications:

1. Ketu is possibly one of the *devas* riding a chariot pulled by a lion.

2. Kubera is possibly in the chariot pulled by his mount, the horse.

3. Nirrti is shown on the shoulders of a *rakshasa* (or *yaksha*) (Fig. 57).

4. Agni is in a chariot pulled by rhinoceros (Fig. 60).

5. Skanda, with six faces and ten arms, stands on his mount, the peacock (Fig. 59).

6. Indra on Airavata, his elephant, who wears a crown and holds an enemy in his four tusks (Fig. 61). The howdah is almost identical to the one bearing Suryavarman II in the relief of the Historic Procession, reinforcing the analogy between the two kings.

7. Vishnu/Krishna is depicted in a prominent central position on Garuda (Fig. 62).

8. Kalanemi/Bana, with many heads (seven visible) and arms (Fig. 58).

9. Yama is in a chariot harnessed to his mounts, the buffaloes (Fig. 56).

10. Shiva is in a chariot pulled by two bulls with humps, similar to his mount Nandin (Fig. 64).

11. Varuna stands on a goose (*hamsa*), his usual mount in Khmer iconography. If, instead, this divinity is interpreted as Brahma, then Varuna may have a *naga* as his mount (Mannikka 1966: Table 8; see 12 below).

12. Surya is in a chariot drawn by four horses and surrounded by the solar disc; his charioteer is Aruna (half-brother of Garuda) (Fig. 63).

13. A deity riding a five-headed *naga* that is harnessed like a horse with a bridle held by a driver (Fig. 65). This deity is difficult to recognise because two other figures in the relief are on chariots pulled by identical *naga* (Fig. 66). The one under consideration is the only one represented in the army of the *devas*. Coedès (1911: 185) suggested that it might be Varuna, the Lord of water and of whom all the *nagas* are subjects

(*Mahabharata*, 2.9). However, in Khmer iconography this god is generally depicted riding a goose; moreover Varuna is already represented in the relief, before Surya. Of the other two *naga*-drawn chariots, the first carries the *asura* warrior facing Agni, and the second belongs to the *asura* opposing Indra – possibly one of his traditional enemies, such as Vala (or Pana) or Vritra.

The sequence in which the deities are displayed does not follow the presumed planetary sequence found in the relief of 'Invitation for Vishnu to descend' (N. 1), even if the relief is read from right to left as Mannikka proposes (1996: 190). However, it is generally accepted that in Khmer pictorial tradition, these deities and their mounts can be represented in a variety of combinations and sequences. Interestingly, the composition is not divided in two symmetric halves around the central motif, in this case Vishnu mounted on Garuda. Throughout the relief, the forces of the *devas* penetrate deep into the inimical ranks of the *asuras*, and vice-versa.

Fig. 55 A princely warrior.

FIG. 56 Yama and his buffaloes.

FIG. 57 Nirrti.

FIG. 58 The *asura* Kalanemi or Bana.

Fig. 59 Skanda on his peacock.

FIG. 60 Agni with his rhinoceros.

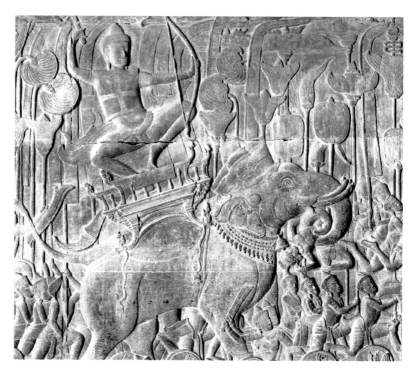

FIG. 61 Indra on Airavata.

Fig. 62 Vishnu/Krishna on Garuda.

Fig. 63 Surya on the solar disc.

Fig. 64 Shiva.

FIG. 65 Unidentified *deva* (possibly Varuna).

FIG. 66 Unidentified *deva*.

FIG. 67 Rama on Hanuman near Balarama and Vibhishana.

This final relief stretches for 51.25 metres along the northern wing of the western gallery. Unlike other battle scenes, it is not subdivided by any pseudo-registers and the primary figures of both armies (that of Rama and Ravana) barely emerge from the mass of fighting figures. Rama and his generals are all on foot, while Ravana and his *rakshasas* stand on ornate war chariots harnessed to horses or lions with dragons' heads (chimera?). Only one elephant is depicted, that of the *rakshasa* Mohadara.

With the exception of himself, Lakshmana and Vibhishana, Rama's army is completely made up of monkeys, their leaders distinguishable by their large size and small conical helmets. The masses of fighting monkeys appear to be the real protagonists of the scene. According to the text, they do not suffer heavy casualties because the wounded use a spell to neutralise the magic arrows of the *rakshasas*, and stand up again and resume fighting. For weapons the monkeys use stones or branches, but they are frequently shown using their sharp teeth and powerful arms and legs to tear apart their enemies. A few have secured weapons from the wounded or the dead *rakshasas*. The *rakshasas'* army is equipped with shields and armed with all sorts of maces, sabres, spears, javelins, clubs and the *phkak*.

It is difficult to pick out from this seething background the individual fighters Coedès believed to be depicted in the relief (1911: 184). Amongst Ravana's army, the commanders lack any personal features, as do the animals pulling their chariots, unlike those described in Valmiki's *Ramayana* (chapters 44-58). Khmer artists seem to have generalised the animals simply into horses or lion/dragons (chimeras). Indeed, the latter are not even mentioned in the text, and their presence in this – as in the other reliefs of this enclosure – is more likely due to local tradition (or perhaps to the use of a local version of the *Ramayana* unknown to us).

FIG. 68 Ravana on his chariot pulled by lion/dragons.

FIG. 69 The monkey Nila killing Prahasta.

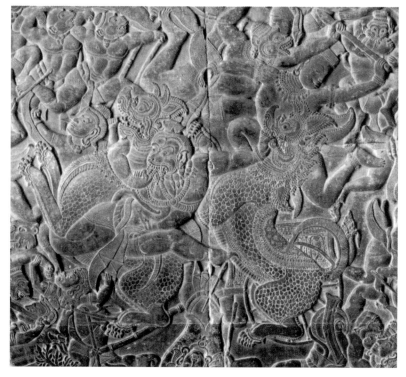

FIG. 70 Angada assaulting Vajradamshtra.

Starting at the relief's northern end, the first important recognisable scene is of Rama standing on Hanuman's shoulders in the middle of a shower of arrows. Behind him is his brother Lakshmana and the renegade prince Vibhishana recognisable by his *rakshasa*'s plumed helmet (Fig. 67). They stand in a static noble pose, in contrast to the surrounding excitement. Not far from them is Ravana with ten heads, 20 arms and four legs. His many arms hold an assortment of weapons, arrows, swords, axes, one *phkak* and two bows (Fig. 68). He is standing firmly on his beautifully decorated chariot, pulled by monsters with the massive heads of lions/dragons. Hanuman and Sugriva are represented several times in the relief. In the first instance, a crowned monkey strikes directly at Ravana's multiple heads, and could be either Hanuman or Sugriva, as described in the initial attacks against the monster (*Ramayana*, chapter 59). The heroic monkey looks of diminutive size when compared to the colossal king of the *rakshasas* (Coedès 1932: plate No. 483). In between Rama and Ravana two dramatic scenes are illustrated: the one in which the monkey general Nila kills Prahasta (Fig. 69) and the scene in which Angada, Valin's son, is hurling himself at the colossal elephant of Mahodara (chapter 70), toppling it and causing Mahodara's death (Fig. 71). To the right, Angada is shown biting the horse of Narantaka (Fig. 70); at the same time, another monkey, having uprooted a tree, hits Mahodara on the head. Proceeding further to the right of Ravana Angada assaults the *rakshasa* Vajradamshtra and his lions followed by Hanuman attacking the *rakshasa* Nikumbha (Fig. 73) while another strong monkey topples his horse. Further to the right, a crowned Sugriva is depicted (Fig. 74) wrenching the arrow from the bow of Kumbha before killing him.

There are too many iconographical inconsistencies to confirm Coedès's identification of Nila grabbing and putting on his shoulders the body of the giant *rakshasa* Prahasta (Coedès 1932: plate No. 481). Also questionable is the scene (to the right of Ravana) of Angada wrestling with Vajradamshtra who menaces him with a spear while another ferocious monkey is slashing at his chariot-pulling lions. Doubtful too is the presence of Angada depicted again in a duel with the *rakshasa* Narantaka, where he first kills the horses. The same low-conical

shaped helmet is worn by other monkeys, and is not exclusive to him, as Coedès believed.

The *Ramayana*'s Battle of Lanka is one of the most savage of Hindu epic literature. It was a subject dear to Khmer sculptors, perhaps because it provided the opportunity to visually develop several sub-plots which demonstrate the dynamism of the heroes of the *Ramayana*. Moreover, the depiction of monkeys allowed the use of emotional representation otherwise unusual in Khmer art, such as grimaces and attitudes of savagery and aggressiveness unsuitable to human warriors and *kshatriya*. The narration of this battle occupies more than half of the *Yuddha Kanda* (6th book of the *Ramayana*), from the first confrontation of Sugriva with Ravana (chapter 40) to the death of Ravana (chapter 110). The most extensive and significant combats of Rama and Lakshmana against Ravana, his son Indrajit and his brother Kumbhakarna are intercalated with comparatively minor fights among the elite of both armies. Rama's allies include Hanuman, Sugriva, Angada and the generals Nila, Rishabha,

FIG. 71 Angada killing Mahodara.

FIG. 72 Angada fighting Narantaka.

Sushena and Jumbavan in addition to many others. All of Ravana's sons – Trishira, Atikaya, Narantaka and Devantaka – reinforce the *rakshasas'* lines, together with Kumbhakarna's sons Kumbha and Nikumbha and several leaders like Mahodara and Matta.

Although the counting of important personages within the intricate mêlée of the Battle of Lanka relief is an arduous task, one can detect the probable presence of 19 *rakshasas* generals, excluding Ravana. Since each of these should be confronting a hero from Rama's army, one may be tempted to confirm a total number of 19 pairs of combatants in the relief as Mannikka has proposed (1996: 196), excluding also Rama on Hanuman's shoulders and Rama and Lakshmana. However, both Hanuman and Sugriva appear several times, accounting for a large number of heroic monkey figures, and thus complicating and perhaps destroying this theory.

Narrative programme of the panels

As mentioned at the beginning of this chapter, although much has been written about the viewing order of these eight panels, we have at present so little evidence of the customs followed by the Khmers that any such theories must remain exactly that. The most critical point on which these theories usually hinge is whether or not XII-century Khmer practice was analogous to that practised in India. In Hindu tradition, processions honouring the deity are an important part of the temple's activity, and the movement of worshippers takes place, in general, in the most open and public part of the temple. Alternatively, it may proceed with a circumambulation following a clock-wise direction, the *pradakshina*. For funerary rites, even in modern times, the opposite direction (counter-clockwise) is followed, the *prasavaya*. It is possible, however, that due to different religious traditions, the Khmers did not follow Indian rules.

With regard to Angkor Wat, we do not know if, at the time when the temple was in use, the galleries of the 3rd enclosure were even accessible to the public, or if they were restricted to the initiated and the elite. Architectural features like the very high steps which devide the various galleries, the massive wooden doors which divide them from the corner and intermediate pavilions, and the numerous statues that were possibly once spread throughout the galleries would have made a processional sequence arduous, if not impossible.

Another problem is that the temple was not finished when Suryavarman II died. Out of the eight large sculptural panels, only five were completed – as noted 'The Churning of the Ocean of Milk' had several details unfinished. Furthermore, the inscriptions naming the monarch in the Historic Procession use his posthumous title 'Paramavishnu-loka'. The general conclusion has been that either the king was already dead when the panel was sculpted or the inscription was added later.

To further complicate the issue, one has to consider that the two panels of the northeastern quadrant were sculpted in the XVI century. Although the reason for their creation is fairly easy to grasp – being part of King Ang Chan I's (and probably his son's) restoration of the 'national' monuments of Angkor after almost two centuries of neglect (Coedès 1962: 235) –, the reason why they were originally left unsculpted is more elusive. What is known is that after Suryavarman II's death in 1150, the Khmer throne went through a thirty-year period of instability until the accession of Jayavarman VII in 1181. Not only were resources for this grand project greatly diminished, but also priorities of state

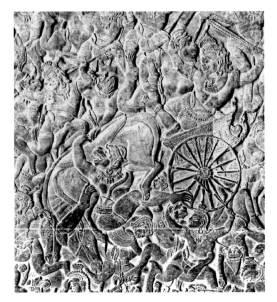

FIG. 73 Hanuman fighting Nikumbha.

FIG. 74 Sugriva killing Kumbha.

had shifted away from its completion. It was a Khmer belief that, after the king's death, the new king would gain more merit by building his own temple than completing that of his predecessor.

Despite these obstacles, many scholars have come up with interesting theories concerning the Large Panels' narrative programme. Both Bosch (1933: 71) and Mannikka (1996) gave particular importance to the counter-clock-wise direction of viewing the reliefs. If for Bosch, Vishnu's reliefs followed a 'solar path' of dawn (rise to power), noon (apogee) and sunset (death), for Mannikka the cycle was more purely astronomical.

According to Bosch, the reading of the reliefs should start in the southeastern quadrant with 'The Churning of the Ocean of Milk' because it is the event when the jewel Kaustubha comes into the sun-king's (Vishnu's) possession allowing him to govern as the *chakravartin* (Universal Monarch). The Churning would then be a metaphor for the beginning of the rule of the Khmer king as an earthly *chakravartin*, and this first relief would represent 'dawn' within Bosch's 'solar path'. The path's 'noons' were the succeeding reliefs of battles (up to and including the Battle of Lanka), which elevated the wars of Suryavarman II against the Cham and Dai Viêt to the same level as these heroic conflicts. In Bosch's opinion, the Battle of

Kurukshetra represents the concluding event ('sunset') in the cycle of Suryavarman II. It is conceivable that the Khmer considered, as did the Javanese, this battle to signify the end of the sun-king (the king who is, for Bosch, a solar god), and therefore it was a sinister and unfortunate event. For this reason it was sculpted within the 'southern region' of the temple, that being the direction of Yama and the dead.

Bosch acknowledged that the last two panels of his cycle – the Historic Procession and Heavens and Hells – didn't really fit in with his 'solar path.' The Historic Procession seemed to be an actual military event, and the Heavens and Hells included neither an image of Vishnu nor of the king. To explain the Procession, Bosch argued that, since the posthumous title 'Paramavishnuloka' is inscribed under the king's images, the relief must therefore refer to an event in the kingdom of the dead. The procession is the solemn 'descent' march of the army, commanded by the deceased king, towards the last judgement represented in the next panel of Heavens and Hells. Bosch resolved the problem of the lack of images of the king or Vishnu by reasoning that while the sinners are placed in hell to expiate their transgressions, the 19 generals and ministers of the Historic Procession are shown being elevated to the heavens. The king himself *is* represented, not as 'Paramavishnuloka', but as Yama, the king of death.

As discussed earlier (p. 37), Yama's domain was the earth as well as the underworld, and as Suryavarman ruled his people in life, he would rule and judge them in their after life as well. Moreover, the *Mahabharata* (109.32, 35) provides a link between the image of Yama and Vishnu in its reference to the latter taking on Yama's duties during the Krita Yuga.

Bosch concluded that since the king was symbolically present as the heroic protagonist in all the reliefs, the cycle was therefore a complete one. It started with the Churning, continued with the dispersing of the demons of darkness and was followed by the great victory of the Battle of Lanka. It began to decline with the Battle of Kurukshetra, and reached its natural end in the kingdom of the dead, from where Suryavarman would re-emerge as Vishnu to be worshipped at the Vishnuloka in the central tower of Angkor Wat.

Mannikka (1996: 161) extrapolates the presence of the sun and the moon in the relief of the Churning in the southwestern corner pavilion (S. 1) to the narrative programme of the 3rd enclosure. In the former, Surya and Chandra, depicted inside a large disc on each side of the churning pivot, indicate a close connection with astronomical matters. On the day of the winter solstice (around December 22nd), the sun is at its southernmost position in the sky, moving gradually northward until the summer solstice (June 21st), after which it moves south again. This polar oscillation ranges between 49 and 43 degrees, and the moon oscillates laterally between north-south extremes along a celestial equator in an arc that can reach an average of 54 degrees. As they were in Indian astronomy, these numbers were venerated by Khmer astronomers. The pulling of the snake Vasuki involved in the Churning causes the sun and moon to move back and forth, north and south, each year covering an arc of at most 54 degrees every six months. In the 3rd enclosure's relief, the position of the pivot corresponds to that of the spring equinox. The 91 *asuras* [11] in the southern portion of the mural represent the 91 days from equinox to winter solstice, while the 88 *devas* in the northern portion represent the 88 days from equinox to summer solstice (in fact there are 88 *devas* aligned in the relief). The oversized northernmost *deva* holding Vasuki's tail, therefore, would represent the summer solstice day, and the southernmost oversized *asura* holding the head would correspond to the winter solstice day. Furthermore, the three oversized figures on each side of the pivot help divide the Churning scene into six segments representing the six months between December 22nd and June 21st (and vice versa). The period of the solstices is also expressed in terms of days: the total of 180 *devas* and *asuras,* plus three days symbolised by the churning pivot at the spring equinox centre of the relief, add up to the 183 days between solstices (182 if the *deva* on top of Mount Mandara is excluded). Both numbers are correct, depending on the year: 183 + 183 = 366 days – the leap year, 183 + 182 = 365 – the normal year. The scene is thus a calendar, a temporal cycle. Suryavarman II himself is like an equinox, but rather than being at the centre of time and space between solstices, he is at the centre of his realm, with the central sanctuary tower of the temple being the conceptual centre of the capital and the nation.

According to Mannikka, the special importance for the Khmers of the myth of the Churning is further emphasised by the calculations the architects of Angkor Wat made for the sun in its annual progression to illuminate different images within the reliefs (1996: 162). During the winter and summer solstice periods, clearly distinguishable shafts of light bracket each side of Mount Mandara and Vishnu at the centre. In effect, the two solstice shafts flank the Churning scene as they flank the centre of the Battle of Kurukshetra on the opposite side of the enclosure. Because the special shaft of light also illuminates the oversized *asura* closest to the central image of Vishnu in the Churning mural, Mannikka hypothesises that this must be another incarnation of Vishnu, his *asura* manifestation, instead of the identification of Ravana given by earlier authors. As a consequence, the corresponding oversized figure on the side of the *devas* with the head-dress of an *asura* must be the 'deva manifestation' of Vishnu. Mannikka extends her theories, of which only two are discussed here, to most of the other seven panels to complete an astronomical-cosmogonical cycle.

Bosch and Mannikka believed that through astronomy and the solar cycle it was possible to unravel an overall narrative programme symbolic of the life and deeds of the king in his earthly life. The reliefs, nevertheless, can perhaps be better understood individually as metaphors of sacred and profane concepts, of the assertion of the Vaishnava principle and of Khmer kingship. The Historic Procession thus becomes a metaphor for and acceptance of the supremacy of the king, and of the loyalty required of his ministers, generals and army. The Heavens and Hells relief that follows, if read in continuity of narrative, may therefore symbolise the righteousness of such loyalty, since his 19 ministers in the Historic Procession are likely the 19 personages comfortably on their way to Paradise. Like Yama, Suryavarman II could be the embodiment of righteousness (*dharma*) and the king of justice (*dharma-raja*). The meaning to the viewer, could also have been intended to be the acceptance of one's own karma and of being judged for earthly deeds by the king of the dead, Yama. In both instances, it is a king who demonstrates his rightful power, both in life and after death, highlighting the intimate association between secular and divine power. The myth that Vishnu had to replace Yama during the terrible times of the *Krita Yuga* (*Mahabharata*: 109.32, 35) would then allude to Suryavarman becoming the ruler of the underworld in times of strife, becoming the Khmer Yama. The same relief, however, also depicts the punishments or rewards to be expected by the layman, not only by the elite, thereby outlining the moral precepts by which all should live.

Helene Legendre De Koninck has proposed (in several short papers published from 1983 to 1996; see bibliography) an interesting hypothesis concerning the bas-reliefs of Angkor Wat. This hypothesis refers to the approach worked out by Madeleine Biardeau on sacrifice in ancient India and on the connections between the *Yuga* time cycle, the sacrificial battle and the royal dharma. The analogy between the battle of the *kshatriyas* and sacrifice, well known in Hindu mythology, is considered essential. In battle, as well as in sacrifice, chaos eventually generates order. As Legendre De Koninck reports: "Situations of imbalance particular to cosmic crisis concern the representatives of Good and Evil and are always consecutive to the usurpation of a fundamental Good due to the Evil taking advantage of a favour. The normal hierarchy that rules mutual relations thus collapses. In these circumstances, the representatives of Evil, usually the *asuras*, always appear stronger. On the other hand, the function of

the *avatara* is to restore harmony in the Three Worlds when the situation appears to be desperate. ... his coming [of the *avatara*] occurs during the dawn between the *Kali* and the *Krita Yuga*." (1996: 283).

A Vaishnava king – continues Legendre De Koninck – had the *avatara* as a model and considered himself a form of terrestrial *avatara*. Therefore, Suryavarman II, who acceded to the throne by usurpation, might have wanted to justify his action by presenting himself, on the eight Large Panels, as the saviour of the Three Worlds and particularly of the Khmers. The illustrations of the antagonism between the forces of Good and Evil and the reconquest, by a Vaishnava heroic figure, of a fundamental Good which brings back universal order, would convey an association between Suryavarman II's reign and his project of time regeneration. On the reliefs of Angkor Wat, he would have stressed the promise of a brilliant future for his people, his territorial project having more or less already reached its limit. The ambitious Suryavarman II would have introduced himself as a master of time, rather than of space, as the hero who could command the golden age, the *Krita Yuga*.

For Legendre De Koninck, the eight Large Panels can be separated into a northern and southern group. The southern half contains four bas-reliefs representing a temporal cycle from destruction to rebirth (from the Battle of Kurukshetra to the Churning of the Ocean of Milk). In between, the panel depicting the Historic Procession and that of Heavens and Hells represent two 'phases' established by a competent king. The northern half's four panels depict a series of combats: of Vishnu against the asuras, Krishna against the *asura* Bana, of the *devas* against the *asuras*, and that of Lanka. These sacrificial combats symbolise the two objectives of the royal function: the drive towards the establishment of a new order and the end of an age of misery, the *Kali Yuga*.

After a revision of the opinions and hypotheses on the interpretation of the Large Panels, the point to be made here is that the Churning of the Ocean of Milk is one of the myths richest in symbolism. In it, one can read the establishment of order out of chaos and the primal act of creation out of separation. But foremost, in the context of Angkor Wat, it may be an allegory of Suryavarman II's successful attempt to unite his various feudal princes who ruled over

the small, semi-autonomous fiefdoms of XII century Cambodia. It would thus refer to the creation of a united peace and prosperity. Furthermore, it has been suggested that the Churning may have been enacted as a ritual tug-of-war for Suryavarman's *indrabhisheka*, as has been the practice at royal accessions in Cambodia in more recent times.[12]

The five large reliefs depicting great battles together symbolise the perils of the *dharma*'s decline and the need to re-establish it by defeating evil forces with the assistance or the guidance of Vishnu, or that of his *avatara* of Krishna and Rama. These reliefs are also indicative of the supreme power of Vishnu and his victorious mission to re-establish the divine law and order. In addition, the Battle of Kurukshetra may have been considered of primary importance to the Khmer for its paradigmatic references to religious and social teachings. The profound meaning of the *Bhagavad Gita* could only be exemplified through an image of the battle of Kurukshetra, during which Krishna propounds its message to Arjuna.

The Khmer kings, steeped in Hindu belief and culture, would not have had much difficulty in identifying themselves and their lives with the heroic princes and warriors from the *Ramayana* and the *Mahabharata*, practising asceticism to win divine support, and waging ferocious battle against the forces of evil in order to re-establish order. The epic world would have been mirrored in Khmer experience, with its conflicts between associated but often disunited fiefdoms, as well as the wars against their enemies, the Chams and the Dai Viêt. At the same time the Epics stress the forging of alliances. The Angkorean kings identified themselves with the gods, and their righteous deeds were equated to those of Rama, Krishna or Vishnu, and their enemies with the *asuras* and *rakshasas*.

Layout of the composition

An analysis of how the visual elements are arranged in the composition of each relief reveals some interesting points:

- In The Battle of Kurukshetra, three main events occur: the gruesome great battle, the death of Bhishma and Krishna expounding to Arjuna the *Baghavad Gita*. All are laid out like a frieze, with the events depicted in linear progression in a single large register. Bhishma and Krishna, although playing important roles, are depicted more as 'cameo' appearances.

- In the relief illustrating the Historic Procession, the story is illustrated in two registers in the initial third of the panel, after which it becomes a single register of the army and court processing. There are four main events depicted:

1. The King attending a ceremony, or giving audience on Mount Shivapada, in which he is surrounded by ministers, brahmins and officers.

2. The women of the court moving in the forest at the foot of Mount Shivapada. towards the point where they will meet/join the procession.

3. The troops descending the mountain.

4. The king joining the procession on his elephant, and the Khmer generals deploying their platoons, preceded by possibly the mercenary forces of the Syam kuk.

Also, the sculptors have represented the various events in linear progression in space and time. Obviously, that was the best solution for filling the enormous horizontal space of the panels.

- In the Heavens and Hells, multiple events are illustrated. Apart from the movement of the souls towards their destination in heaven or hell and the depiction of the heavens, there is the scene of Yama's judgement which is the pivotal event, and determines the subsequent depiction of 32 hells. Each of the hell scenes is a sub-plot of the main story and is described in a linear sequential mode.

- In the Churning of the Ocean of Milk, if one believes that the same serpent (Vasuki) is represented twice, then several different events in the myth are being represented on the same field. First, Vasuki sleeping at the bottom of the ocean, then his participation in the Churning action, with the creation that follows. Alternatively, the lowest *naga* resting at the bottom of the Ocean could be Vasuki, while the upper one used for the Churning is Shesha (or Ananta), the other king of the *nagas*.

- The Victory of Krishna over the *Asura* Bana has many sub-plots, the most evident of which are the seven appearances of Krishna on Garuda. However, the scene with greatest visual impact is that of Garuda extinguishing the fire, rather than a more traditionally key episode such as the meeting of Krishna and Shiva. These events, however, do seem to be narrated not only in linear sequence (from left to right), but also in chronological sequence, as the text places the scene of the extinguishing of the fire at the beginning of the story and the meeting of gods at the very end.

- An analogous situation occurs in the Battle of the *Devas* and *Asuras*, where each frontal confrontation of the various deities is in itself an event, a sub-plot within the broader story of the mythological battle. The scenes are illustrated in linear sequence, like in a frieze.

- In the Battle of Lanka, the savage assaults of the monkeys on the *rakshasas* are minor sub-plots within the general picture. The only outstanding events are, in the left side of the panel, Rama standing on Hanuman, flanked by Balarama and Vibhishana, at the beginning of the battle, and the central confrontation between Rama and Ravana. The entirety is narrated in linear mode and in temporal sequence.

- In conclusion, it seems that in all the large panels more than one event, or several sub-plots are visually represented. The only exception is 'The Victory of Vishnu over the *Asuras* where only one event is depicted: that of the god, at the centre of the composition, surrounded by the attacking armies of the *asuras*. It is illustrated in a simple linear mode.

In the Large Panels, the visual narrative discourse takes place in the single composition depicting the actions or episodes logically referring back to earlier episodes, describing the particular of the present and indicating the direction that the narrative may take in the future. The narrative image is open-ended,

leading forward, backward, or to other actions or stories, whether these appear in another relief or in the viewer's memory. Furthermore, the various single acts of narration of the eight Large Panels form patterns that provide consistency to the pictorial narrative of the Angkorean period. This takes place independently from the identity of the viewer, the viewing circumstances and the possible differences in the composition of the group of sculptors (the workshops) that worked at the various panels.

Directional composition

Another approach for investigating the structure and meaning of the Large Panels is an analysis of the directional composition. In six of the eight reliefs, arrangement of the main protagonists in the scene follows the converging movement of forces engaged in battle or contest. An analysis of the graphic distribution of these opposing forces may elucidate the meaning of the concept of symmetry-asymmetry and its close relationship with the balance between the forces of good and evil.

In the Churning of the Ocean of Milk, Vasuki is being pulled along a north/south axis to the apparent disadvantage of the *devas* in the north, who are fewer in number. This explains the need for the intervention of Vishnu. The numerical advantage of the *asuras* further accentuates the subtle asymmetry of the components of the relief. The *asuras* are placed to the south according to Indian iconographic rules respecting the significance of the cardinal points – the south being the direction of the underworld and its inhabitants. This applies also to the relief of the Churning in the inner gallery of Bayon.

In the Victory of Vishnu over the *asuras*, the movement of the troops converges symmetrically on the central image of Vishnu on Garuda. This is not the case in The Victory of Krishna over the *Asura* Bana, where the movement of the *devas* from east to west (left to right) overpowers that of the *asuras* moving towards them from the opposite direction. The overall composition is therefore asymmetric. A similar situation is displayed in the panel depicting the Battle of the *Devas* and *Asuras*, except this time to the *asuras*' advantage. The balance of forces is uncertain in the Battle of Lanka. A very slight advantage seems to be given to Ravana's forces coming from the south (which is also the direction of Lanka) and directed towards Rama's troops coming from the north. However, the monkeys' ferocious attack on his forces obscures a clear indication of a south to north progression. It seems a case of asymmetry with the balance in favour of the forces of the bad. In contrast, the Kauravas and Pandavas converge in equally-sized groups in the panel of the Battle of Kurukshetra, thus creating a symmetric composition.

In the panel depicting the Historic Procession, no opposing forces are depicted since we are dealing with the uni-directional parade of Suryavarman II's army. Also in the Heavens and Hells there is no confrontation of forces. In both panels, the movement of the elements of the composition flows from west to east, in linear progression, creating thus an asymmetric layout.

When considering these eight panels within the rectangular plan of the galleries of the third enclosure (*see Table 1*), the two panels of the southern gallery display a definite progression from the west to the east, while the northern gallery places a more subtle emphasis on movement from the east to the west. In either case, however, for the viewer, the action appears to proceed from left to right. In the eastern gallery, The Churning of the Ocean of Milk depicts a temporary advantage for the *asuras* who are pulling towards the south, thereby creating a north to south movement. This may be correlated diagonally by what happens in the Battle of Lanka in the western gallery, where the larger forces of Ravana push up from the south creating a south to north movement. Finally, the fighting forces represented in the Battle of Kurukshetra converge symmetrically at the composition's centre, which is mirrored in the composition of 'The Victory of Vishnu over the *Asuras*'.

For these reasons one might conclude that the directional composition of the eight panels seems to follow a pattern of symmetry and asymmetry. Furthermore, the way the elements of the relief are arranged and displayed in these eight panels does not always reflect the prevailing force of good over the demons, giving the initial impression that evil forces are going to win, and that good is in danger. This imbalance is a moment of crisis bringing about the need for a sacrifice. In its broader sense, such a crisis calls for a sacrificial combat involving Vishnu, his *avatara* or even the king, for the re-establishment of the dharma, revolving in cycles of destruction and recreation. Cosmic destruction is considered a sacrifice needed for the recreation of a new world in a new era. The *avatara* intervenes in time of crisis, appearing at the passage from one *yuga* to another. In graphic terms, the imbalance between the forces of good and evil is expressed thorough the asymmetric layout of visual elements.

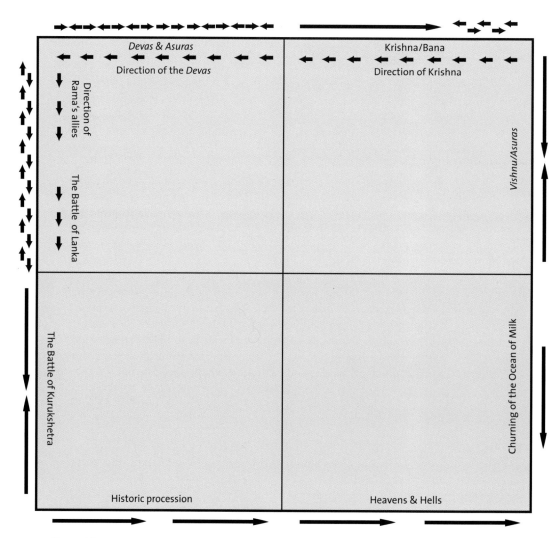

Table 1 Directional composition of visual elements in the large panels.

TABLE 2 LARGE PANELS OF THE THIRD ENCLOSURE GALLERIES.

No.	STORY'S TITLE	TEXT	DEITY	SYMBOLISM
LP. 1	THE BATTLE OF KURUKSHETRA	*Mahabharata*	Krishna	- Dharma's re-establishment - Nature of action & sacrifice - Social & religious duties - Obedience to god's instructions
LP. 2	THE HISTORIC PROCESSION	--	--	- Supremacy of the king - Loyalty to the king - Symbolism of the mountain
LP. 3	HEAVENS & HELLS	--	--	- Reward or punishment of earthly deeds - Acceptance of own karma
LP. 4	THE CHURNING OF THE OCEAN OF MILK	*Ramayana, Mahabharata and Bhagavata Purana*	Vishnu	- Beginning of all events - Dharma's re-establishment - Divine intervention - Future benefits - Obedience to god's instructions - Symbolism of the mountain
LP. 5	THE VICTORY OF VISHNU OVER THE *ASURAS*	*Harivamsa*	Vishnu	- Victory over enemy - Victory over evil forces - Dharma's re-establishment - Divine physical strength
LP. 6	THE VICTORY OF KRISHNA OVER THE *ASURA* BANA	*Harivamsa, Bhagavata Purana*	Vishnu/ Krishna	- Victory on evil forces - Accomplishment of karma
LP. 7	THE BATTLE BETWEEN THE *DEVAS* AND *ASURAS*	*Vamana Purana*	Vishnu	- Victory over evil forces - Dharma's re-establishment
LP. 8	THE BATTLE OF LANKA	*Ramayana*	Rama (Vishnu)	- Dharma's re-establishment - Victory over evil forces - Accomplishment of karma

OVERLEAF, FIG. 76 View of the southwest Corner Pavilion and the gallery with the Large Panel of the Battle of Kurukshetra.

Chapter 3

The Reliefs from the Corner Pavilions

Introduction

The reliefs from the western corner pavilions do not seem to have stimulated the same scholarly attention that has been focused on their greater counterpart, the enormous reliefs of the galleries of the 3rd enclosure. Comparatively little has been published since the seminal work of George Coedès on the 'bas-reliefs' of 1911, based on his analysis of the plaster casts produced in Cambodia by Doudart de Lagrée in 1863-66. He put together – for the first time – the scanty suggestions and interpretations previously put forward by F. Garnier (1869-83), L. Delaporte (1880), J. Moura (1883), A. Bastian (1886), and E. Aymonier (1901-4), based on comparisons with the Sanskrit texts of Indian epics and *Puranas*.

In his above-mentioned publication, Coedès noticed that the arrangement of the reliefs' topics did not seem to follow any apparently 'logical' order, and that the subjects of the corner pavilions were placed haphazardly. Coedès' great knowledge of, and insight into, Indian and Southeast Asian cultures facilitated his accurate interpretation of the stories. These identifications have formed the basis on which subsequent authors have been able to recognise the original texts of almost all but the handful of stories that he left un-named. In this book, the completion is proposed by the identification of two reliefs as representing the story of 'Krishna and the *Gopis*' (N. 11) and of 'Akrura's Vision' (N. 4). A third proposed interpretation as 'The Betrothal of Shiva' or the more generic 'Shiva Receiving Homage'(S. 2) is still tentative.

Very little has been written since the 1960s on the reliefs in the corner pavilions. Albert Le Bonheur in his comprehensive work on Angkor of 1989, did not provide any description or critical comments on the various panels of the corner pavilions, which he called 'Cruciform Pavilions'. However, he stressed the dilemma of the arrangement of the themes of the various panels. Firstly, not all the themes depicted in the reliefs have been identified; secondly, if there is a 'logic' in the arrangement, each individual pavilion has its own, which is also independent from that of the Large Panels of the galleries. He also proposed a correspondence of subjects between the diametrically opposed arms of the cross, as well as between some panels located on each side of the transverse arms (*see Chapter 8*). Le Bonheur added further details to his views on the corner pavilions' reliefs in the 1995 publication with photographs by Jaroslav Poncar (p. 84).

At the same time, Chandra M. Bhandari presented some summary descriptions of the corner pavilions' reliefs in his book *Saving Angkor* of 1995. Interestingly, he provided some opinions which are probably based on southern Indian traditions; they are critically discussed in the sections dealing with the reliefs S. 5, S. 11 and N. 10.

Recently, in 1996, Eleanor Mannikka in her previously mentioned book on the astronomical and cosmological meaning of Angkor Wat's architectural measurements, went through the narrative reliefs of the 3rd Enclosure, including the ones in the corner pavilions. In her reading of the latter, she followed the traditional iconographical interpretations of French scholars (with the sole exception of the relief of the Viradha/Kabandha story (*see description of relief*

S. 12). She is the first author to believe that there is some logical pattern in the sequence by which the stories are arranged, according to a 'geometrical outline' in the placement of the reliefs.

The Reliefs

Each pavilion – having a cruciform plan – has 12 panels, some occupying the full wall (c. 4.5 m high and 3.5 m wide), others only the wall over the window (c. 3 m high and 3.5 m wide) and the pillar at the side of the window (c. 2 m high and 2-2.3 m wide).

Over the lintel of each of the four doors, the walls are decorated with a horizontal flat pediment (c. 2-2.5 m high and 3 m wide), composed of a flat fronton (tympanum) framed by an arch made by an undulating *naga*, as in all Khmer pediments. The reliefs are sculpted on the wall's large stone blocks laid over the structural lintel, itself unadorned.

Order of Visiting (*see Plan 10 and 11*)

When visiting the western corner pavilions, it is difficult to detect – at first glance – any order by which to proceed in the reading of the reliefs. A path to follow when walking around the pavilions is proposed here. It is a 'visiting order', and not necessarily a narrative order. It does not imply correspondence to a visiting or ceremonial order of the Khmer, nor that the corner pavilions have necessarily to be visited by entering from the long galleries. This same order is adopted in describing the reliefs of the corner pavilions. In front of the progressive numbers, the letters 'S' and 'N' appear, to indicate if the reliefs are from the southern or the northern corner pavilion. In the list opposite, italics refer to the flat pediments over the lintels; the list to the right mentions the Sanskrit texts and the number of the book from where the stories have been taken.

It is suggested here that the visiting should start from the south in accordance with a convention established by the early scholars of Angkor. Puzzled by the apparent lack of narrative order of the large sculptural panels of the galleries of the 3rd enclosure, Coedès' hypothesis (1961: 34) was adopted, by which the panels must be read while circumambulating

the enclosure counter-clockwise. This was in line with the consideration that Angkor Wat was the funerary temple of Suryavarman II. For other reasons, Bosch (1933) and Mannikka (1996) were of the opinion that the *prasavya* direction was required to follow the symbolic cycle of the life of the sun-king Vishnu which was equated to that of the Khmer king, beginning with the Churning of the Ocean of Milk.

All the above are working hypotheses, since there is no proof from inscriptions of the order actually followed by the Khmers, nor – even more importantly – that any such procession took place. The descriptions of the reliefs of the two corner pavilions are thus given in isolation, independently from the visiting/reading order of the large panels of the 3rd enclosure, because the twelve stories narrated in each of the pavilions do not seem to follow any narrative sequence. That the western corner pavilions are to be visited by themselves is supported by the absence of any reliefs in the corner pavilions of the eastern side of the enclosure; this fact precludes the full reconstruction of a possible narrative sequence. It is reasonable to assume that the Khmers originally intended to decorate also the eastern corner pavilions, and that they had to leave them incomplete – for political and economical reasons – as they did the walls of the long galleries of the northeastern quadrant of the 3rd enclosure.

Angkor Wat is the most important Khmer Vaishnava temple, the supreme visual apotheosis of Vishnu's divinity. Vishnu is depicted in hundreds of reliefs, more often in his *avatara* form of Krishna than Rama. Furthermore, Vishnu with his usual four arms frequently replaces Krishna in the depiction of many of the Krishna myths (*see page 55*). Therefore, in view of the fact that the greatest visual emphasis is given to Vishnu, it is here suggested to start the reading of the reliefs from the two most primordial events of Vaishnava mythology: 'The Churning of the Ocean of Milk' for the southwestern corner pavilion (Fig. 78), and from the 'Invitation for Vishnu to descend' for the northwestern corner pavilion (Fig. 118).

TABLE 3

SW Corner Pavilion

S.1 – The Churning of the Ocean of Milk	*Bhagavata Purana* VIII (7)
S.2 – Krishna lifting Mount Govardhana	*Bhagavata Purana* X (24)
S.3 – Rama killing Marica	*Ramayana VIII*
S.4 – Shiva in the pine forest	*Linga Purana* II (9)
S.5 – Ravana shaking Mount Kailasa	*Ramayana*. VII
S.6 – Krishna as a young boy dragging a heavy mortar	*Bhaghavata Purana* X (9)
S.7 – Shiva reducing Kama to ashes	*Shiva Purana* XVI
S.8 – The death of Valin	*Ramayana* IV
S.9 – The Murder of ?Pralamba and the dousing of a fire	*Bhagavata Purana* X (18)
S.10 – Dvaravati water festival	*Harivamsa* II
S.11 – Shiva receiving homage	*Vamana Purana* XXV (26)
S.12 – Krishna receiving the offerings destined for Indra	*Bhagavata Purana* X (24)

NW Corner Pavilion

N.1 – Invitation for Vishnu to descend	*Vishnu Purana* V (1)
N.2 – Krishna bringing back Mount Maniparvata	*Bhagavata Purana* VIII (6)
N.3 – Rama's alliance with Sugriva	*Ramayana* IV
N.4 – Akrura's vision	*Brahma Purana* X (39)
N.5 – Sita's ordeal by fire	*Ramayana* VI
N.6 – Viradha's attempt to abduct Sita	*Ramayana* III
N.7 – Rama on the Pushpaka chariot	*Ramayana* VI
N.8 – Sita meeting Hanuman	*Ramayana* V
N.9 – Rama's alliance with Vibhishana	*Ramayana* VI
N.10 – The *svayamvara* of Sita	*Ramayana* I
N.11 – Krishna and the *gopis*	*Baghavata Purana* X (29)
N.12 – Rama killing Kabandha	*Ramayana* III

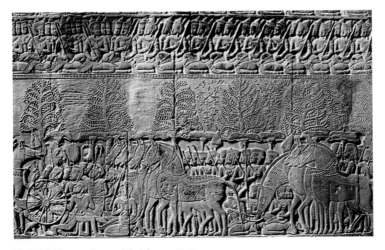

FIG. 77 Soldiers, squires and their horses. N.10

FIG. 78 The Churning of the Ocean of Milk. S. 1

FIG. 79 Kurma, Lakshmi and Ucchaihshravas. S. 1

FIG. 80 *Devas* and *asuras*. S. 1

Description of the Reliefs

The Southwestern Corner Pavilion

S. 1 - The Churning of the Ocean of Milk

This relief, placed over the window of the western wall of the northern arm, is divided into two pseudo-registers, with the upper one in a very poor state of preservation affecting the central figure of Vishnu on the churning pole. At the very top of the pole, in an almond-shaped area, only the legs of a seated personage are still visible, perhaps belonging to another image of Vishnu or Brahma. On either side of the pole where Vishnu acts to balance it, are two large discs. In the one to the left is a seated figure in royal attire, holding a rosary. This figure represents the Moon, while the similarly-apparelled personage in the right-hand disc represents the Sun. The pole itself is covered with a design of overlapping lozenges which elsewhere in Angkor's reliefs are meant to represent stone, but which in this case could also refer to the bark of a tree.

In the lower pseudo-register, separated from the scene above by the representation of a dense forest (with vines climbing some of the tree trunks), is a row of *asuras* (wearing the *rakshasa*'s crown) and *devas* (with the usual Khmer conical crown) each pulling at either end of the snake Vasuki who is wound around the churning pole pivoting on Kurma's back (another of Vishnu *avatara*). Also neatly sculpted is the head of Lakshmi and the horse Ucchaihshravas who are created by the churning of the Ocean (Fig. 79), while there are no signs of the other products mentioned in the Hindu texts. The Ocean's waters are inhabited by a multitude of fish swimming mainly from right to left. Vasuki is represented with a scaly body and his five heads are on the side of the *asuras*, while the tail, now missing, is held by the *devas*, as in the Churning depicted in the Large Panels (LP. 4).

The panel to the left of the window is decorated with four superimposed registers of 23 seated *devas* and 22 *asuras* symmetrically arranged facing each other. The *asuras* hold clubs in their right hands, while the *devas* have their arms resting on their chests (Fig. 81).

The mythic event of the Churning is amply discussed in relation to its depiction in the Large Panel, with references to the textual sources for the *Mahabharata*, (I, chapters 15-17), the *Ramayana* (Book I, chapter 45) and the *Bhagavata Purana*. Here, attention is paid to the fact that in Khmer iconography of 'The Churning of the Ocean of Milk' a surprising confusion is often created by the depiction of Mount Mandara – the churning pole – and the personage on top of it. When the churning pole is shown simply as a pole terminating with a capital, the dynamic figure of Vishnu is depicted over it. When it is depicted as a branching tree, it is a lotus with multiple buds, and on the central bud the small static figure of Brahma is sculpted. We have thus the possibility of two different types of churning pole with two distinct deities at its top. The second type is totally out of context with the myth of the Churning. Brahma on a lotus stem belongs to the myth of 'Vishnu *Anantashayin*' (reclining on the snake Ananta). In the latter event, from the umbilicus of Vishnu rises a lotus stem on which Brahma, the architect of the universe is sitting; for this reason the

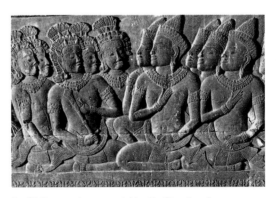

FIG. 81 *Devas* and *asuras* watching the Churning. S. 1

myth is also alluded to as 'the birth of Brahmā'. Nevertheless, although both myths deal with the concept of creation, they are quite distinct.

To elucidate this situation, it is necessary to look at Khmer reliefs of the Churning in more detail. In the case of the relief under consideration (S. 1), the churning pole looks like a thin pole made of rock or covered with bark. It ends with a large capital with two rows of lotus petals on which is seated a figure of whom only the feet remain. However, given that he is seated, it seems more likely that the figure represents Brahmā.

In the Large Panel of the Churning (*see p. 44*), the unfinished churning pole has more the shape of a phallic mountain. The figure 'flying' horizontally on top is more likely to be Vishnu. This is also the case in the reliefs of the inner enclosure of Bayon (northeastern side facing north), where the churning pole is once again like a column ending with a capital (with two rows of lotus petals and a thin plinth) on which the figure of Vishnu seems to be crawling. In a pediment of Banteay Samré [1] the churning pole is instead in the form of a tree ending with three branches on which the central one supports Brahmā and the two lateral ones, each support a small running or dancing figure. Brahmā is clearly depicted with four heads and four arms.

In comparison there are a few reliefs of Vishnu lying on Ananta (in some cases identifiable with 'Vishnu *Anantashayin*'). The relief depicting this scene in the northwestern corner pavilion (N. 1) is very badly damaged and little can still be seen of the branching lotus at the back of Vishnu's figure; in the eroded area, however, there is room for a figure of Brahmā. The lintel of the western central door of the Western *Gopura* shows a thick lotus stem emanating from an eroded reclining Vishnu that ends in a lotus flower supporting a four-headed and four-armed Brahmā. Of his two lower arms one is on the chest and the other on the knee. At Banteay Samré the three branches of the lotus stalk protruding from Vishnu's umbilicus sustain, at the centre, a four-armed deity of whom the head is missing, seated on a lotus flower. At both sides are the usual running or dancing personages. At Preah Khan, [2] the relief shows the lotus stem emanating from the umbilicus of Vishnu ending with three lotus buds but without any personage, not even that of Brahmā.

The placement of Brahmā's image on top of the churning pole is a juxtaposition or a contamination of elements of two myths, and it would be interesting to know how this entered the Khmer repertory. It is a surprising feature since all the reliefs were presumably planned by brahmins and executed under their supervision. Theological matters of this type could not have been overlooked. One can only speculate that perhaps both myths were perceived as intimately connected to each other, combining the larger Vaishnava concept of creation. Finally, it is possible that Khmer artists had confused the churning pole with the Parijata tree produced during the Churning (Giteau 1951: 145). In Vedic formulation, the 'Tree of Life' emerges into space from the umbilicus of the god recumbent on the waters, its trunk representing the axis of the Universe, its branches all the possible different ways of being. In the Puranic tradition, this tree became eventually the lotus generated from Vishnu's umbilicus, bearing Brahmā on its opened blossom.

The story of the Churning of the Ocean of Milk is a vivid example of multiple meaning. Besides being a myth of creation it carries also other meanings: that of the importance of divine intervention expressed by Vishnu incarnating as a tortoise to support Mount Mandara; of the need for the faithful to obey Vishnu's instructions in order to achieve a goal (the *amrita*, elixir of immortality); and the promise that future benefits will derive from the *amrita* and great prosperity from Lakshmi.

S. 2 – Krishna lifting Mount Govardhana

Occupying the entirety of the eastern wall of the northern arm, this relief is divided into several pseudo-registers. In the top pseudo-register Krishna, in the company of his brother Balarama, is depicted holding up the mountain with his right arm to protect the shepherds and their flocks from the torrential rain released by Indra's fury (Fig. 82). As executed by Khmer sculptors, it looks as if Krishna is lifting Mount Govardhana the way "a little boy picks a mushroom" (*Bhagavata Purana*, chapter 25), and the cowherds (*gopas*) and their cattle are reassured and calm. There is some doubt as to whether the small personage behind Krishna is actually Balarama, since Krishna's brother is not mentioned in the text.

Fig. 82 Krishna lifting Mount Govardhana. S. 2

FIG. 83 Rama killing Marica. S. 3

FIG. 84 Detail of Rama shooting an arrow into the base of Marica's neck. S. 2

However, in Hindu iconography, the two are almost always inseparable.

The scene takes place in a park, amongst shepherds and domestic animals (Fig. 85). Despite their rich apparel, the two protagonists are cowherds themselves, as indicated by the herdsman's crook that Krishna holds with his left hand, and that Balarama has on his shoulder. Krishna's hair is arranged around a *mukuta* surmounted by long braids tied up in three knots from which pointed tufts emerge; that of Balarama differs only in not having a *mukuta*. These hairstyles typify Krishna and Balarama as youths, when they are closely associated with the cowherds. Above them, the sculptors have represented the mountain by the conventional use of a grouping of small lozenges. Ascetics, sitting in the customary crossed-leg position inhabit all the surrounding forest behind and above the two main personages. Wild animals are scattered around the forest.

The vertical line that passes through the left hand of Krishna and the centre of the rows of royal personages of the lower pseudo-register dominates the compositional layout of this relief. This line defines the centre of symmetry affecting also the grouping of flying *apsaras* in the topmost part of the relief.

This episode of Krishna's childhood is narrated in the *Bhagavata Purana* (X, chapter 25), *Vishnu Purana* (V, chapters 10-11), and the *Harivamsa* (Book 2, chapter 15).

In the Bhagavata Purana *it is told that Krishna did not approve of the* gopa *presenting offerings and making sacrifices to Indra, doing the so-called Indra-yuga. Krishna instead advises them to make these offerings and sacrifices to Mount Govardhana (the summit of Mount Kailasa). The cowherds, headed by Nanda, oblige and make the offerings by circumambulating Mount Govardhana, always keeping it on their right. At this moment, Krishna announces that Mount Govardhana is in fact himself and that the mountain can take any form he likes. Observing this, Indra becomes enraged and directs down to earth a host of the terrible* samvartaka *clouds that are intended to bring about the destruction of the Universe. He declares that he wants to annihilate Nanda's friends and their cattle, and will pursue them with his elephant Airavata together with his troop of* maruts *of enormous prowess. The terrified cowherds beg Krishna for help. At once Krishna, with a childlike ease,*

FIG. 85 *Gopa* and their animals. S. 2

uproots Mount Govardhana with his left hand and holds it up easily for seven days without moving his position. Noticing this miraculous event, Indra – his pride broken and plans shattered – ends his attack. Once the sky is cleared of clouds and the sun is shining, Krishna pacifies and preaches to his crowd, who thereafter happily return to their camps, full of praise for the Lord. Later (chapter 27), Indra admits his perversity, ignorance and stupidity, and asks pardon from Krishna, who he crowns as the Supreme Ruler by proclaiming him as the 'Govinda' (divine 'cowherd') in this world.

From the text it becomes apparent that in dissuading the cowherds from venerating Indra, Krishna wants to override the old Vedic gods and local divinities, and introduce the Vaishnava cult. In another part of the text, it is written that on this occasion Krishna makes a sermon that emphasises that it is the Supreme God who decides the *karma* of people. Secondary divinities like Indra cannot be mistaken for the Supreme, and one should perform one's duties prescribed by caste (*varsa*) and stage in life (*ashrama*).

S. 3 – Rama killing Marica

The relief is sculpted in a single register within the flat pediment framed by *nagas* above the pavilion's northern doorway. At the centre of the composition stands the figure of Rama, in the characteristic position of an archer in action – bow held in the right hand, several arrows held in the left hand and with flexed legs – depicted a few instants after having shot an arrow (Fig. 83). To his right is Marica in his metamorphosis as a beautiful fawn with large eyes and in a leaping position; the animal has a small floral cloth on its back, wears a necklace and has horns studded with gems. An arrow is piercing its back at the base of the neck (Fig. 84).

To understand the magic of this event, one has to refer back to the original text of the *Ramayana* (Book III, *Aranya Kanda*, chapters 42-44).

As they enter the forest, the exiled Rama, Lakshmana and Sita encounter many strange adventures. The first is the meeting with Shurpanakha, sister of Ravana, who attempts to seduce the brothers but is mutilated by Lakshmana who cuts off her ears and nose, on Rama's orders. When Ravana hears of this outrage, he schemes to kill Rama and kidnap Sita. For this he asks the help of the rakshasa *Marica, son of Tataka whom Rama killed in an episode narrated in an earlier part of the* Ramayana *(Bala Kanda, chapter 23). Ravana and Marica fly away to Rama's hermitage on the magic Pushpaka chariot. Once there, Marica transforms himself into a wonderful fawn ornate with colourful jewels, straying here and there to capture Sita's attention. At first glance, Sita becomes infatuated and points out the gracious animal to Rama and Lakshmana. The latter is the first to suspect the fawn is the product of trickery, but Sita begs them to capture it. Rama, also amazed by its beauty, decides to follow it into the forest either to "slay it or bring it back alive", but first makes Lakshmana promise never to leave Sita's side.*

Marica, by using magic, keeps appearing and disappearing, leading Rama away from the hermitage. Eventually Rama releases his flaming arrow, like a lightening flash, piercing the heart of Marica, who, on the point of death, returns to his monstrous aspect. He still has the strength to call "O Sita, O Lakshmana!" imitating Rama's voice, thus luring Lakshmana to his brother's assistance, effectively taking him away from Sita. Immediately Ravana appears before her, disguised as a venerable brahmin, and Sita offers him the traditional hospitality. Her beauty enchants him, and struck by Kama's arrow [of love], Ravana reveals his godly origin and asks her to prefer him to Rama who is only a mortal and not even worth one of his fingers. Sita, roused to anger, defies him with strong words. Hearing this, Ravana strikes one hand on the other and resumes his original gigantic monstrous form, resembling death itself. With his left hand he grasps the hair of Sita and with his right, her thighs; he ties her up and takes her away on his Pushpaka chariot.

According to the narrative sequence, the killing of Marica takes place after Viradha's attempt to kidnap Sita – illustrated in the relief in the northwestern corner pavilion (N. 3) – and before the successful abduction by Ravana, sculpted in half pediments at other sites of the temple. The symmetry of the composition of this relief is striking, emphasised by Rama's arrows pointing at the central indentation of the *naga* frame, and by three identical trees on either side of Rama.

S. 4 – Shiva in the Pine Forest

The top pseudo-register of this relief sculpted over the northern window of the pavilion's western arm stands out for its triangular shape which dominates the entire composition with its teeming rows of figures. The wives of the brahmins (*rishi patani*) are arranged in two rows rising towards the figure of Shiva standing at the centre of a door (Fig. 87). To Shiva's left is a woman reaching out to touch his loincloth while, at the right another woman attempts to touch him with a twig. Such gestures would have been common acts of veneration and perhaps of dance (*rasa*). The women ranged in two rows seem to be gesticulating, and some are depicted in a state of high agitation with their faces and gestures raised towards the god. Many have one hand on the belt holding up their flowery sarong, as if they were releasing it. Others are embracing each other. The women to the left of the viewer wear three-pointed conical crowns, perhaps reflecting hierarchical differences between their husbands and those of the others.

FIG. 86 Shiva at the portal decorated with a crocodile. S. 4

Fig. 87 Shiva in the Pine Forest. S. 4

FIG. 88 *Rishis* in the forest (below) and rejoicing *gopis* (above). S. 4

At the mountain's summit, Shiva is framed majestically against the portal of a temple or a palace with a richly decorated base and long banners streaming from its roof. Above the portal is the image of a reptile (Fig. 86). Judging by the large scales on both sides of his tail and by the long mouth, it is a crocodile and not a chameleon or other lizard. Shiva has a serene and happy expression on his youthful face. His *sampot* is of minimal size, without extending flaps, just with two short ends at the front. The background is composed of a forest on a hill. The lowest pseudo-register contains a thin horizontal strip of thick vegetation inhabited by animals and groups of ascetics practising penance (*tapas*).[3] To the right are two groups of two or three ascetics (Fig. 88) who seem to be running towards a group of *gopis* (notice the typical hairstyle of the cowherds' women), creating their own story within the main narrative.

On the panel to the right of the window (Fig. 89), three high registers are sculpted, instead of the usual four or five, in order to accommodate images of standing women wearing very high, pointed crowns. In the topmost of these registers, they all face up towards Shiva's apparition. In the other two registers they are posed facing each other and gesticulating.

The fact that Shiva is bigger than any other figure in the relief, and that he is framed within the empty door at the top of a pyramidal composition of agitated personages, confers the scene with an almost magical atmosphere – the apparition of a supreme deity in all his splendour causing ecstatic excitement in his devotees. One unusual feature is that the banners flying from the sides of the temple are higher than the *apsaras*, perhaps further emphasising the presence of a very important god. The wives of the *rishis* are all running up towards him, expressing their joy by their body movements. In comparison to their wives, the *rishis* have an almost insignificant role. Much smaller in size and number, they meditate in the forest, unaware of what is going on. The story unwinds in a series of different temporal situations giving rise to a short narrative: Shiva appears, the wives of the *rishis* move towards him, while, at the same time, the *rishis* meditate in the forest. The gaze-directing attitude of the ladies at the top register flanking the window, as well as the many gestures pointing upwards, give further impetus to the vertical thrust of the entire composition towards the crowning image of Shiva.

The story of Shiva, the *rishis* and their wives is found in the *Linga Purana* (II, chapter 29) under the title 'Victory over death'. It is, however, more commonly known as the story of 'Shiva in the

Pine Forest' (Doniger 1981: 172) mentioned also in the *Vamana Purana*. The form that Shiva assumes in this episode is that of the 'Bhikshatanamurti' (Giteau 1964: 131). The story runs thus:

To propitiate Shiva the sages perform a terrible penance in the Daru forest (or Devadaruvana), accompanied by their wives, sons and sacrificial fires. Shiva is delighted, but wants to test their sincerity and turn their mind from the observance of sacrificial rites towards the path of pure devotion. Therefore, in order to test their faith, he playfully assumes a deformed but attractive appearance, with three eyes and two hands, nude, of dark complexion. Even in this form, he is extremely handsome and sexually arousing to women. On seeing him, all the women of the village stop their activities (like in the story of the Rasalila; *see N. 11) and follow him singing, not caring for their loosened garments and ornaments. Some brahmins' wives, finding that their own garments are loose, cast off their bangles and join in. Some sing, some dance while others roll on the ground; some talk loudly, others embrace themselves. Even caste ladies fall down in awkward postures with their clothes loosened and their tresses dishevelled; all in the presence of their husbands. They detain Shiva, gesturing lewdly, and asking him who he is, where he is going and why he would not stay with them. But the god remains silent.*

Witnessing their wives' distraction, the brahmins begin to insult and criticise Shiva, but they have no power over him. They seek Brahma's help who quickly informs them that the intruder is none other than lord Shiva, and that they should honour guests even if they happen to be deformed, dirty or illiterate, such observance being a way of self-expiation. Brahma quotes the perfect example of Sudarshana who with a single act of piety towards a guest conquered death. He advises the brahmins to do the same and return at once to the forest and seek refuge in Shiva. The brahmins ask Brahma the procedure for renunciation in order to become acceptable to Shiva, to which the god obliges by listing all the tasks. One endowed with devotion may attain immediate liberation, because it is only by means of devotion to Shiva that death can be conquered.

The state of nakedness in which Shiva appears to the women is not unusual for the ascetic who has renounced all. The name *Bhikshatanamurti*, usually attributed to this figure, refers to *bhikshu*, a religious mendicant who subsists entirely on alms, and not to his naked state, as the term for that kind of mendicant who wears no garment is *ksapanakam*. Shiva's presence here, magically appearing at the door of an imaginary building, contrasts with the agitated/activated figures of the women, dancing and playing below him, highlighting the contrast between sacred and profane. Besides Shiva's iconographic codes (*sampot*, crown, rosary, etc.) which are easily observable in the relief, one must look for the 'signs' of the god standing 'high' in the scene indicating his divine superiority, and of his direct, self-assured and clear pose revealing the determination of his mission.

The reason why Shiva has to become a *bhikshu* is explained in the *Linga Purana* (I, chapter 7). It started when Shiva argued with Brahma on who was the real creator of the Universe and Brahma told a lie. This impelled Shiva to behead one of Brahma's five heads, earning thus the sin of murdering a brahmin (*brahmahatya*). To expiate this sin, he became a beggar (*bhikshatanamurti*), and roamed naked for twelve years. Since total nudity is absent in Khmer iconography, Shiva is shown in the relief instead wearing a smaller than usual *sampot*; this is sufficient to account for the frenzy and excitement of the women, the most striking feature of the relief.

The crocodile over the door where the god appears is the relief's most curious element, the true meaning of which has continually eluded modern scholars. In Hindu iconography, the crocodile is the emblem on the banner of the God of Love (see the story of Shiva reducing Kama to ashes [*Shiva Purana*, chapter 16-19, and also relief S. 7]). In Khmer reprsentations of the myth of Shiva *Bhikshatanamurti*, the crocodile, usually of comparatively small size, is depicted on top of a door, as in the relief under consideration. It appears also in the rock sculptures of the K'bal Spean in the Kulen mountains,[4] in one medallion of the tapestry relief of a door of the Western *Gopura* of Angkor Wat (*see page 218*), and in one of Bayon's inner galleries (south of the eastern entrance). The relationship between Shiva and the crocodile is further mentioned in the *Brahma Purana*[5] narrating the story of Shiva taking the form of a brahmin boy caught by a crocodile in order to distract Parvati from meditation and penance. The story is an allegory of the devotion needed to achieve victory over the senses.

In Vaishnava iconography the crocodile, usually of larger size, appears in reliefs depicting Vishnu *Trivikrama*, where, together with other animals, it stands as a symbol of the realm of Earth and its waters. It appears at Banteay Samré's western *gopura* I (S face), at Angkor in a lintel of monument 'W' of Prah Pithu, of the Thomannon's *antarala*, and in a pediment on the ground around Prasat No. 486. However, the most striking appearance of the crocodile is in the central tower reliefs of Prasat Kravan (first quarter of the X century) where the reptile is sculpted above the eight-armed Vishnu within a pattern reminiscent of a temple's door, similar to its location in the Shiva *Bhikshatanamurti* relief.[6]

George Coedès has quoted yet another interpretation. For him the main protagonist of this relief was not Shiva, but Ravana appearing as a handsome young man at the entrance of Indra's gynaeceum, after having taken the shape of a chameleon (or lizard) to sneak under the door. This story, not found amongst Indian legends, is narrated in a modern Cambodian text entitled *Traiphet* (Coedès 1912: 26) and it is still used by the tourist guides of Siem Reap to explain the reliefs. However, it may be that the reliefs, in fact, inspired the story.

In conclusion, the depiction of a reptile over a door in the representations of the stories mentioned above applies to reliefs of Shaivite, Vaishnava and Buddhist myths. Since it is unknown in India, it indicates the great popularity that the reptile enjoyed amongst the Khmers for reasons that are not clear to us. Perhaps we are dealing with different reptilian forms in different stories; sometimes it is a crocodile and in others a chameleon or a lizard. One may also hypothesise that the crocodile may have been perceived by the Khmers as the embodiment of a local genie (*neak ta*) of the waters, since crocodiles may have been the 'guardians' of the irrigation system and of sacred waters.

The myth of 'Shiva in the Pine Forest', discussed by Wendy Doniger O'Flaherty in her comprehensive study on Shiva (1973), is a typical example of paradoxical mythology. Although eroticism and acts of seduction permeate the story, it is primarily concerned with the sages' transformation, and Shiva is the centre around whom the other characters revolve. His seduction, or attempt to seduce the wives of the sages, has the objective of demonstrating a metaphysical truth. The error of the sages is based on conflicts of power, or conflicts of social roles that Shiva wants to correct.

Shiva opposes the *tapas* of the sages not out of fear of their power, but out of belief that *tapas* alone were insufficient as a path to Release. He also wanted to punish the hypocrisy of sages who pretended to perform *tapas* while enjoying their wives. He – the supreme ascetic – considered them false ascetics, ignorant of the *dharma*, and not free from lust, being fools that have undertaken the vows out of senility! The episode of Shiva's apparition in the Pine Forest is followed by that of the curse of the angry *rishis* causing Shiva to lose his penis[7] and at the same time reveal their true nature and loss of dignity because of their mad lust. Their hatred of Shiva's virility may reveal their own repressed sexuality, and this is what Shiva wants them to admit. Shiva designed the lesson, and purposely came into the pine forest to test them, and bring them into enlightenment.

To be a trickster and have 'burlesque ideas' is an innate part of Shiva. The trickster appears in myths and folk tales of every traditional society; his figure links culture, sex and laughter, shaping the perception of reality (Pelton 1980; Joung, 1972). This is clearly revealed in this myth in two ways: sometimes Shiva pretends to seduce the sages' wives in order to reduce the power of their *tapas*, sometimes in order to teach them a lesson. Seduction is a variation of the general method of subverting virtue or *tapas*. Shiva retains his ambiguous status as the god who is both seducer and seduced. As a true ascetic, he is only tempted by the wives of the sages, and as a hypocritical ascetic he seduces them, while as a supreme god, he brings about the seduction of the sages.

Shiva enters the pine forest as a Pashupata, a member of the sect (also called Kapalika) which believed that anyone injuring another would lose his good karma to the injured person. By false accusation, the accused would get the merits of the other, and his bad karma would go to the accuser. Therefore, Shiva plays 'the lecher' in order to stimulate slander, acquiring *tapas* by this means, and transference of the karma. Brahma elucidates this, in another way, when the sages go to seek his advice. He tells them that they have ill-treated Shiva himself, and that one should never do that to a guest, for the guest then takes the good karma of the host and leaves his own bad karma behind. The sages were performing *tapas* without knowing the true nature of God; they were obtaining great powers by prayers and sacrifices, competing with Shiva. By seducing their wives, Shiva not only causes them to lose their powers, but also transferred those powers to himself.

The symbolism of the episode of 'Shiva in the Pine Forest', is encapsulated in the *Brahmada Purana* (Book 1, chapter 2), when Brahma reveals to the petitioning *rishis* that there are three recognisable forms of Shiva (Rudra): 'his dark form as Agni, his passionate form Brahma, and the form of goodness known as 'Vishnu'. The *Puranas* expand the perception of the Trinity (Shiva, Brahma and Vishnu) by adding the cosmological and cosmogonical concepts of the three realms of the triple universe (earth, ocean, sky-paradise; men, *asuras* and gods). The universe is destroyed by fire at the end of each *yuga* and remains submerged in the cosmic waters until it is time to be created anew. According to the Pancharatra doctrine of Creation, it is Vishnu who brings about the dissolution of the Universe and its recreation after his long periods of sleep. From this one can see how the episode of Shiva in the Pine Forest is related – albeit indirectly – to Vaishnava beliefs.

S. 5 – Ravana shaking Mount Kailasa

In this relief the story is displayed in two main pseudo-registers on a rectangular wall area above the southern window of the western arm; a small part of the wall to the right below Shiva has crumbled away, unfortunately affecting Shiva's image (Fig. 91). As in previous reliefs, the layout of the visual narrative is pyramidal in nature, with Shiva's image at the top beneath a single large triangular tree. Shiva is placed at the centre, seated in a yogic position on a low plinth, his right hand on his chest, the left resting on his lap. He does not appear to be holding a rosary, and is wearing the customary jewellery, as well as a peculiar, lobed *mukuta* from which hang two thin plaits. He is meditating in the forest at the top of the mountain, which is surrounded by flying *apsaras*. The degradation of the relief's stone does not allow a reading of the position of Shiva's legs, in particular if his toe is pushing down the mountain to squash Ravana and stop his shaking it.

FIG. 89 Women with tall pointed hats. S. 4

FIG. 90 Ravana. S. 5

To the left of Shiva one can barely see the image of a female figure holding a lotus, and who is likely intended to be Parvati, while to his left is a male figure holding a trident. This arrangement is closely reminiscent of the one in the relief of Kama attempting to disturb Shiva (see S. 7). As in that case this male figure probably represents Shiva himself, the *Shulandhara* Shiva (holding the *shula* or trident), or a human form of his door guardian Sailadi (*see relief S. 7*).

There is a noticeable contrast between the peaceful atmosphere of the upper pseudo-register and the violent action depicted below. The middle pseudo-register is the largest of the relief and where the representation of Ravana dominates (Fig. 90). He is sculpted with ten arms on each side, and with four very large heads surmounted by four of medium size, which in turn are surmounted by two smaller ones – making for a grand total of ten, as prescribed by the text. His face has bulging eyes, continuous eyebrows, a large grimacing mouth, and the stylish moustaches

that are common in Khmer sculpture of the time. His legs are spread apart in a weight-lifting attitude. The ten arms at either side of his head are supporting Mount Kailasa, clearly shown as composed of rocks (in the traditional superimposed lozenges effect) and forest vegetation. Closely surrounding his body, in the empty space between him and the forest, are strange round objects with a single small tail, like a flame or leaf.[8] Many wild animals, all of which are frightened, including the snakes, populate the dense forest surrounding Ravana. Also present are some fleeing ascetics, a few holding long sticks in defence against the animals. At either side of Ravana are ascetics in the act of praying or squatting under trees. The panel to the side of the window displays seated royal figures which seem to be detached from the event taking place above (Fig. 92).

The story of Ravana shaking Mount Kailasa can be found in the *Ramayana* (Book VII, *Uttara Kanda*, chapter 16).

FIG. 91 Ravana shaking Mount Kailasa. S.5.

Fig. 92 Members of the royalty. S. 5

One day, the ten-faced rakshasa Dashanana (Ravana), Lord of Lanka, takes his magic Pushpaka chariot over the Saravana forest of reeds surrounding Mount Kailasa. Suddenly, his cart comes to a stop at the base of the mountain where Shiva is frolicking with Parvati. Nandi (Shiva's guardian) appears to inform Ravana and friends that the mountain is a forbidden area. Ravana becomes furious and ridicules the situation and the simian look of Nandi. On hearing this, Nandi feels provoked and curses him prophesying that one day monkeys will destroy him[9] and his race (of rakshasas). Enraged by this prophe-

cy, by being denied access to the mountain, and – not least – by Shiva's great power to continuously 'sport' with Parvati, Ravana decides to uproot Mount Kailasa. He then seizes the mountain in his arms and shakes it violently causing the mountain to tremble. The attendants of the god (gana) shiver and Parvati, terrified, clings to the neck of Shiva. Then, as if part of a game, Shiva, with his toe presses down on the mountain crushing the arms of the rakshasa, who emits a terrible cry causing the Three Worlds to tremble. Having heard this in the skies, the gods supplicate Shiva to release him. Shiva obeys and lets him go, but declares his name to be Ravana, "the one who causes the worlds to cry out". Ravana then begs Shiva to grant him the boon that no gods, anti-gods or monsters will ever kill him – he does not consider men as they are too insignificant.[10] Shiva condescends, and Ravana, leaving on the Pushpaka after paying obeisance to him, returns to the worlds where he will spread misery and death.

A totally different interpretation is provided by C.M. Bhandari (1995: 68) which may originate from the local traditions of Southern India. Ravana, although king of the *rakshasas*, was a great scholar and devotee of Shiva. He desired Shiva to live in his kingdom on the isle of Lanka instead of on Mount Kailasa. Since Shiva would not move, Ravana tried to lift the entire mountain to transfer it to Lanka.

Referring to the *Ramayana's* narrative, it is impossible to specify if the scene depicted in this relief has taken place before, during or after Shiva has taken action to punish Ravana. The god is represented sitting quietly, without showing any sign of exercising pressure on the mountain with his toe. Nor would he necessarily be so shown, as the whole point of the story is that Shiva crushed Ravana with the slightest movement. However, in the relief Shiva is not shown extending a leg towards the ground, as in the relief from Banteay Srei. The artists may have represented the moment after Ravana had disturbed Shiva, when the gods of the Hindu pantheon, together with Yaksha, Vidyadhara and Siddha exhort Ravana to propitiate Shiva by singing hymns and reciting sacred texts (Przyluski 1921-23: 319). Therefore Shiva is relaxed, and immobile. Nevertheless, according to the text, at this point Ravana's arms must have been crushed under the mountain, a thing that the relief does not show. On the contrary, Ravana is shown actively shaking the mountain. So it is more likely that the artists have depicted the very beginning of the story, when Shiva is still merrily sitting in the company of Parvati.

In the episode of Ravana shaking Mount Kailasa, the connection with Vaishnava doctrine lies in the fact that the misadventures of Ravana are not narrated in texts other than the *Ramayana* which is after all about an *avatara* of Vishnu. Furthermore, the *rakshasas*, so often depicted in Angkor Wat and of which Ravana is the supreme king, were amongst the most renowned enemies of Vishnu. Vishnu accepted the gods' invitation to descend to earth for the very purpose of slaying these demons (Bana, Kalanemi and Ravana).

S. 6 – Krishna as a young boy dragging a heavy mortar

The relief is sculpted in a single register in the flat pediment within the *naga* frame over the lintel of the western door. The layout involves, at the centre of the relief, a main group of two standing figures and Krishna crawling on the ground (Fig. 93). The first are women wearing only long sarongs, with a curious hairstyle of long vertical loops, common to Khmer depictions of *gopis*. They are looking at the young Krishna, one pointing at him with her hand.

The toddler Krishna is crawling on the ground with the rope holding him to the mortar clearly visible in between two trees; of the mortar itself, only one part is observable behind the right tree, with the rope around it. Krishna is wearing a low crown, heavy earrings, a necklace with a large heart-shaped pendant, and several thin bracelets and anklets. His *sampot* is not visible, being eroded by weathering. His face is childish, with thick lips, slanted eyes and continuous eyebrows in the Khmer style of the time. He stares at the viewer, as if in pride. In front of him are three ascetics seated in the ceremonial fashion, the nearest pointing his finger at Krishna. They have the typical chignon of the *rishis* and carry delta-shaped fans made of peacock's feathers.

The story is one of the most popular anecdotes of Krishna's childhood, and is related in many texts, including the *Harivamsa* (64), *Vishnu Purana* (V, chapter 6) and *Bhagavata Purana* (X, chapters 9-10). From the latter (Shastri 1994) the following is abstracted:

Yashoda, Krishna's foster-mother, tired of the young boy's (Bala Krishna) mischief-making, ties him with a rope to a heavy wood mortar (not of stone). Krishna, however, perceives that the two nearby arjuna trees are in fact two guhyaka *(celestial musicians) and sons of Kubera (the god of wealth), Nalakubara and Manigriva,*

Fig. 93 Krishna dragging a heavy mortar. S. 6

who had been imprisoned in arboreal form. The reason
for this punishment was that one day, the two, totally
drunk and in the company of celestial singing nymphs,
entered the Ganga's waters for amorous games. But the
sage Narada saw them, and the nymphs, devoted to
Vishnu, quickly got dressed, but not the two boys. They
remained stark naked despite the persistent pleas of the
nymphs. Noticing that Kubera's two sons were so inebri-
ated with wine as to not be aware of their nudity,
Narada decided that they deserved to remain naked and
immobile as trees, but retain the memory of their guilt.
After one hundred celestial years, they would regain their
original forms. Having pronounced his curse trans
forming Nalakubara and Manigriva into twin arjuna
trees, Narada retired to the hermitage of Narayana.
Deciding to complete the prophecy, Krishna drags the mor-
tar to the two trees, crawls in between them, and with the
rope tied around his hips drags the mortar and violently
uproots the trees. They fall down with a terrible crash and,
in a dazzling flash the two brothers emerge. Immediately
they bow down to Krishna, and – freed by their penance
from egoism – profess unswerving devotion to him. Then,
they both circumambulate the Lord tied to the wooden
mortar, and leave in the direction of the North (the
direction of Kubera).

Exceptionally, in this relief the figures are not arranged in the usual symmetrical way. Because Krishna has to be represented horizontally on the floor, the empty space above him has been filled with trees. This, however, is not enough to complete-ly balance the scene and a sense of asymmetry predominates.

S. 7 – Shiva reducing Kama to ashes

In this relief crowning the western window of the southern arm, Shiva is depicted at the centre of the uppermost register, with, at his right Parvati, and to the left a male personage holding a trident (*trisula*) like the one seen in the relief of Ravana shaking Mount Kailasa (S. 5; Fig. 94). Shiva is represented as an ascetic, but a richly adorned one, as suits a king amongst the gods. He is seated on a plinth decorated with floral motifs, and with both hands he holds a rosary. His face, with closed eyes, seems to be absorbed in deep meditation (Fig. 98). Given the

condition of the relief, it is uncertain as to whether the third eye is sculpted on his forehead. Parvati, wearing the royal three-pointed crown, is holding in her left hand a lotus bud, while the trident holder is seated at a lower level than Shiva, although slightly higher than Parvati. A dense forest populated by small groups of *rishis* surrounds the three figures. In the uppermost portion of the relief are flying *apsaras*.

The middle pseudo-register is comparatively thin, occurring in between the one with the large image of Shiva above, and one depicting Kama below. The most puzzling aspect of it is the presence of another, much smaller and unadorned image of Shiva standing on a high plinth finely decorated with floral motifs (Fig. 97). He is surrounded by a flaming aureole, perhaps representing the heat of penance (*tapas*). In his right hand he holds some elongated objects, while his left is extended to receive (or give) a round gift held by a worshipper kneeling in front of him. To either side are *rishis*, some facing each other, others facing the centre of the panel. All are placed against the lozenged background indicating rocks with scattered images of trees. Presumably this locates the scene atop Shiva's mountain retreat.

The bottom pseudo-register contains the illustra-tion of two 'culminant' events of the story. On the right Kama is depicted with his bow armed, standing in a flexed position, ready to shoot Shiva with the arrow of love, while, on the left, is the dead Kama on the floor, his head tenderly supported by his wife Rati (Fig. 96). Alternatively, this last scene can be interpreted as Kama's reincarnation as Pradyumna, with his head supported by his mother Rukmini. Although the incinerating ray that emanated from Shiva's third eye – the killing agent – is missing, the representation of the dead body is highlighted, perhaps because it implied future resurrection or reincarnation of Kama as Pradyumna, the son of Krishna and Rukmini (*Bhagavata Purana*, X, chapter 55).

In the panel to the right of the window are sculpted five small registers; the top four depict women wearing high crowns, symmetrically facing each other. The bottom, fifth register, displays groups of women with their children (Fig. 95). Since they are modestly dressed, do not wear crowns, and have their hair simply arranged, it seems likely that they represent common people.

Fig. 94 Shiva reducing Kama to ashes. S. 7

Fig. 95 Women and children attending the event. S. 7

The details of the story of Kama, the God of Love,[11] are narrated in the *Shiva Purana* (chapter II, 16-19), in the *Saura Purana* (chapters 53-54), and mention of his misfortune is also made in the *Ramayana* (Book I, chapter 23).

In the Shiva Purana *it is said that the demon Taraka, having propitiated Brahma by means of asceticism, obtains the boon that he could not be killed by any of the gods, but only by someone who was born from the seed of Shiva. He brings havoc amongst the gods, including Vishnu. In order to restore peace, Indra summons Kama, the God of Love ('He who is born in the mind'), and charges him to distract Shiva from his meditation and turn his mind towards lovemaking with Parvati.*

Kama armed with his flower-bow, and crocodile-bearing banner, reaches the place where the Great Lord is absorbed in meditation. At the door stands the guardian Sailadi, who is described holding a trident, and adorned and resplendent like a second Shiva. To bypass him, Kama transforms himself into a fragrant breeze, gentle and cool. Finally he comes into the presence of Shiva. Standing on his left side, with his bow fully drawn, he is ready to discharge the arrow of mango blossoms. Shiva notices him and is instantly angered. Kama discharges the arrow, but the infallible weapon becomes futile on the great Lord; Shiva's third eye in response shoots a great flame that reduces Kama to ashes. Parvati faints, and when she regains consciousness, she asks Shiva to resuscitate Kama, because without him there would be no feeling between man and woman, no happiness.[12] Also Rati, Kama's wife, implores Shiva to bring her beloved back. Shiva then makes Kama arise from the ashes in a disembodied form, indefinable, "going here and there like the wind" with his bow and arrow.[13]

The representation in the relief of a male figure holding a trident sitting to the left of Shiva could be attributed to Sailadi, a form of Shiva holding the *sula* (or *trisula*), named also Shiva *Suladhara*. Sailadi, however, is better known as Nandi.[14] In the *Vishnudharmottara*, Nandi is described as a man with three eyes and four arms, wearing a tiger skin, holding in one of his hands the *trisula*, the typical Shaivite emblem. However, Nandi is more often represented as the sacred bull of Shiva. In the *Ramayana* (Book VII, *Uttara Kanda*,

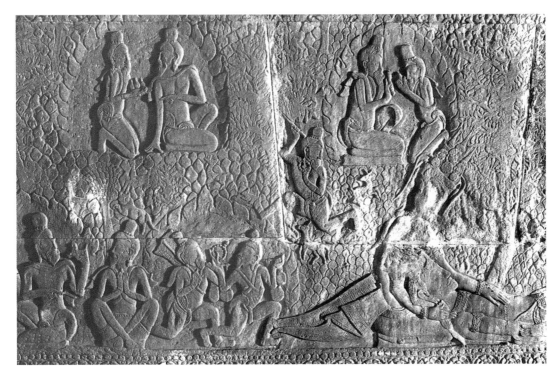

FIG. 96 The dying Kama supported by Rati (right). S. 7

FIG. 97 A smaller figure of Shiva (left) surrounded by *rishis*. S. 7

chapter 16) Nandi is said to be another manifestation of Shiva and that he was the guardian of Kailasa at the time Ravana was flying over it with the magic Pushpaka chariot he had just stolen from Kubera. Nandi is said to look like a dwarf, hold the trident, and to blaze with light like a second Shiva. Ravana was so enraged by Nandi's command not to approach the top of the sacred mountain, that he grabbed the mountain at its base and started to shake it violently, frightening the attendants of the gods and Parvati herself. This is the starting point of the episode of 'Ravana shaking Mount Kailasa' (see S. 5).

It is important to notice that Kama's arrow is not directed at the large image of Shiva of the top pseudo-register, but to that of the middle pseudo-register. Therefore, the action occurs between the middle and the lower pseudo-registers, with the top register depicting the beginning (Shiva in meditation) or the end of the story (the triumph of Shiva over desire and love). The episode of Kama shooting at Shiva depicted in this relief is not the only such occasion. In the *Vamana Purana* (Book 6, chapter 25) we are told that there were two previous occasions in which Kama attempted to hit him and drive him mad. The final episode, however, is this one. Another interesting feature, given its appearance in the relief of Shiva in the Pine Forest (S. 4), is the textual emphasis on Kama's banner bearing the image of a crocodile.

In the myth 'Shiva reducing Kama to ashes', the conflict between Shiva and Kama is central. Shiva is the natural enemy of Kama (god of desire) because he, Shiva, is the epitome of chastity, the eternal *brahmacharin* (the ascetic who has renounced everything). But, as a typical paradox of Hindu mythology, Shiva's chastity is set against his own lust; it is almost impossible to find a myth in which Shiva remains chaste after the original promise to be so. Although the original significance of Shiva burning Kama is unequivocally anti-sexual, immediately after it Shiva is seduced by Parvati and by the *tapas* she has performed in order to seduce him (Doninger 1973: 141). Yet, in terms of opposition and reversal, Kama is chastised in his own right, not for interrupting the love play, but for attempting to stimulate it and, as soon as Shiva burns Kama, Shiva does what Kama was tempting him to do anyway.

The interaction between Shiva and Kama is that of two supposedly opposed fires: the fire of desire and the fire of asceticism. But the ascetic fire from Shiva's eye merges with the fire with which Kama pierced Shiva, and finally penetrates the hearts of lovers. As Shiva and Kama are both creators, their roles are closely intertwined in the creation myths and can be interchanged. However, though Kama is merely one aspect of Shiva, the reverse is not true. Shiva is the god of virility, Kama the god of sensuality. Shiva burns Kama because of Kama's frivolous approach to a matter that for Shiva involves the procreation of the cosmos, rather than mere titillation which is Kama's stock and trade.

On the assumption that the interpretation of Shiva's myths is correct, it seems that they are all allegories of sensuality and eroticism, in keeping with Shiva's association with fertility. In the first, Shiva appears as a naked young man to seduce the *gopis* in the Pine Forest (S. 4); and in the second (S. 5), Ravana is prevented from travelling to Mount Kailasa, where Shiva and Parvati are making love. The third story (S. 7) relates to Kama's attempt to make Shiva unite with Parvati to procreate; finally, the fourth (S. 11) may deal with the betrothal of Shiva and Parvati which anticipates their love and union (and not with Shiva receiving homage). To be considered in conjunction with this topic is the fact that Shiva myths include the motif of interruption (Doniger 1973: 308). Kama interrupts Shiva's yogic trance to make him copulate with Parvati; Shiva is stopped by the sages from seducing the *gopis* of the Pine Forest; Ravana is prevented from interrupting Shiva's and Parvati's lovemaking. In Indian mythology, the interruption of a sexual scene is regarded as a sin. Metaphorically, however, the interrupter is considered a messenger who unites the worshippers with their gods.

The symbolic connection between Shaivism and Vaishnavism is subtle in this episode of Shiva reducing Kama to ashes. Kama, after having been reduced to ashes by Shiva, was reborn as Pradyumna, son of Krishna and Rukmini. And as previously discussed (*page 9*), according to the Pancharatra belief, Pradyumna is one of the main emanations (*vyuha*) of Vishnu. Furthermore, the relief of 'Shiva receiving homage' or 'The betrothal of Shiva and Parvati' (S. 11) may be the prelude to the formal union of Shiva with Parvati, as 'The Svayamvara of Sita' is of Rama and Sita (N. 10).

Concerning the layout of this relief, the arrangement of the various figures follows a hierarchical ordering. In the upper register, the various groups of ascetics are placed at three different levels, reflecting thus an internal order of merit. Also in the five registers to the right of the window, the village women are at the very bottom, below the ladies of the court. The women with their children depicted in the lowest register convey the happiness of family life that seems appropriate given the procreative theme of the story.

As shown, the relief's narrative technique is far from linear, narrating as it does the episode in four stages arranged according to the 'ellipsic method'.[15] The story is not entirely recounted but instead suggested through a couple of scenes, giving a synthesis of the plot. However, the visual sequence is woven into one organic entity with a clear sense of continuity of time and space.

S. 8 - The Death of Valin

Situated above the eastern window of the southern arm, this representation is divided in two main pseudo-registers. To the left of the upper register Rama and Lakshmana are represented holding bows and arrows and standing amongst seated monkeys (Fig. 102). Both are dressed in royal attire, with chest crossbands and cylindrical crowns with a cone at the top, the *kirta mukuta*. While Lakshmana is shown erect, Rama stands with flexed legs as if in the action of shooting an arrow, or more likely, having just shot an arrow (Fig. 100). Rama holds several more arrows as if in readiness to re-arm the bow. As the brothers are represented to the left of the central conflict between Valin and Sugriva, they are curiously shown as being left handed.

To the right are Valin and Sugriva in the grip of hand-to-hand combat. Valin is identifiable on the left with Rama's arrow in his chest, depicted an instant after Rama shot the arrow on the indication of Sugriva. To the right side of the two fighting monkeys is a seated crowned monkey watching the combat, who perhaps could be Hanuman interested in the fate of his master Sugriva.

FIG. 98 Shiva (detail). S. 7

FIG. 99 Grieving monkeys. S. 8

In the lower pseudo-register, the left half is occupied by the seated Sugriva flanked by Lakshmana (left) and Rama (right). The two brothers are standing, holding their disarmed bows and arrows. Rama is clearly displaying a pointed arrow, and looking down at Sugriva who is also looking up at him, even though time has heavily weathered his face. Lakshmana's attention is detached. One can conclude that the relief represents a conversation between Rama and Sugriva. On the right side of this register are several figures, but the most salient are the dying Valin and his wife Tara (Fig. 101). Valin lies on the ground, stiff, grim faced, his two arms aligned lifelessly along the body, Rama's arrow still in the right side of his chest. His head is supported by Tara (with queen's *mukuta*) who kneels on the ground and places her left arm around Valin's right shoulder in a tender gesture of affection. Several figures kneel around the royal couple; most are recognisable as monkey princesses from the conical pointed high crown, and refer to Valin's harem wives and court ladies. Those at Valin's feet hold and caress their dying lord, lamenting with open mouths.

The panel to the left of the window is sculpted with four rows of kneeling and grieving monkeys (Fig. 99). According to Ramayanic narrative, after Valin expired, a great tumult arose amongst the monkeys who lamented the loss of their valiant king and leader, and they feared that without his protection they would lose their security within the predator-infested forest.

The episode referred to here, also known as 'The duel between Sugriva and Valin', or 'Rama's murder of Valin', is taken from the 4th book of the *Ramayana*, the *Kishkindha Kanda*, so-called because it is set largely in the monkey citadel of Kishkindha. It continues the fairy-tale atmosphere of the preceding book of the adventures of Rama, Sita and Lakshmana in the forests. The conflict between Valin and Sugriva occupies a third of the book (26 chapters out of the 76), and in summary is as follows (*see page 135 for an account leading up to the scene depicted here*):

Exiled by Valin, his brother and king, Sugriva lives in constant terror of being pursued and murdered by him, as Valin is so powerful that he has never been defeated in combat (chapter 11). Sugriva admits being a coward and unacquainted with the skills of a warrior. At

Fig. 100 Rama shooting an arrow in Valin's back. S. 8

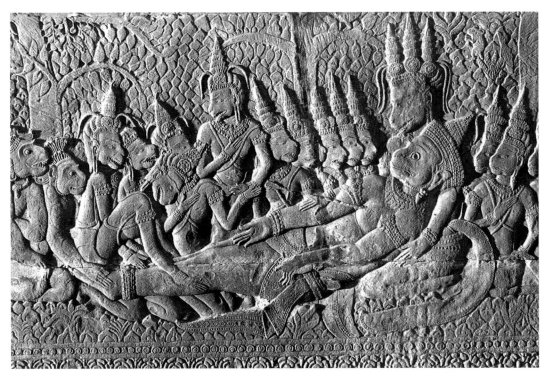

Fig. 101 Valin dying in the arms of his wife Tara. S. 8

this, Rama incites him to trust his courage and be confident. Sugriva, however, begs Rama to help him to assassinate Valin (as he had promised earlier in chapter 4) and he asks Rama to demonstrate his superior strength. Rama proves it by shooting an arrow that first pierces seven sala trees before burying itself in a mountain (chapter 12). Encouraged by this, Sugriva decides to confront Valin. A frightful fight between the two brothers follows, but Sugriva is defeated and, wounded, he escapes to the mountains where he meets again with Rama and Lakshmana. He is upset that Rama did not keep his promise to kill Valin, but Rama explains that he was unable to distinguish between the two brothers as they fought and therefore refrained from shooting. Later, Sugriva, once again incited by Rama, challenges Valin to fight, this time wearing a flower garland as identification.

The two monkey brothers become engaged in a fierce combat (chapter 16), furiously searching for each other's weak point, inflicting violent blows and becoming covered in blood. Rama and Lakshmana, concealed behind trees, see Sugriva becoming weaker and losing his courage. When Rama realises that Sugriva is exhausted and about to be overcome, he pierces Valin's chest with one of his formidable arrows. The valiant king of the monkeys falls to the earth, his voice strangled with sobs which gradually fade away.

Valin reproaches Rama for striking him when engaged in combat. He asks, "What merit do you hope to earn by this?" (chapter 17). Valin calls Rama a perverse creature, outwardly virtuous but in reality a scoundrel, a man who has killed him without reason. Moreover, Valin asks why a member of the warrior caste would commit such a wicked deed, break the laws of virtue, disregard justice, and become covered with the guilt of infamy. Valin also tells Rama that, if he had confided his purpose to Valin, then it would have been the work of a day for Valin to have destroyed Ravana and rescued Sita. He would also have allowed Sugriva to succeed to the throne legitimately after his death. Rama (chapter 18) justifies himself by telling Valin that he (Valin) was ignorant of his own dharma, *and accused him of 'simian folly' being a heedless monkey surrounded by irresponsible simian counsellors. He was also perverse in having marital rela-*

Fig. 102 The death of Valin. S. 8

tions with Ruma, Sugriva's wife – lust with a sister-in-law being an offence punishable with death. It was not for personal gain that he killed Valin "while engaged in combat with another" but in conformity to the ancestral ethics. Rama adds "There are Gods who, assuming human form, dwell on earth!" and he, Valin, has insulted him in anger. The dying Valin admits Rama is right, and, giving his son Angada into Rama's protection, falls into a coma.

Tara laments the death of her king and embraces her dying husband, deciding to die of hunger together with the other beautiful wives of Valin (chapter 19 and 20). But Hanuman tells her that she is now the protectress of all monkeys (chapter 21) and she has to ensure that prince Angada (her son with Valin) should be installed as king. Valin whispers his last words (chapter 22) to his brother and to his son, and dies (chapter 23) when general Nala draws the arrow from his chest. Tara then washes the corpse with her tears. Following this commotion, a remorseful Sugriva feels (chapter 24) that he does not merit the throne and is no longer worthy to live; after the funeral rites (chapter 25) he is eventually installed as king (chapter 26). He then passes his time in "drunken stupor and sexual indulgence" with Tara (chapter 31) to the point that he is severely reprimanded by Lakshmana. He has forgotten his promise to Rama, and allows four months to pass without making ready for the expedition to find and release Sita (chapter 30).

The tragic event displayed in this relief is underlined by the layout and the attitude of some of the personages. For instance, Valin's position in the relief is higher than Sugriva, connoting his superiority as well as his being a fighter overpowering his contestant. Altogether his body gives the impression of being more massive, stronger, and his jumping reveals more energy at that point of the fight. In the layout of the lower pseudo-register, the long arrow sticking out from the chest of the dying Valin is aligned almost exactly with Rama's left hand on the bow, and the central jewel of his necklace (the most important part of the ornament). Perhaps, in order to deflect attention from Rama's treacherous behaviour, the sculptors have depicted the arrow stuck in Valin's chest and not in his back as stipulated in the *Ramayana*.

Rama's arrow performs a discursive or perlocutionary act, telling us to look at a specific point within in the relief – that of the relationship between Rama and Valin. Many other figures are also displaying body gestures revealing a close participation in the event. For example, the hands of three of Valin's wives holding his feet are aligned, emphasising the action. The hands of the other grieving wives seem to be painting towards Valin's face; only one has her hand on her chest. Also noticeable is the direction towards the dying king of the gaze and the pointing fingers of the many kneeling monkeys in the registers to the left of the window. A few of them (second row from the bottom) have one arm over the head in a gesture of desperation, while others have one arm, or both, bent on their chest.

The core-issue of the episode of the death of Valin, is not why Rama killed Valin (to re-establish the *dharma*), but the way he killed him, as Valin repeatedly points out while dying (*Ramayana*, Book IV, chapter 17). The whole story is quite intriguing since it discloses the intimate characters of its protagonists. The details that Sugriva recounts to Rama about his enmity with his brother Valin are somewhat odd; Sugriva suffers from paranoia (Masson 1975: 95), he lives in constant fear of being persecuted and murdered by his brother. But in fact, Valin never intended any harm to his brother, deliberately refraining from killing him during the several confrontations they had. Even Sugriva (chapter 24) tells Rama that Valin has refused to kill him in battle, simply asking him to go away, almost in a paternal manner, and Sugriva goes so far as to admit that Valin acted justly and that he, Sugriva, acted out of anger, like a monkey. Although Valin had stolen Sugriva's wife, Sugriva always fancied Tara, Valin's wife, who he hurried to marry immediately after Valin's death.

Rama's character reveals two great flaws: to have killed Valin from a concealed position, contrary to the laws of war that he, as a *kshatriya* prince was morally bound to uphold, and of which he considers himself to be the great protector (*Ramayana* IV, chapter 18, addressing Valin). Then, to have decided precipitously to kill Valin, before listening to Sugriva's full story or indeed that of Valin. It is Rama who first mentions murder as a solution, Sugriva only requests help. Almost as an afterthought Rama asks Sugriva what was the reason for the enmity (chapter 8) although he – at the same time – also assures Sugriva that he has already decided upon

Valin's guilt. For Rama, the time taken to hear the story will be just sufficient for deciding to string his bow (chapter 8).[16]

The underlying symbolism of this event is the liberation of Valin from his unfortunate incarnation, his bad karma, and Rama (a manifestation of God) giving him a chance to return on earth as a rightful being. With his action, Rama re-establishes the *dharma* on earth. However, in the visual representation of this story, the Khmers may have deliberately shifted the attention away from Rama's murder of Valin to the figure of the dying Valin, not so much in a gesture of compassion, but mainly because Suryavarman II and his brahmins were convinced that Rama acted rightfully. The Khmers perceived Valin as a usurper who wanted to regain his kingdom from Sugriva, denying the fact that Sugriva had taken Valin's kingdom without checking if his brother was actually dead. For the Khmers, Sugriva was the rightful king, implying that – similarly – Suryavarman II's grandfather (Jayavarman VI) was the rightful successor of Khmer royal ancestors, and not a usurper expanding a new dynasty, and that anybody who attempted to usurp Suryavarman II's kingdom deserved death.

The layout of this relief also follows the 'ellipsic' method described in the previous relief. Therefore, it is impossible to determine the occasion of the conversation between Rama and Sugriva in the lower pseudo-register. We know from the text that there is a discussion well before the fight and another just after it. The first (chapter 11) is the one that brought Rama to commit himself to kill Valin; the other – after the murder – when Sugriva expresses his remorse (chapter 24). In the reading of the relief, two interpretations are possible. In the first, the depiction of Sugriva seated on the floor, his right arm on his chest, might suggest a person in a physical and emotional state of distress. In this case the conversation depicted would have taken place after the fight. Alternatively, one might consider the body language of Sugriva squatting on the ground, an indication of sadness at being exiled and losing his wife. He is represented in a similar attitude on two occasions in the panels of the Baphuon temple. In this case we may be dealing with the dialogue that takes place at the first meeting of Sugriva and Rama, when he tells Rama his lengthy story of enmity with Valin. In tune

with this interpretation is the gesture of Rama displaying his arrow by placing it in front of his face (the pointed tip in front of his eyes) and in the direct line of Sugriva's gaze. It is obstructing eye contact between the two, making sure that Sugriva notices it. Rama reaffirms thus that the arrow is the material pledge of the alliance. In this case the conversation has taken place before the fight.

S. 9 - The murder of Pralamba & The dousing of a fire

The identification of this relief sculpted over the southern door is unclear (Fig. 103). Although it seems to represent at least two Vaishnava stories, as yet no reference has been found to a particular event in the life of Krishna or Vishnu, nor – in the case of two events – how they are interconnected. Coedès tentatively attributed the grouping of figures in the right half of the relief to 'The Murder of Pralamba', while the scene on the left he designated 'Krishna Extinguishing a Fire' (1932: plate 305). In full awareness that these matters of identification need further study, Coedès's attributions are accepted for the purpose of this discussion.

Both scenes are contained in two pseudo-regiters, the lower one being filled with landscape scenery of rocks, vegetation and some animals (lions, deer and birds). In the right portion of the upper pseudo-register, two figures are depicted what appears to be a mountain. The left-hand one, located at a higher level, is Krishna (or Vishnu) in royal attire. With one of his four arms he is holding a mace (or axe). With his upper arms, Krishna/Vishnu holds a conch, and the discus (*chakra*). His unarmed victim is dressed in a short vest and has a simple hairstyle. He appears to be frantically gesticulating, and it is difficult to say if the object in his right hand is a tool or a branch of the nearby tree.

To the left, this same, or perhaps another, man is displayed walking through a fire with his arms folded in the attitude of respect or prayer. He is approaching the figure of an ascetic seated ceremonially in front of another image of Krishna/Vishnu. Once again, the latter is represented with four arms, this time holding the mace, conch, discus and possibly a lotus. If the reading of the attributes is correct, the image could represent Vishnu *Janardana*, Giver of Rewards (Rao 1914, I: 230).

The episodes of 'The Murder of Pralamba' and 'The Dousing of a Fire' proposed by Coedès are to be found in the *Bhagavata Purana* (X, chapters 18-19) and in the *Brahma Purana* (II, chapter 78). In the former text we read:

Krishna, Balarama and their cowherd friends enter the forest and indulge in playing, wrestling, singing and dancing (chapter 18). One day, the demon Pralamba, having assumed the guise of a cowherd, joins the group with a view to kidnapping the boys. Aware of this evil scheme, Krishna decides to trap Pralamba by allowing him to join their games. Pralamba becomes irritated with Balarama, and assuming his original demonic form "like a cloud illuminated with flashing lights" snatches up Balarama and flies away with him into the sky. Balarama strikes the demon's head with his fist, shattering it to pieces. Vomiting blood profusely Pralamba emits a terrifying roar and falls dead. Balarama is praised by his friends as well as by the gods who shower him with wreaths of flowers.

Later, while Krishna, Balarama, the cowherds and their cattle are in the forest (chapter 19), a fire breaks out, and is spread by the wind. Everybody runs to Krishna asking for help, and he says 'Don't be afraid. Please close your eyes'. As they do so, the Supreme master of Yoga swallows the menacing fire and saves them from calamity.

There is no doubt in the text, that it is Balarama and not Krishna that kills Pralamba thus making the relief's identification with this episode problematic. Furthermore, in the text Pralamba assumes the form of a gigantic monster while in the relief a quite unremarkable man is represented. The interpretation of the second part of the narrative, dealing with Krishna swallowing the fire of the forest, is also questionable because Krishna is not depicted in the act of doing so. Furthermore he is shown hieratically seated behind a *rishi*, a personage not mentioned in the text. It is also not clear why the man is attempting to walk through the fire, and why he is going towards Krishna in what seems to be an act of contrition.

Fig. 103 The murder of Pralamba (right) and the Dousing of Fire (left). S. 9

Although its links with Krishna dousing the fire are weak, this scene is even less likely to be that of the 'Burning of the Khandava Forest' narrated in the *Mahabharata* (I, The Book of the Beginning, 214-219). According to this tale, the fire god Agni, having exhausted his strength by devouring too many sacrificial offerings, determines to set on fire the entire Khandava forest and devour it as a means of regaining his power. He is prevented from doing so by Indra's torrential rain, but obtaining the help of Krishna and Arjuna, he baffles Indra and accomplishes his objective. This story is beautifully rendered in a pediment of Banteay Srei (eastern pediment of northern Library) although it has usually been identified as the Puranic story of 'The Rain of Indra' (Jacques 1997: 110). As concerns the present relief, it seems almost impossible that it refers ro the *Mahabharata* episode. The strongest reason for this is that according to Khmer iconography, Krishna and Arjuna should appear on chariots, the former holding the discus and the latter the bow, the magic weapons they received as rewards for helping Agni. Not only is Arjuna unidentifiable in the present relief, but Krishna is certainly not riding a chariot.

S. 10 – The Dvaravati water festival

Although for years French scholars – George Coedès (1911) and Maurice Glaize (1963), for instance – have suggested analogies between this relief and the Dvaravati water festival,[17] it is not clear whether it was meant to depict an earthly event or the mythological enactment of that event. The relief contains clear references to the description of the festival in the *Harivamsa* but it also includes local, Khmer elements such as the poses and detailing of the main figures, as well as abundant fish and crocodiles in the water, which are not mentioned in the text.

The scene is arranged in two main pseudo-registers. In the upper pseudo-register (Fig. 106), the full width of the wall is sculpted with the image of a large boat made in the shape of a mythological animal with the prow in the shape of a dragon's head. Built over a

FIG. 104 The Dvaravati Water Festival. Detail of chess (?) players. S. 10

FIG. 105 Parents holding their children. S. 10

base is a cabin, with a windowed extension at each side, and a double-tiered roof with pointed finials. At the top, on the roof, is a pointed dome. This construction is more likely meant to represent one made of wood, and possibly decorated with gold. Under a canopy are two personages, male judging from the hairstyle, without crowns, playing a chess-type game with counters on a low table (Fig. 104). They are surrounded by women: the ones to their left, in a small group, are arranging something (flowers?) in a pot. Another group is shown with children and boys, while some of the figures seem to fall overboard. Above this last group are four men with blowpipes, two of which are aiming at something hidden in the dense foliage of a tree. On the other side of the cabin, is a group of seated personages, mostly ladies with high *mukuta*. Tall trees on the shore form the background, some of them are being climbed by men in search of coconuts.

In the lower pseudo-register (Fig. 107) is another large boat, similar to the one above, but with its prow sculpted as the head of a *hamsa* (badly preserved; compare with Varuna's mount in the relief of the 'Invitation for Vishnu to descend', N. 1). At the stern, above the rowers, is a group of four or five people, two of whom hold parasols and another something resembling a flywhisk. At the centre is a complex construction on a high and richly decorated plinth, with a central domed cabin with an extension at each side. The two-tiered roof terminates with finials, and is covered by a dome on top of which is a smaller baldaquin. Here, under rich draperies made of floral fabrics, are a woman (important, judging from her large size) with a baby on her lap, and, to the right of the viewer, a man holding a child in his raised arms (Fig. 105). He seems to have a short beard and hair arranged in a single chignon; he is dressed in a long rich gown hanging down almost to his feet. Women in the adjacent rooms surround these two main personages. At the boat's aft is again a group of people with two parasols crammed together, watching a cockfight (Fig. 108). This boat, as well as the one above, floats through waters indicated by wavy lines and teeming with fish and crocodiles (Fig. 109), and the occasional bird on the surface (mandarin duck?). The banks of the river or lake have lush vegetation, with some trees with climbing vines on their trunks.

This extravagant and luxurious scene does have some parallels with the *Harivamsa*'s description of the Dvaravati water festival (II, 45-46).

Fig. 106 The boat in the upper part of the relief. S. 10

Fig. 107 The boat in the lower part of the relief. S. 10

FIG. 108 People watching a cockfight. S. 10

Dvaravati is the city of Vishnu, and from there Krishna makes a maritime pilgrimage (called Samudrayatra) to Pindaraca. On this occasion, everybody leaves town, with Krishna's compatriots, the Yadavas, leading their children and wives. Beautiful women of pleasure and singing apsaras accompany Krishna and Balarama. First, they enter the forest for love games, and towards the evening, they board marvellous boats to continue to indulge in pleasures. These ships carry large buildings with porticoes, verandas, and gardens with wild animals and birds, in an arrangement that simulates Mount Meru. All the pavilions are ornate with gold, precious and semi-precious stones, besides being crowned with garlands, birds and swarms of bees; all trees are in bloom. The climate is mild so that nobody is sick, restless, worried or thirsty. The great architect Vishvakarman has created a sort of Nandana, the celestial grove of Indra.

The boats, shaped like geese, peacocks and sea monsters, are steered by able pilots, and cut elegantly across the waves of the sea. One boat alone is for the use of Krishna and his retinue. Singing and dancing enhance the festival, the apsaras praising Krishna's adventures; the orchestra plays without interruption; the guests enjoy all sorts of pleasures. Krishna multiplies his forms in order to please his 1,600 wives, who, lightly dressed, recline in sensual attitudes; in making love to them, he makes sure to vary their enjoyment. Balarama drinks kadambari (a liquor obtained from Kadamba flowers mixed with autumn rain) in the company of Arjuna and his wife Subhadra, Pradyumna and others. Narada acts the clown.

FIG. 109 A man fishing. S. 10

There are other less plausible interpretations of the event narrated in this relief. One involves combining the story of Rama's return to Ayodhya as narrated in Valmiki's *Ramayana* with a local belief that this must have taken place by sea, and not by using the magic flying Pushpaka chariot that Rama had gained upon defeating Ravana. Another interpretation would be that it represents Vibhishana's return trip to the isle of Lanka with his wife and entourage after Rama's coronation (*Ramayana*, book 6, chapter 130). Today, the local guides at Angkor believe that the scene is a sumptuous festive occasion of rich local Chinese merchants on the *barays* or the Tonlé Sap. In fact, it was Moura in 1883 who first suggested that the main figures in this relief were Chinese, but the idea was refuted early by Coedès (1911: 99). Later, Bernard Philippe Groslier (1973: 172) pointed out that the boats and all the occupants are Khmer in appearance. Only the orchestra of one boat of the relief is identical to that of the boat of the Bayon's relief (SE outer gallery) presenting a lord wearing a 'Chinese' hat and dress (an ambassador?), probably attending a royal ceremony. Groslier was convinced that this relief depicted a scene evoking the pleasures of the celestial city of Dvaravati, symbol of the royal capital (of Angkor). At Bayon, the Chinese pleasure boat is accompanied by a large Chinese junk with sailors playing chess. This raises questions as to the importance and role of the Chinese at Angkor. It may have been purely commercial, involving the arrival of a Chinese ambassador for important events, like the investiture of a Khmer king.

The orientation and arrangement of the many oars, differing in angle between the two boats, seem to increase the sense of action and movement that pervades this relief. By following the laws of spatial representation in use at the time, the boats are sculpted as if they were one above the other. From this it follows that only one water surface (river, lake, or sea) is depicted here, with two boats floating on it. The boat in the lower pseudo-register is possibly more important than the one in the higher pseudo-register, a fact confirmed by its larger pavilion and by the presence of such royal emblems as the parasols and flywhisk. When read according to the *Harivamsa*'s description, this lower register's boat with royal insignia and larger size would be for Krishna and his wives, accompanied by a noisy brigade of court maidens and servants,

while the other boat is for Balarama, playing chess, surrounded by his courtesans. This interpretation, although tentative, seems more likely than the inclusion of a single secular scene of a Khmer water festival amongst the programme of otherwise mythological scenery.

S. 11 – Shiva receiving Homage or The Betrothal of Shiva and Parvati

This relief is sculpted above the southern window of the eastern wing. Unfortunately, the degradation of the rock has defaced most of its upper part, including the main personages, with the exception of the central figure of Shiva, whose identity is confirmed by the beard visible on close inspection. Because of this poor state of preservation, the relief's reading is quite elusive (Fig. 112).

The story is narrated in three pseudo-registers. Although heavily damaged, one can discern in the topmost a central figure of Shiva with the beard of a *rishi* sitting on a high base in the *yogasana* position (Fig. 110). However, his aspect is not that of a *rishi*. He is wearing a *mukuta* surmounted by a thin conical end from which two tufts of hair protrude, and he is richly adorned with heavy jewellery. Instead of the usual rosary, in his left hand he holds a piece of fine jewellery in the shape of a lotus bud with a tapering flexible stem (almost identical to the object that Suryavarman II is holding in the Historic Procession [LP. 2]).[18] Shiva is depicted turning to his right, with his right arm raised, of which unfortunately the hand and its *mudra* have eroded away. He is facing four male personages, wearing crowns and adorned with jewels. They are seated or squatting slightly below the deity, and some hold a hand raised to their chest. The figure closest to Shiva seems to have both arms raised in the direction of Shiva, perhaps making an offering of a container (eroded) with a lid that has a still-visible disc or wheel finial.

The middle and lower pseudo-registers are composed of bands of trees amongst which ascetics sit with crossed legs and joined hands (Fig. 110), possibly in prayer or meditation. In one instance in the lower pseudo-register is a small scene with ascetics climbing a tree in order to escape an atrack by a wild animal (Fig. 113), while others are on the ground in

Fig. 110 *Rishis* in caves. S. 11

Fig. 111 Shiva in *yogasana* position. S. 11

various activities: holding fans made from peacock feathers (deltoid-shaped), conversing or in meditation.

The panel to the right of the window is sculpted with four registers (Fig. 114) with further seated royal figures, most with one hand on their chest, while others hold the stem of a large lotus bud; a few *rishis* are also displayed in the top register.

In the relief under consideration, Shiva either seems to be formal receiving homage from royal personages, or he may be addressing people around him, preaching a sermon. The scene takes place in a forest at the top of a mountain, probably the mighty Mount Kailasa, Shiva's abode, with its caverns where ascetics sit in penance and meditation. In general, this event is reminiscent of Shiva's meetings with great sages and important personages as recounted in a few Shaivite stories, of which the most popular are that of 'The Birth of Parvati' (*Vamana Purana*, XXV.1-75, towards the end) and 'The Betrothal of Shiva and Parvati' (*Vamana Purana*, XXVI.1-71). The narrative of the

latter has several points in common with the story displayed in this relief. In it, it is narrated that:

One day, Shiva summons the seven great seers (and Vasishta, the wife of one of them) to Mount Mandara, inviting them to enjoy the beauty of the location. He then addresses the assembled and seated sages, requesting them to go to the king of the Himalayas to ask – on Shiva's behalf – for the hand of his daughter, Parvati. Known under a variety of names (Uma and Devi being the most common), she was born from the union of the king Himavat and his wife Mena. The last of three girls, she had developed such an intense beauty from the practice of tapas *that the gods could not approach her, overcome as they were by her brilliance. But then, one day she was met by Shiva who repeatedly tested her devotion, before asking her hand in marriage. King Himavat was pleased by the request of Shiva, but would take the final decision only after discussing the matter with the kings of all the other mountains. These quickly assembled, aware of the importance of their task; they were twenty-three in total,*

Fɪɢ. 112 Shiva receiving homage. S. 11

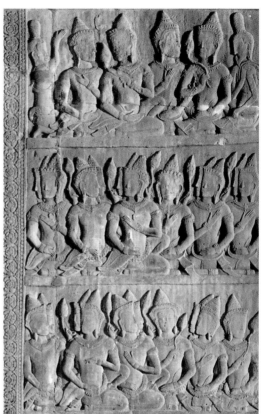

FIG. 113 An ascetic climbing a tree to escape a tiger. S. 11   FIG. 114 Courtiers witnessing the event. S. 11

including Mount Mandara, Mount Kailasa and Mahendra (Maniparvata). They sat on golden seats in the assembly hall, together with lesser mountains and hills. After hearing Himavat, they agreed unanimously that Shiva would be a suitable son-in-law to them all. The betrothal was thus arranged.

The kings of the mountains of the text are perhaps the numerous crowned personages assembled at the top of the mountain in this relief. The figure to the left of Shiva would then be King Himavat, making a formal offering to Shiva of a vase or container symbolic of his daughter. Parvati's presence is not mentioned in the Indian text, and perhaps in a relief illustrating the story she would also be absent. (However, as mentioned, the present relief's erosion precludes a complete reading). Parvati's absence would account for French scholars choosing not to propose any specific episode, but simply refer to the

relief generically as 'Shiva Receiving Homage'. Accordingly, interpreting the relief as 'Shiva's Betrothal' is highly conjectural.

C. M. Bhandari (1995: 70) believes that the relief illustrates a particular episode from the teachings of Shiva, when some *rishis* wanted to learn the *Vedas*, and went to Shiva for help. The god agreed to help them and sat in meditation facing south, hence the origin of the name Shiva *Dakshinamurti* (*Dakshinayana* is the southern transit of the sun, from Cancer to Capricorn). At once the *Vedas* became illuminated on his meditating body, and the *rishis* could learn them by seeing and reading rather than by the verbal teaching of Shiva. Besides Shiva *Nataraja* (Lord of the Dance), Shiva *Dakshinamurti* is the most important manifestation of Shiva as a personal god. However, in the case of this particular aspect of Shiva, his posture and *mudras* can only be of a certain variety and this is not the case here.[19]

FIG. 115 Krishna receiving the offerings destined for Indra. S. 12

FIG. 116 The offerings (detail).

S. 12 – Krishna receiving the offerings destined for Indra

The relief is sculpted within a *naga* frame in a flat pediment over the door of the eastern wing of the pavilion. In the central part of the single pseudo-register that composes this relief, the image of Vishnu (or of Krishna assimilated to Vishnu) is represented standing amongst kneeling figures (Fig. 115). He wears a tall crown and traditional body ornaments. The god is represented with four arms: the upper right holding the disc (*chakra*); the upper left the conch; the lower left a conical object, and the lower right in the attitude of receiving an offering from a worshipper. On either side of Vishnu is a seated worshipper with both arms raised to make an offering (a lotus bud?) to him. Behind the worshipper to the right of the viewer is a bearded figure with an elaborate hairstyle and wearing a long shirt/vest, probably signs of high rank. He is depicted with upraised arms in offering to the god another small conical object (Fig. 116). At both sides of Vishnu/Krishna are figures carrying trays on their heads with offerings in three pointed containers (or cakes?). The scene is depicted as taking place in a forest or in a garden, and in the sky fly celestial beings who seem to be male, with crowns and carrying garlands of flowers or jewels (pearls?).

French scholars, with some reservations, have identified this relief with the story of Krishna receiving the offerings originally destined for Indra as narrated in the *Bhagavata Purana* (X, chapter 24) and discussed in relation to the relief of 'Krishna lifting Mount Govardhana' (S. 2).

One day, Krishna is observing the cowherds on the move to bring offerings and make sacrifices to the god Indra; he questions them, "What does the great Indra have to do with it? Therefore let a sacrifice be dedicated to Mount Govardhana, the Brahmanas and the propitiation of the cows be initiated" (stanza 23). Krishna tries to dissuade them from adoring Indra in order to introduce the Vaishnava cult, because – he explains – Mount Govardhana is a form of himself. Having convinced the cowherds to do so, they bring him the offerings that were destined for Indra. Inevitably, Indra becomes enraged and releases the famous downpour of rain.

The text mentions offerings being carried to Mount Govardhana[20], and not to Krishna or Vishnu. However, as Krishna declared that the mountain was the same as himself, the offerings are ultimately destined for him. Although we know very little about the original form of the Krishna cult, it was probably a strongly monotheistic religion, worshipping Bhagavat, 'the adorable one'. It taught *bhakti*, or the single-minded devotion to the supreme deity as the best means of salvation. Krishna gradually came to be identified and venerated as Bhagavat. There is a precedent to the relationship between Krishna and Indra. According to the *Harivamsa* (Vol. II, 68, 33), Krishna describes himself as a younger brother of Indra, presenting thus himself as the ultimate fulfilment of Indra's manifestation (S. Bhattacharji 1970: 306).

PAGE 132, FIG. 117 Part of of the Northwestern Corner Pavilion and the exit to the Gallery with the Long Panel of the Battle of the *Devas* and the *Asuras*.

N. 1 – Invitation for Vishnu to descend

This relief over the northern window of the pavilion's eastern arm is in very poor condition with some of the key elements being completely obliterated or rendered unrecognisable. It is still possible, however, to discern that it is divided into two main pseudo-registers, in the upper of which one can still make out the body and the hood of the very large snake Ananta (or Sesha). Reclining on him is Vishnu (whose torso and head have also eroded away) sleeping on his left side in the traditional position, with his feet in the lap of his spouse Lakshmi (Fig. 118). This is almost identical to the image of Vishnu *Anantashayin* – one of the most popular in the Khmer repertory – but there are several elements that make it distinct from that. The first of these are the large branching lotuses reaching up to the sky, none of which emanate from his umbilicus, as in the myth of the creation of Brahma. By the time of the event depicted in this relief, Brahma[21] was, of course, already in existence, and the leader of the 30 gods participating in the delegation to invite Vishnu to descend to Earth. To either side of Vishnu, are two superimposed rows of religious, royal and celestial personages, amongst a forest of parasols and fans. The great Ananta rests on a sea (the Ocean of Milk) full of fish and reptiles; trees distinguish the more distant shore.

In the lower pseudo-register is displayed the second element that distinguishes this relief from that of the myth of Vishnu *Anantashayin*: a parade of the eight deities on their way to invite Vishnu to descend on earth as an *avatara*. They are, from right to left: Ketu (the comet), holding a mace and a lotus bud, and riding a lion; Agni with one arm on his chest, mounting his rhinoceros; Yama, also armed with a mace, riding on his buffalo; Indra on his crowned elephant (Airavata); Kubera, holding a whip, mounted on a horse; Skanda with many arms, holding the trident as son of Shiva, on a peacock; Varuna, holding a *pasa* or noose, riding on his *hamsa*, and Nirrti on the shoulders of a *yaksha*, with a mace in one hand and a flywhisk in the other. At the top of the relief is the usual storm of *apsaras*, while the panel to the right of the window is composed of two registers illustrating two further deities making up the delegation to Vishnu: Chandra, the Moon (top), and Surya, the Sun (bottom), depicted as two male gods seated on chariots backed by a large disc (Fig. 119). Each chariot is pulled by two horses (both with a single head), unusually represented frontally, riding towards the viewer, amongst flags, parasols, fans, trees and surrounded by kneeling personages in prayer.

In the layout of this relief, the vertical axis of symmetry is passing through the middle of Vishnu's body (the navel?), behind which a lotus branches out creating a strong visual feature. Of the ten gods, eight are arranged in a linear sequence going from left to right of the viewer, while two (the sun and the moon) progress out of the relief, towards the viewer.

The episode of Vishnu's invitation to 'descend' as an *avatara* occasions the god's incarnation as Krishna. It is recounted in the *Vishnu Purana*, (V, part 1, chapters 5-33; 56-86; and part 2, chapters 1-6) and in the *Bhagavata Purana* (X, chapter 1, 17-23). The latter is a shorter version in which, when the gods first ask Brahma for advice, Mother Earth takes the shape of a cow, but the detail of Vishnu taking two hairs and splitting them to create Krishna and Balarama is omitted. The most relevant elements of the version in the *Vishnu Purana* are as follows.

The Earth goddess, oppressed by heavy burdens complains to Brahma that the Daitya (asuras), led by Kalanemi, have overthrown the world of mortals and are oppressing all humans. Kalanemi had once been slain by Vishnu but was reborn as Kamsa. The Earth begs the gods to release her from the problems caused by Kamsa and his demons. Having heard this, Brahma and the Thirty Gods propose to go to the shore of the Ocean of Milk and pray to Vishnu in the hope that he will hear their request.

The Earth, Indra, Nasatyas and Dashra (the two Asvins), Rudras and Vasus, the Sun, the Wind and Fire, accordingly give praise to Vishnu who pulls two of his hairs from his head, one white, one black, and tells the gods that these hairs will descend to earth to save the world. One will become the eighth embryo in Devaki's womb and will be born as Krishna who will kill Kamsa. The other hair will be the seventh embryo of Devaki (the previous six having been destroyed by Kamsa); although aborted he will survive to become Samkarshana (Balarama), the elder brother of Krishna.

The narrative in the relief, therefore, follows a fairly linear sequence, starting from Vishnu sleeping or dreaming on the great snake in the top register, proceeding to the delegation of deities inviting him to become an *avatara* in the lower register. The whole necessity for Vishnu to 'descend' as Krishna is imposed by the need to put an end to the terror and chaos created by the monster Kalanemi.[22] Krishna's origin as an *avatara* is an unusual choice for a relief in this pavilion where the majority of images relate to the *Ramayana*; Rama would have been a more appropriate *avatara*.

In view of the fact that some of these gods or demi-gods appear in reliefs from many other sites of Angkor where their identification is not always entirely clear, their main characteristics are here described (*see drawing of Table 5 on page 137*).

1. Vayu

The god of wind, he is considered to be the guardian of the Northwest. He is a youthful strong person, carrying a banner and a *danda* (command stick). He may be seated either on a prancing lion (*simhasana*) or a deer, and be shown moving quickly. According to Hindu texts, he also rides a chariot with wheels of wind, pulled by 1,000 horses.

2. Agni

He is one of the three great Vedic deities, together with Indra and Surya, respectively representing earth, air and sky. Agni is considered the guardian of the Southeast. He is described as having four hands, with smoke for his standard and crown, and carries a flaming javelin. He travels on a chariot pulled by red horses, with the seven winds as the wheels. A ram, which sometimes he rides, accompanies him; but his mount varies and in Khmer iconography he is seen on a rhinoceros.

3. Yama

He is the god of the dead, with whom the spirits of the departed dwell. He is also their judge in which task he is assisted by Citragupta (see I.P. 3, Heavens and Hells). Yama is the regent of the South, and as such is called Dakshinapati. He is represented riding a buffalo or on top of a *simhasana*, armed with a heavy mace and a noose to secure his victims.

4. Indra

One of the triad with Agni and Surya, he was originally a god of the first rank, but gradually lost importance. He is considered the guardian of the East. King of heaven, he sends the lightning and hurls the thunderbolt, and the rainbow is his bow. He is frequently at war with the *asuras*, of whom he lives in constant dread. As a libertine, he enjoys sending *apsaras* to excite and distract holy men. He is known for his sensuality and seductions. Once he slew the demon Vritra, who being a brahmin, obliged him to make penance and sacrifices until his guilt was purged away. Indra, protector of heroes, is the father of Arjuna. In the *Ramayana* we are told that Ravana's son defeated him in a sky battle thus acquiring the name Indra-jit, conqueror of Indra. In the *Puranas* he appears as a rival of Krishna (see relief S. 12). Krishna also won the fight against him for the possession of the Parijata tree.

Indra is represented as a white man riding a horse (Ucchaihshravas) or an elephant (Airavata), bearing the *vajra* or thunderbolt in his hand or a sword (Pananja). In Khmer iconography he is usually mounted on his three-headed elephant.

5. Kubera

The lord of riches, king of men and genies, he is considered the guardian of the North. He is half-brother of Ravana who expelled him from Lanka, his initial abode. Mount Mandara is his residence, where he is assisted by *kinnaras*. Having performed austerities for 1,000 years, he obtained from Brahma the boon of immortality, and the magic aerial chariot Pushpaka. He is represented as a white man with deformed body, having three legs and only eight teeth. Bedecked with ornaments, he holds a sword or a mace while riding a horse. In a pediment of the northern central pavilion of the 1st enclosure, Kubera is represented surrounded by mongooses, symbols of wealth and abundance and therefore associated with him.

FIG. 118 The invitation for Vishnu to descend. N. 1

6. Skanda

Also known by the name of Karttikeya because he was reared by the six Pleiades (Krittikas), developing six faces to drink their milk. The son of Shiva (or Rudra) without the intervention of a woman, he was born as the god of war in order to slay the anti-gods Taraka and Mahisha, who challenged the gods with the power obtained from austerities (*tapas*). He is represented riding a peacock (Paravani), dressed in red, with one or six heads, two or twelve arms, holding a bow in one hand and an arrow in the other, or a sword, a thunderbolt and an axe. His spear, which never misses its mark, returns to his hand after killing the enemies. His banner, a gift from Agni, is red as the fire of destruction. In Khmer iconology he is represented – as in this relief – holding a trident.

7. Varuna

He is one of the oldest and most powerful of the Vedic deities, the personification of the all-investing sky, the maker and upholder of heaven and earth. As such he is the king of the universe, of gods and men, possessor of unlimited knowledge, the supreme deity to whom especial honour is due. In the *Puranas*, he is the sovereign of the waters, with a *hamsa* as his mount, a *pasa* or a noose in his hand, and sometimes an umbrella. Guardian of rites, he dwells in the West. Varuna should replace the identification of Brahma in many previous interpretations. Occasionally, a three-headed *naga* is depicted as his *vahana*.

8. Nirrti

Nirrti is the regent of the Southwest, representing misery, lord of the elves (*nairrta*), ghosts, night

FIG. 119 Chandra (above) and Surya (below). N. 1

wanderers (*rakshasas*), and of the Lords of the directions (*Dikpalas*). In this relief Nirrti is shown on the shoulder of a *rakshasa* or *yaksha*,[23] holding a mace in one hand and a lotus bud in the other. This *deva* was unidentified until Mannikka (1996: 187) proposed Nirrti on the grounds that he is the *deva* suitable to fill – in this relief – the only gap left amongst the *dikpalas*, that of the Southwest.

9. Chandra

In Puranic literature, the Moon appropriated the name and some of the characteristics of *soma* (the juice drunk by the brahmins); he is the son of Atri (detachment, born from Brahma's mind) and Anasuya (benevolence). When the Ocean was churned, the Moon sprang forth joyfully, just after Lakshmi, spreading a cool light (*Mahabharata*, I, 18.34). His chariot has three wheels and is drawn by ten horses of the whiteness of jasmine. Together with the Sun, the Moon spotted Rahu stealing some of the *amrita* produced by the Churning and informed Vishnu, who punished him severely (see S. 1). This is perhaps why, in Khmer iconography, the moon and the sun appear at the sides of the pole of the Churning of the Ocean of Milk, like in S. 1 and many other reliefs, with the exception of the Long Panel (LP. 4). In this relief, Chandra and Surya are holding lotus flowers in their right hands.

10. Surya

The sun is one of the three main deities of the *Veda*, and is the great source of light and warmth, considered, in the *Ramayana*, to be the son of Brahma. He is represented in a chariot drawn by four or seven horses, or a single horse with seven heads, surrounded with rays, with Arunba (or Vivaswat) as the charioteer. The horse with seven heads has a predominant position, together with the three-headed elephant, in the reliefs of the Terrace of the Elephants in the northern part of Angkor Thom.

The deities taking part in the procession illustrated in this relief raise the problem of their correct individual identification. This problem possibly goes back to the Khmer depiction of the so-called *navagraha*, the Nine Gods of Hindu mythology (K. Bhattacharya 1956: 183, and L. Malleret, 1960: 205) that include (from left to right) Surya, Chandra,

Yama or Skanda, Brahma, Indra, Kubera, Agni, Rahu and Ketu. It is difficult to identify them because – firstly – they are represented with personal attributes and *vahana* that are not always those prescribed by the Hindu texts. Secondly, they are shown in a variable order of arrangement, although usually the couple representing Surya-Chandra is to the left, and Rahu-Ketu to the right end of the relief. The five gods at the centre are, however, arranged at random with Indra usually in a central position, Skanda/Varuna and Yama to the left, and Kubera and Agni to the right.

At some point in Khmer history, some of the deities of the *Navagraha* became the object of a cult addressed to the regents and guardians of space, the *Dikpalas* of the four cardinal directions and of the four inter-cardinal directions. They are (Table 4):

TABLE 4

Deity	Direction	Indian mount	Khmer mount
Kubera	North	ram	?horse
Shiva/Skanda	Northeast	peacock	peacock
Indra	East	elephant or horse	elephant
Agni	Southeast	horse or ram	rhinoceros
Yama	South	buffalo or simhasana	buffalo
Nirrti	Southwest	man or lion	*yaksha*
Varuna	West	fish or goose	goose (*naga*)
Vayu	Northwest	simhasana or deer	lion

TABLE 5

Nirrti	Varuna	Skanda	Kubera	Indra	Yama	Agni	Ketu

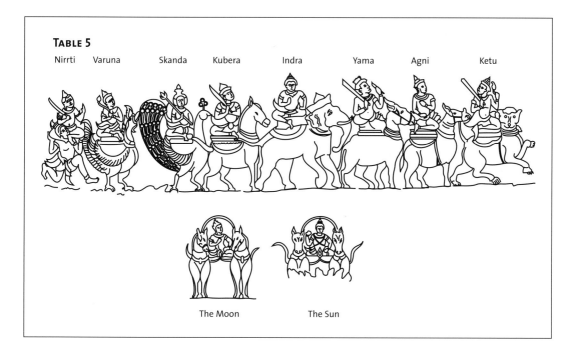

The Moon   The Sun

The *Dikpalas* excluded Surya and Chandra of the *Navagraha* but introduced Shiva, Nirrti and Vayu to complete the list of the guardians. Unfortunately, among the *Dikpalas* there are also iconographic inconsistencies mainly regarding the mounts that should characterise each of them, and in the attributes they should be carrying. When comparing the Indian characteristics with those of Khmer reliefs, some discrepancies become evident (*see above list*). Some light has been shed by the translation of a passage of the Cambodian *Ramaker* by F. Martini (in Bhattacharya 1956: 183) in which the gods and their respective mounts are described when attending Sita's *svayamvara*. Briefly, they are: Indra on the elephant, Agni on the rhinoceros, Vayu on a horse, Varuna on a *naga*, Skanda on a peacock, Brahma on the *hamsa*, Nirrti on a *yaksha*, Vaishravana (Kubera) on a *vimana* (chariot), and Ishvara (Shiva) on the bull.

Later, it was suggested that in Khmer iconography Brahma could be replaced by Varuna riding a *hamsa* rather than a *naga*, and the doubt was raised about who was pulling Kubera's chariot. On the assumption that some of the above deities are the same ones depicted in our relief, the identity of the personage on the lion remains unresolved. He should be Vayu, being the deity needed to complete the *Dikpalas'* group. Also the identity of Kubera in this relief is unclear and he is here tentatively placed on a horse, while according to Hindu canons, he should be seated on a ram or on a chariot pulled by a man. The anomalous presence, amongst the *Dikpalas*, of Skanda can be explained by him having the function of replacing his father Shiva, the guardian of the Northeast. Finally, concerning the problematic identification of the personage riding the lion, it is here suggested that he may be Vayu since he is sometime illustrated seated on a *simha*, the prancing lion. However, in other reliefs, the lion is the mount of Ketu despite the fact that no *Dikpala* is known to have such an animal as his mount (Rao 1914: 515; Malleret 1960: 206).

Reverting now to the main figure of the relief, that of Vishnu reclining on Ananta, there is some doubt about the identity of the female deity holding his leg. Even the work of Gopinantha Rao published in 1914, one of the few authoritative studies Hindu iconography in English, is of little assistance. In fact,

the author mentions that in the depiction of the story of Vishnu *Bhogasayanamurti*, the god is surrounded by his two consorts when reclining on the snake Sesha. Bhumidevi is holding Vishnu's right leg and foot, while Lakshmi is close to Vishnu's head, the two goddesses being distinguishable – in statuary – by Lakshmi holding a lotus flower (*padma*) and Bhumidevi the blue lily (*nilotpala*). This would conform to the textual reference of the *Vishnu Purana* (I, 9, 100) indicating that, in 'The Churning of the Ocean of Milk', as soon as she rose from the Milk, Lakshmi "went to Vishnu's chest". However, in the same volume, Rao indicates that in the image of Vishnu *Jalashayin*, where the god is lying on the serpent Adishesa, one leg of the god rests upon the lap of Lakshmi "as required in the Sanskrit authorities" while Bhumidevi seems to be seated near his head. There is thus a contradiction concerning the position of the two wives of Vishnu in Indian reliefs, perhaps related to an iconographic and ritual difference between Vishnu *Bhogasayanamurti* and Vishnu *Jalashayin*. In Khmer iconography, in the representations of Vishnu reclining on Ananta (*Anantashayin*) only one wife is depicted and, according to popular convention, she is considered to be Lakshmi, the goddess of good fortune and prosperity, rather than Bhumidevi, the goddess of the Earth.

N. 2 – Krishna bringing back Mount Maniparvata

Occupying the entire south wall of the pavilion's eastern arm, this relief is also the victim of severe erosion and staining, making the reading quite difficult. It is composed of seven pseudo-registers, five of which are dominated by the central figure of Krishna, standing on the shoulders of Garuda who is carrying Mount Maniparvata. Krishna is represented in his divine form with four hands holding the sword (or mace), the conch, the discus and a small spherical object (the Earth). Garuda is depicted as a massive and powerful eagle-like bird, with a long feathery tail, outspread wings and arms, and legs apart suggesting a motion towards the right. Also wearing jewellery and a cylindrical crown, he carries in his right hand a minute female figure with a three-pointed *mukuta* and holding a lotus (Fig. 120). Presumably she is either his consort Satyabhana or that of Vishnu, Lakshmi. The Maniparvata (the summit of Mount Mandara) has a squat conical shape; towards its base are seven tiny female figures in royal attire with tall conical *mukutas*, sitting facing towards the right side. A few *rishis* are also present. On the slopes are several trees, with the largest at the summit.

Below this main composition are two pseudo-registers with further figures of servants and attendants carrying round containers (jars) covered with tall conical lids, again progressing to the right. In the lowest pseudo-register is a densely-packed row of soldiers armed with a spear or sword, marching to the right in a forest, together with three groups of mounted cavalry. As usual, at the very top of the relief is a row of dancing *apsaras*, mostly facing right.

The general layout of this wall panel is characterised by a sense of movement towards the viewer's right, intensified by the energetic stride of Garuda. Moreover, vertical lines are emphasised by the representation of a multitude of legs and spears surrounding the over-sized figure of Krishna standing on the shoulders of Garuda. The mushroom shape of Mount Maniparvata does not alleviate this effect with its horizontal volume because it is not carved in that deep a relief.

Several versions of this event are known: from the *Harivamsa* (II, 121), and the *Vishnu Purana* (V, 29), and perhaps the most popular of all from the *Bhagavata Purana* (VIII, chapter 6). They all converge in two tellings: either the mountain is the Maniparvata stolen from Indra, or it is a part of Mount Mandara to be used for the Churning,[24] as it appears in the texts below.

In the Bhagavata Purana, *Indra pleads for help in subduing the* asura *Naraka who has not only kidnapped almost all the beautiful spouses of gods and kings, but threatens to steal his own three-headed elephant, Airavata. He has also stolen Mount Maniparvata, the peak of Mount Mandara. The task of retrieving it falls on Krishna who does so while mounted on the powerful Garuda, who, on this occasion, is accompanied by his wife Satyabhana. Krishna is aided by his army of servants who also bring back the remains of the defeated Naraka.*

The more recent compilation of the *Srimad Bahagavata* (VII, chapters 5-11) tells another story:

When the devas *and* asuras *lift Mount Mandara from its base in an attempt to take it to the sea to start the Churning of the Ocean of Milk, they cannot bear its weight and drop it, injuring and killing many amongst them. The compassionate Krishna intervenes, lifts the mountain with a single arm, puts it on Garuda, and mounting him, carries it to the sea, surrounded by the* devas *and* asuras. *Garuda then unloads them both from his shoulders onto the seashore and, with the permission of Krishna, flies away.*

In this relief, there are many indications pointing to its illustrating the version of the story in the *Bhagavata Purana*. Firstly, the presence of female personages in royal attire at the base of Mount Maniparvata must be Indra's kidnapped wives, and the accompanying soldiers and servants also indicate Krishna returning from a war expedition. In particular, the large jars and containers of various size and shape carried by the long file of servants, must

FIG. 120 A female *deva* on the hand of Garuda. N. 2

FIG. 121 Krishna on the shoulders of Garuda. N. 2

presumably contain the treasures taken from the defeated Naraka and other *asuras*. Furthermore the small, richly dressed female figure, standing on Garuda's right hand side is mentioned in the *Harivamsa* and the *Vishnu Purana* as Satyabhana, Garuda's spouse, who accompanied him on this occasion.

N. 3 – Rama's alliance with Sugriva

The *naga*-framed pediment over the eastern arm's door is a single register with a large figure of Rama seated at the centre flanked by the slightly smaller figures of Lakshmana on the right and Sugriva on the left (Fig. 122). Rama holds the bow in his left hand and a set of arrows in his right. He wears the customary jewellery and a cylindrical crown. Lakshmana is similarly adorned, and holds a mace in his right hand while his left arm is raised to his chest. Rama faces Sugriva who wears the composite conical crown of a king. He is seated at some distance from Rama, with his mouth open in the act of talking, his eyebrows enhanced, and both his arms are folded on his chest. Behind the figures of Sugriva and Lakshmana are two pairs of seated monkeys, all with one hand raised to their chests, and the other in their laps. While the foreground is barren and rocky ground, the background is a lush forest, with vines climbing some tree-trunks.

It is easy to recognise in this composition the episode narrated in the 4th book of the *Ramayana* (*Kishkindha Kanda*) where Rama forges an alliance with Sugriva, with the resulting murder of Sugriva's brother Valin that can be found in the relief of the southwestern pavilion (*S. 8, page 109*).

Rama and Lakshmana, in their search for Sita in the forest, one day enter the territory occupied by Sugriva, the king of the monkeys (chapter 1), who had been deprived of the throne and of his wife by his brother Valin. Sugriva, anxious and perturbed, fears that the two skilful archers are sent by Valin, and asks Hanuman to discover their intentions (chapter 2). Hanuman, in the guise of a wandering monk, approaches them (chapter 3) and informs them he is sent by the exiled Sugriva to seek their friendship. Rama and Lakshmana agree to follow Hanuman to meet Sugriva.

In the next chapter (4), Lakshmana recounts to Hanuman their exile and the loss of Sita. Therefore Rama, overwhelmed with sorrow, is, in fact, coming as a supplicant to Sugriva. The astute Hanuman, realising that Rama could be a means for Sugriva to regain his kingdom, resolves to bring about an alliance between Rama and his master. At the meeting (chapter 5), Sugriva offers his support and that of his monkey tribe in search of Sita; in return he asks Rama to help him to gain justice from Valin, who stole his wife, and put an end to his life in exile. Rama, acknowledging the fruitfulness of mutual aid, promises to slay Valin with his powerful arrows, concluding thus the alliance with Sugriva. Then (chapter 6) Sugriva tells of having seen and heard Sita when Ravana kidnapped her, and that he was holding the cloak and jewels she threw to him. Rama, after pressing the cherished jewels to his breast, is impatient to discover the monster's residence where his chaste spouse is imprisoned. Sugriva, however, does not know the whereabouts of Ravana (chapter 7) and consoles Rama by promising to make all efforts to find him, and renews his request to Rama (chapter 8) to help him against Valin.

After concluding the alliance, Sugriva tells his own story (chapter 9). Valin, the elder of two brothers, became the rightful king when his father died. One day, Valin was challenged to battle by the demon Mayavin. Together with his brother Sugriva, he confronts the monster, who escapes into an underground cavern. Valin orders his brother to wait at the entrance until he returns, then follows the demon into the narrow cave. More than a year passes, and Sugriva fears that his brother might be dead. Some time after this, blood and foam begin to flow out from the cave, and the screaming of demons could be heard, but no cries of Valin. Sugriva concludes that his brother has been killed, and plugs the entrance of the cave with an enormous boulder. He then returns to the city, where the ministers 'force' him to accept the throne of his presumably dead brother. But Valin was not dead, and returns to find his brother occupying his place. He reproaches Sugriva, refuses to pardon him, and binds his ministers in chains. Sugriva attempts to explain what happened (chapter 10), but Valin, enraged, banishes him from the kingdom and deprives him of all his possessions. Valin explains that, after having slain the demon and his entire family, he could not find the exit of the cave because the entrance had been blocked, and he called Sugriva in vain many

Fig. 122 Rama (centre) with Lakshmana (left) and Sugriva (right). N. 3

times. Finally he managed to roll back the rock that was closing the entrance, emerge and return to the city, only to discover that Sugriva had taken the throne and his wife Tara. In his fury, Valin chased him from the kingdom with but a single garment, having ill treated him and carried off his wife.

Central to this narrative is Rama's agreement to kill Valin and thereby re-instate Sugriva as ruler of the monkey kingdom in exchange for help in finding Sita. After Sugriva's statement, it is obvious that there are striking parallels between his and Rama's circumstances (Lefeber 1994: 41): each is in exile, each has lost his wife and each has been deprived of a kingship that has gone to a brother. However, what is totally unalike is the manner in which they, and their respective brothers and wives behave, and in this lies the difference between humans and monkeys. Rama has calmly accepted his fate, without resentment towards his brother who has taken his place, as he has no fear or dislike of the difficult life in the forest. He suffers terribly only from the abduction of his wife who, we are assured, remains loyal and chaste even when a captive of the lascivious Ravana. Sugriva, on the other hand, has no true right to the kingship in the first place, since Valin himself was still alive when Sugriva blocked the exit of his cave, and later appropriated Tara, Valin's 'widow'. When Valin returned from the dead, he rejected Sugriva's excuses, denounced him publicly and not only took back his wife Tara but also his brother's wife Ruma.

In truth, however accidentally, Sugriva was the usurper, not Valin. Sugriva was madly in love with Tara, Valin's beautiful wife. It is with her that he continued to be infatuated after Rama has killed Valin, to the point of forgetting his promise to help Rama to find Sita. The story becomes even more problematic because Rama murders Valin in an ambush, a very unchivalrous action for a *kshatriya*.

Finally, a comment has to be made on the *vanaras*, the monkey tribe which is introduced into the story at this point through the alliance of Rama with Sugriva, their king. Some scholars believe that they are not actually monkeys but tribal people.[25] In general, however, it is clear that whether monkey or human, the *vanaras* are outside the society to which Rama properly belongs and, in a sense, scarcely worthy to be his allies. But even the sharp difference between the human and the monkey world is bridged by Rama's manner in killing Valin, an action that introduces to the epic issues of moral ambiguity.

N. 4 – Akrura's vision

Sculpted over the eastern window of the northern arm of the pavilion, the relief centres on Krishna and Balarama seated together under parasols in the upper pseudo-register (Fig. 123). Krishna is seated in *lalitasana* on a slightly higher plinth, adorned with jewellery and dressed with a *sampot* ending in long flaps.

Fig. 123 Akrura's vision. N. 4

Fig. 124 The presumed ablutions of Akrura. N. 4

FIG. 125 A princess with her attendants. N. 4

His hands seem to be empty. Behind a tiara, his long hair – in the fashion of the *gopas* – is tied up in three knots from which pointed tufts emerge. Although Balarama's dress and jewellery are the same, he differs in not having the tiara, but only long hair tied up in a single knot and a pointed tuft. The other personages in this register are crowned men in royal attire, sitting or squatting mostly in pairs, under parasols and flywhisks, some with their hand to their chest.

In the middle pseudo-register is depicted a row of male personages in royal attire and conical crowns; most of them are holding a sword and all are seated under parasols and in between fans. The majority of the latter are made of fabric but some suggest peacock feathers. At the centre of the pseudo-register and just below Vishnu and Balarama, are two figures who seem to be either floating in water or gliding in the wind (Fig. 124). Most likely male, they lie with outstretched arms, loosely-flowing hair, and flapping *sampots*. One of them has his face turned down, while the other looks toward the viewer. Their possible identity will be explained below.

The lowest of the pseudo-registers displays another row of seated male personages wearing the usual conical crown, jewellery and *sampot*. They face the viewer, and mostly hold their arms raised to their chests, although some have an arm raised with the hand in a gentle gesture of a respectful salute.

The relief on the panel to the right of the window has three superimposed registers with female figures (Fig. 125). In each, an elegantly dressed princess is seated on a low dais, wearing a high *mukuta* with three long points, jewellery and a flowery sarong. Each holds a lotus bud, and their attendants fan them, or carry caskets possibly for jewels or gifts. They are protected by a multitude of parasols.

The main composition of the relief is of well-defined pseudo-registers that because of their clarity invite a linear reading. The horizontal lines overwhelm the vertical axis of symmetry, which passes through the shaft of the parasol between Krishna and Balarama. The three registers to the side of the window have their own central axis of symmetry passing through the bodies of the princesses – independent from that of the main story.

144

Such a hieratic depiction of Krishna and Balarama sitting over two unidentified bodies stretched out on the ground or under water, in addition to the rank of royal figures in attendance, imbue the relief with a deep sense of mystery. Tentatively this author proposes to dispel the mystery by relating the entire image to a particular event in Krishna's life, that of Akrura's vision, which appears in several of the *Purana*. In the *Brahma Purana* (X, chapter 39):

Krishna's uncle, Akrura, has the task of escorting Krishna and Balarama to the city of Mathura to meet Kamsa. Before entering the town, the trio stops on the banks of the sacred Yamuna, which purges those who bathe in it of their sins. After washing themselves, Krishna and Balarama return to their chariot parked in a shady grove. With their permission, Akrura also goes for the ritual ablution. He immerses himself and, while reciting the appropriate mantras, has a vision of Krishna and Balarama under the water. Amazed, he surfaces to ensure that they are both still in the chariot. He submerges himself a second time and has a vision of Vishnu sitting on the great snake Sesha (Ananta). [The text gives us an exhaustive description of the beauty and graciousness of the god as his avatara *Krishna, and a long list of gods and goddesses praising him]. In witnessing this extraordinary vision of Krishna revealing his divinity, Akrura is overpowered by the highest delight and devotion; his hair stands on end, and – crying – he prostrates himself to recite a hymn to the Lord.*

A shorter version of the same story is told in the *Vishnu Purana*, Book V, chapter 18, in the translation of H. H. Wilson of 1860, with Wilson's comments that Akrura's hymn is typical of the Vaishnava eulogy of the *Purana*, never present in the *Harivamsa*. Furthermore, in this text, Akrura addresses Krishna, or Vishnu, as identical with the four *vyuhas*: Krishna, Balarama, Pradyumna and Aniruddha (*see Chapter 1*).

In this author's opinion the two prone figures under the image of Krishna and Balarama represent a single personage, Akrura, immersing himself twice in the water.[26] There would have been no other way for the sculptor to represent the two immersions but to depict Akrura's body twice. Further, the host of royal personages and worshippers surrounding the hieratically seated pair quite possibly represent the deities listed in the *Brahma Purana*. Similarly, the elegant ladies sculpted on the side panel, assisted by their handmaidens, are likely to be the goddesses mentioned in the text. Finally, Krishna's and Balarama's hair arranged in the *gopas'* fashion indicates that the two brothers are still youths. Comparing the headgear of the two main personages with that which Krishna and Balarama have in the relief of the story of 'Krishna lifting Mount Govardhana' (N. 2), it is evident that they are one and the same.

Figures horizontally placed in space are rare in Khmer reliefs, with the exception of those of worshippers in front of their deity or the statue of their deity. The images of figures who seem to float, like in this case, seem most suitable to the depiction of an abstract concept, as proposed here, that of divine revelation.

The story of Akrura's vision (N. 4) is very important because it reveals the divine origin of Krishna. What Akrura miraculously saw during his immersions was a vision of Krishna in his divine form assimilated to that of Vishnu. Before this episode, Akrura considered Krishna to be a mortal youth and a friend of the cowherds; now Krishna revealed his divine status as a god and *avatara* of Vishnu. This story reinforces the divinity of Krishna implicit in the myth of the 'Invitation for Vishnu to descend' (N. 1), and of the crucial divine intervention/s by Vishnu in 'The Churning of the Ocean of Milk' (S. 1). In this way, the creators of Angkor Wat's reliefs were adding further references to Vaishnava (Pancharatra) texts to complete the visual expounding of essential precepts.

N. 5 – Sita's Ordeal by fire

Above the western window of the northern arm of the pavilion is an almost square relief with ranks of figures arranged in several pseudo-registers, all in an extremely poor state of preservation. The central portion has been practically obliterated by water infiltration, making the identification of the scene difficult but not impossible. At the centre, all that can now be seen is a pyre on a decorated plinth with flames extending up more than half of the height of the relief. On the right are vestiges of the pointed drapery of Sita's sarong that must have been arranged in the flaps of Khmer tradition. Beyond this, under parasols, is a row of kneeling figures dressed

FIG. 126 Sita's ordeal by fire. N. 5

FIG. 127 Royal personages observing the ordeal. N. 5

in royal attire; the most important one is on a plinth and with his raised hand indicates Sita (Fig. 127). On the left of the pyre, the outlines of three important personages can be discerned: the nearest holds the bow in his left hand and arrows in his right– the usual attributes of Rama. Then to his right, are two smaller figures, badly eroded and unrecognisable, although one, or both, carry arrows, suggesting they might be Rama's brothers, according to Khmer iconography. Close to the left edge of the relief are two squatting monkeys wearing crowns, most likely Sugriva and Hanuman. The background of the scene consists of trees with birds.

The pseudo-register below is composed of two ranks of squatting figures, which on the left half of the composition are monkeys, and on the right are human. The latter, mostly wearing various types of crowns, are probably *rakshasas*, as explained in the text below. Several monkeys carry a tree branch in one hand while all make the gesture of one hand raised to the chest or of both hands united in prayer over the head. All of these gestures seem to illustrate great concern for what is going on in the main register, even possibly representing despair. We know from the text that at the moment of Sita's ordeal a terrible roar arose from the spectators. In the top part of the relief there are several groups of flying *apsaras* who, as usual in Khmer reliefs, sanctify the event. They are arranged in two superimposed pseudo-registers.

The relief on the panel to the left of the window – below the large relief described above – is composed of five rows of kneeling monkeys. Unusually, they do not gesture wildly, nor have pointing arms or hands. Instead, they stand quietly with their gaze directed at the pyre.

Sita's ordeal by fire occurs in Book VI (*Yuddha Kanda*, chapters 117-119) of the *Ramayana*.

After the furious battle of Lanka and the death of Ravana, Rama sends Hanuman to bring Sita to his presence (chapter 116) and is finally reunited with his spouse. However (chapter 117), he soon tells her that amongst his people doubts have arisen about her conduct while living in captivity with Ravana, and asks her – in an abusive way – to leave. The distressed Sita, trembling and crying, laments (chapter 118) that she has been loyal to Rama all the time, having remained a stranger to Ravana, and that he was passing a premature judgement, like a worthless man. Rama had forgotten that she, born from the earth, was of noble conduct. In desperation, she asks that a pyre be built for her to endure the ordeal by fire to prove her purity. She then circumambulates the pyre and with a fearless heart enters the blazing flames. A great multitude of people witness the scene horrified, and a terrible cry arises from the rakshasas *and the monkeys.*

When the gods (the best amongst the Thirty-three) hear these lamentations (chapter 119), they descend to Lanka, approach Rama and reveal to him that he is a god, not a mortal, and reproach his acting as a common man. Rama replies "I consider myself to be a man, Rama, born of Dasaratha; who then am I in reality?" Brahma tells him that he is the god Vishnu, Krishna and Prajapati (Lord of Beings) and that it was in order to slay Ravana that he entered a mortal human's body.

On hearing these auspicious words (chapter 120), the god of fire Vibhabasu restores to Sita her beauty, and himself taking human form, presents Sita to Rama, telling him she is pure and untainted. After this, Rama is reunited with "his beloved, and experiences the felicity he merited."

This episode is meant to trigger Rama's revelation and epiphany, in that it is to the god-mortal himself that his divinity is revealed. In all the *Ramayana*, Rama is presented as a man of both physical and moral perfection, and his exaltation as a perfect man may be seen as an ideal image of an earthly manifestation of god. Nothing is said of his divine origin in the first five books. It is only late in the 6th book that the revelation takes place, when Krishna is also mentioned, introducing thus the concept of the *avatara* (see discussion in N. 1).

Nevertheless, despite the overwhelming force of Rama's love and devotion to Sita, for the sake of whom he suffers such great grief and hardship, his character is marred by a marked ambivalence revealed on two distinct occasions. Firstly, during the event of the ordeal by fire, when he abuses Sita by telling her that "the purpose for which I won you back was to gain my own fame, since I have no attachment to you, and you may go from here as you wish". Moreover, he maliciously suggests that she has set her eyes on Lakshmana or Bharata, or the king of the monkeys Sugriva, or even the king of the *rakshasa* Vibhishana, now that Ravana is dead.

He adds another rude touch by saying that she looks to him "like a lamp to one whose eye is diseased". Despite loving Sita enormously and being convinced of her innocence and loyalty, he is willing to publicly humiliate her and make her suffer. To justify himself, however, he blames his father, the cause of all misfortune, the old king who was guilty of putting lust before polity, who denied him the throne and was the cause of his exile.

Towards the end of the *Ramayana* (Book VII), the ambivalence and complexity of Rama's character proves tragic. While happily reigning in Ayodhya with Sita at his side, he is confronted again with the old problem, and under the pressure of the nobles at his court, decides to repudiate her, despite being convinced of her innocence (Book VII, chapter 44). At the very end of the story, Rama wishes to be re-united with his wife, but it is now too late. Asserting once more her devotion to her lord Rama, Sita calls on her mother, the Earth, to receive her, and disappears in glory into the earth (note that Sita was born from the earth, hence her name 'The furrow'). This cruel, selfish, arrogant treatment of people by Rama is not exclusive to this episode. Previously Rama reveals an even greater lack of chivalry, with his unprovoked mockery and disfiguring of Shurpanakha (Book III, chapters 17-18), Ravana's sister, who attempted to seduce him and his brother Lakshmana. The unchivalrous murder of Valin in an ambush (*see S. 8*) contributes to Rama's complexity.

On a basic level 'Sita's Ordeal by Fire' is a cruel test which is imposed on Sita by her husband Rama, who needed proof she had kept her chastity when held prisoner by Ravana, even though the latter had abducted her with the intention of possessing her. Sita comes out of the pyre's flames untouched and even more beautiful than ever; thus, at a deeper level, the story of the ordeal is a symbol of Sita's loyalty and innocence, and ultimately love. Symbolic references to loyalty and love are also evident in the episode of Sita meeting with Hanuman (N. 8), where Sita demonstrates her loyalty and love to Rama by quietly withstanding the horrors of her captivity by the devilish Ravana. Hanuman's behaviour too is an perfect example of loyalty towards his patron, as he obediently carries out Rama's difficult orders.

Concerning the narrative technique, this relief represents the culminant event of an episode of the *Ramayana*, a moment of suspense, of wonder over the outcome of the fire ordeal or of expectation of justice because everybody knows Sita is pure and innocent. The layout of the relief's composition reveals – although not directly visible because of the poor preservation – that the axis of symmetry passes through the middle of the pyre, which is slightly off the centre of the wall. It separates the pseudo-registers with the monkeys from those of the presumed *rakshasas*, at the base of the relief.

N. 6 – Viradha's attempt to abduct Sita

Carved in a single register in the unusually flat tympanum delineated by a squat frame over the doorway of the northern arm', this relief is in very poor condition, water infiltration having caused many details to flake away (Fig. 128). At the centre, however, can be made out the *rakshasa* Viradha[27] holding, in his left arm, a diminutive Sita wearing a tall crown (Fig. 129). The monster's enormous size is suggested by the comparatively small size of Sita as well as by his head touching the frame of the relief. Standing with flexed legs, he is in the act of throwing a spear at the figure of Rama to the left. Viradha's hairstyle with a high chignon without crown is typical of the *rakshasas*. He is dressed with a simple *sampot*, and wears a necklace, armlets and anklets. With the bow bent to breaking point, Rama is about to release his arrow at the demon. Although badly preserved, one can see his elaborate *sampot* and the belts crossing the chest. A crown of flared cylindrical shape, ornate with gems, complements the customary jewellery. On the other side is Lakshmana, placing an arrow in his bow. His condition of preservation is worse than that of Rama, although it is clear that he is similarly apparelled to his brother. The scene takes place in a forest with a rocky foreground.

This episode occurs in the 3rd book of the *Ramayana* (*Aranya Kanda*, chapters 2-4) which deals with the adventures of Rama, Sita and Lakshmana during their years of exile in the forest.

One day, when the trio [Rama, Sita and Lakshmana] is in the thick Dandaka forest, a gigantic rakshasa

Fig. 128 Viradha's attempt to abduct Sita. N. 6

Fig. 129 Viradha and Sita (detail). N. 6

appears. He is hideous, massive, "sunken-eyed, huge-mouthed, pointed-eared, his belly deformed." Clad in a tiger skin, dripping with grease and spattered with blood, he makes a great uproar, seizes Sita in his arms and starts to carry her away, cursing the intruders, proudly declaring himself to be Viradha, the master of the impenetrable forest. He tells them he will marry Sita and kill the two men who he does not fear, having obtained Brahma's boon to be invulnerable to any weapon on earth.

The angered Rama replies by speedily placing seven sharp arrows into Viradha who falls to the ground letting Sita loose. The two brothers continue to transfix him with flaming arrows, but he vomits them out by virtue of the boon he had received. Then Rama breaks Viradha's right arm and Lakshmana the left, hurling him to the ground; aware of his boon, they decide to cast him into a pit. On hearing this, Viradha tells his story. In reality – he says – he is the gandharva (celestial being) Tumburu who incurred the wrath of Kubera for having made love to the apsara Rambha. From this boon he will be released by a fight with Rama, assume his natural form, and return to the celestial regions. Having been asked to put an end to his suffering, the brothers bury him in the pit.

Although Viradha's details as described in the text are hardly present in the relief (sunken eyes, huge mouth, pointed ears and deformed belly), there is no doubt that this scene illustrates the abduction of Sita. We know that this happened twice: first by Viradha who failed and was killed, then by Ravana who was successful and ran away with his prey, commencing the main storyline of the whole *Ramayana*. Represented here is the beginning of the story, immediately after Viradha grabs Sita and tries to escape into the forest with her, whereupon Rama releases one of his seven lethal arrows, while Lakshmana is only arming his bow. Notice that Lakshmana's arrow/s extend outside the space of the relief through the sculpted frame, a device employed sparingly in the Large Panels of the same enclosure sculpted in the XII century, and more commonly in those of the XVI century. As in all pediments of the corner pavilions, symmetry is strictly applied in here, with the two brothers being almost mirror images around the axis of Viradha.

N. 7 – Rama on the Pushpaka Chariot

Exceptionally among the wall panel reliefs of the Corner Pavilions, the entirety of this relief above the northern window of the western arm is depicted in a single register (Fig. 130). Illustrating Rama flying back to Ayodhya in the Pushpaka chariot, it is composed of three elements, from top to bottom:

- A tall richly-decorated pavilion in which Rama is seated, and two smaller almond-shaped pavilions at either side, each sheltering a seated personage, both now totally eroded – presumably Sita (to his left) and Lakshmana.
- A row of almond-shaped pavilions in which several figures are seated; some with a clearly simian face, thus Hanuman and Sugriva; one with the *rakshasa's* hairstyle, thus Vibhishana; and others so effaced that they cannot be recognised, but who may be the monkeys' leaders mentioned in the text below.
- A row of very large *hamsas* (mythical geese) supporting and propelling the chariot in the sky.

The magic chariot is surrounded by a forest of banners carried by soldiers, high in the reliefs, and by a thick crowd of jubilant monkeys. Some of the latter carry, in pairs, wooden sticks holding coconut and banana bunches. They seem to run in the street pointing with their arms and fingers towards something higher up in the sky. The uniqueness of the compositional layout of this relief is due to the design of the Pushpaka dominating the entire wall. The top part of the chariot is squashed against the frame, leaving little space for the *apsaras*. Exceptionally therefore, they are reduced to a single row and not arranged in the usual superimposed storms.

The relief on the panel to the right of the window is composed of four pseudo-registers, thematically belonging to the overlying scene (Fig. 131). The highest depicts the same fruit-carrying monkeys, while three monkeys are beating on small drums, and playing hand-bells and brass gongs. One seems to be blowing a conch.

The relief's layout is asymmetric, with the axis of symmetry that passes through the centre of the Pushpaka slightly shifted to the left. The reading of this relief, despite its poor state of preservation, is done in a single view, the attention being con-

Fig. 130 Rama on the Pushpaka chariot. N. 7

centrated on the majestic Pushpaka. Then, one's gaze is drawn to the multitude of dancing monkeys that extend down the side of the window. There is a general sense of movement but without a temporal sequence of events.

Clearly the relief is the visual rendering of the story narrated towards the end of the *Ramayana* (Book VI, the *Yuddha Kanda*, chapters 123-125).

After Sita went through the ordeal by fire and reunited with Rama, Rama decides to go back to his family and people. He accepts Vibhishana's gift of the extraordinary Pushpaka chariot[28] with its many white banners. It can fly anywhere at one's will, is indestructible, with many rooms like a palace, gilded and covered with precious stones and pearls, enriched with golden lotuses hung together with bells diffusing a melodious sound. Looking like the peak of Mount Meru, it is harnessed to hamsas *(geese). The monkeys and their leaders, Sugriva and Vibhishana, insist on accompanying Rama. They all embark on the chariot and, together with Rama, Sita and Lakshmana leave Lanka, comfortably flying towards Ayodhya where Rama will be enthroned king.*

The presence of only jubilant monkeys and not of royal personages and dignitaries suggests that the scene depicted is the departure from Lanka, and not the arrival at Ayodhya where he was met by his brothers, court and citizens of the city (*Yuddha Kanda*, chapter 129).

N. 8 – Sita meeting Hanuman

Above the southern window of the western arm of the pavilion is a relief composed of several registers (Fig. 133). The topmost featuring Sita seated under an acacia tree[29] being attended by a kneeling Hanuman is also the most severely damaged. One can hardly make out the beautiful foliage of the tree of the other trees in Ravana's garden, where She is held captive. Sita is seated on a high base, a sort of throne with legs, and she has long hair tied in a single knot, long earrings, jewellery but not the crown as she lost it during her abduction by Ravana), chest crossbands, and a *sarong* ending with a very long pointed flap. She is facing right, holding

Fig. 133 Sita meeting Hanuman. N. 8

Fig. 134 Hanuman presenting Rama's ring to Sita (badly preserved). N. 8

her arm towards the smaller figure of Hanuman kneeling on the ground, clearly identifia-ble by his monkey's face and vertical tail,[30] raising his arms towards Sita (Fig. 134). The area where the hands of Hanuman and Sita reach out to each other has completely crumbled away, so that it is impossi-ble to confirm the nature of their gesture. From the original text, however, one can guess that they are handling a jewel. Close to Sita, to the right of the viewer, a woman sits on a low plinth: she is Trijata, the only *rakshini* (female *rakshasa*) kind to Sita. Although dressed like Sita, her hair is arranged with a thin crown surmounted by three knotted locks of hair; she holds a lotus in one hand. On both sides are rows of *rakshini* with monstrous animal faces with pointed snouts, their hair coarsely arranged like bristles or wearing the spiky *rakshasa* helmets; all hold a sword and squat in military formation.

The register below contains two more ranks of *rakshini*. Some have the same animal faces seen in that above: a pig's snout or a bird's beak. Although symmetrically arranged, half sit with the right side of their torso facing the viewer while the other half display the left side of their torso. Their swords, however, all point in the same direction – to the right. Below this is a single row of warriors with human faces. They have unusual conical crowns with overlapping vegetal elements, probably indicating that they are also *rakshini*. They squat on the ground, some holding javelins and round shields.

The panel to the left of the window contains four more registers displaying warriors. The topmost includes warriors identical to the ones described above them. In the other three, however, the warriors hold swords and rectangular shields, and although they are interpreted as *rakshini*, they do not have breasts. This iconographical feature is applied here to the *rakshini* in order to emphasise that, although of female genre, these monstrous creatures had none of the feminine human qualities.

The episode depicted is narrated in the *Rama-yana* (Book V, *Kishkindha Kanda*, chapters 13-40).

When Hanuman reaches Lanka, he begins search-ing for Sita who was being kept prisoner by Ravana. He enters a beautiful acacia grove (chapter 13), and reducing himself to a very small size so as not to be detect-ed, decides to hide in a tree and wait for signs of action. Soon he sees Sita, although she is in a misera-ble state, saddened by the separation from Rama and tormented by the rakshini. *Then the horrible Ravana enters the grove demanding that Sita marry him. On being rejected, he threatens her with death, but then he asks the* rakshini *to induce Sita to reconsider. They fail and Sita prophesies that Ravana will be slain by Rama. Ravana leaves in fury. One of the* rakshini, *the aged and prudent Trijata, sympathises with Sita and promises to protect her; but Sita is desperate and con-siders killing herself.*

Hanuman, who has been hiding in the tree, decides to approach her by reciting melodious praises of Rama, to her great surprise. She is also frightened by such a terrible looking monkey, and even thinks he is Ravana in another of his disguises. Hanuman then makes him-self known and gives her the precious ring engraved with Rama's name (chapter 36) that was given to Hanuman so she would trust him (chapter 44). Sita, however, refuses to be rescued by Hanuman, considering the fury this may cause amongst the rakshasas, *which would jeopardise both herss and Hanuman's life. She asks, instead, that he tell Rama to hurry to her rescue because Ravana will kill her within a month, and to give Rama the pearl that adorned her forehead (chapter 38). Hanuman reassures Sita, listens to her instructions and takes leave (chapter 40).*

In the *Ramayana* it is made clear that only female monsters (*rakshini*) from different tribes guarded the prisoner Sita. There is also a complete detailed description (chapters 22-23) of the animal ugliness of their faces and bodies, which is not reproduced by the Khmer sculptors; they limited themselves to depicting animal faces as if that would suffice to illustrate their monstrousness. The *rakshini* Trijata is mentioned in the *Uttara Kanda* (chapter 12) to be the wife of Vibhishana. The sculptors wanted to distin-guish the benevolent *rakshini* from her terrible com-panions by giving her a human face.

Despite Hanuman being the key element of this story, he is represented in unusually small propor-tions, probably because the Khmer sculptors imag-ined him as retaining in the tiny shape he had trans-formed himself into at the beginning of the story (chapter 13).

Concerning the layout of the composition, the asymmetrical arrangement of the weapons of the *rak-shasas* and soldiers contributes to the lack of symme-

Fig. 135 Rama's alliance with Vibhishana. N. 9

try of this relief that is then viewed in a linear fushion. This is another formal device that adds to the lack of organisation of the composition, probably with the intent, on the part of the sculptors, of giving a bad impression of Ravana's court and entourage.

N. 9 – Rama's Alliance with Vibhishana

Within the *naga*-framed tympanum over the western door, this relief depicts in a single register Rama and Lakshmana welcoming – amongst an assembly of monkeys – a warrior wearing the hairstyle of the *rakshasas*. The latter, his arm raised to his chest, seems to swear fealty to his interlocutor. It is likely that this meeting represents the reception of Vibhishana by Rama (*Ramayana*, chapters 17-18). Behind the two brothers is a monkey with a *mukuta*, who could be Hanuman or Sugriva, since both took part in the meeting. The other figures behind the *rakshasas*, although heavily damaged, are monkeys. There is no sign of the four *rakshasa* who, according to the text, were accompanying Vibhishana.

The episode illustrated is taken from the *Yuddha Kanda* of the *Ramayana* (Book VI, chapters 14-19).

The mighty rakshasa *Vibhishana, Ravana's younger brother, tries to persuade Ravana (chapter 14) to return Sita – the cause of all their problems – to Rama, on the grounds that nobody can beat Rama. Indrajit, Ravana's son (chapter 15) accuses Vibhishana of being a coward, while Ravana considers him to be a snake and a traitor. Vibhishana cannot tolerate this outrage and announces his departure (chapter 16). He goes, together with four of his generals, to the camp of Rama and Lakshmana (chapter 17), where he seeks refuge, having had to abandon his wife and son due to Ravana's hostility. Because Sugriva mistrusts Vibhishana, a meeting is held to discuss the case, during which Hanuman suggests asking Vibhishana directly what are his motives and asking the rakshasa of what value he would be as their ally. Lakshmana wants to slay Vibhishana (Chapter 18) but Rama maintains that Vibhishana is not a threat, Rama being able to kill him with the tip of a finger. Finally, after the great Sage Kandu says it is a crime not to give shelter to those who seek it, Rama – convinced of Vibhishana's integrity – allows Vibhishana to join them. They meet courteously (chapter 19) and Vibhishana tells Rama of the terrifying powers of Ravana's brigade. On hearing this Rama virulently commits himself to Ravana's overthrow and installation of Vibhishana as king. Vibhishana, on his side, promises to help him to capture Lanka. The alliance is thus concluded. Immediately they start to plan the attack, which includes throwing a bridge over the sea to reach the island of Lanka.*

In reading the text, one might think that Rama reacted with some impetuosity to Vibhishana's account of Ravana and his army. He is taken by a homicidal rage; he wants to annihilate Ravana, his sons, his kinfolk and his entire army before he returns to Ayodhya. Afterwards he will install Vibhishana as king. It looks as if, in his fury, he has forgotten about liberating and reuniting with Sita. The situation and his reaction are not dissimilar to those when Sugriva asked him to help in the murder of Valin (*see S. 8 and N. 3*).

With regard to the compositional layout of this relief – as usual – the main personage is on the vertical axis of symmetry, with Vibhishana at one side and Lakshmana at the other, complemented by a small group of minor figures at each side. The space between Rama and Vibhishana is larger than that between any others, indicating either circumspection towards a guest whose intentions were not known, or ceremonial deference towards a visitor.

N. 10 – The *Svayamvara* of Sita

Located on the east wall of the southern arm, this relief depicts the test that would be suitor must undergo in order to win her hand (*svayamvara*). It is the second of only two reliefs in the pavilion to occupy the entire wall space without being broken by a window (*see also N. 2*). Divided into five registers, the uppermost of these takes up fully half the space, with, at its centre, a young man of larger size than any other personage. This is Rama (Fig. 136), with his bow upraised in his right hand while the left is about to place one arrow into position.[31] He wears a conical crown, jewellery, a richly decorated *sampot* flapping at the back as well as a thin vest around the shoulders. The position of his right arm and the direction of his gaze create a vectorial movement in the composition towards a wheel on a post with a bird on top – the target at which he is aiming.

To the left of Rama is a princess depicted wearing the three-pointed *mukuta*, typical of a lady of royal status (Fig. 137). Obviously a representation of Sita, she is seated on a richly decorated throne; to her side there is a large casket in the shape of a lotus. She is adorned with jewellery and her sarong ends in a pointed flap. In her left hand she gracefuly holds a lotus bud. She does not seem to be watching Rama, but instead gazes at the viewer. Many court ladies surround her, some holding fans, others with one arm over their chests. They too wear a three-pointed crown, but not as complex as Sita's.

On the other side of Rama is a brahmin identifiable by his bun-like chignon and goatee (Fig. 138). He is Vishvamitra, Rama's personal guru, followed by three seated male figures (and a possible fourth, barely visible) wearing crowns and jewellery, and with their hands raised to their chests. It is not possible to distinguish Lakshmana amongst them. All the protagonists of this scene are protected by a multitude of parasols and fans, including one made with peacock feathers for Vishvamitra. In the background are regularly spaced trees.

In the register below, it is probable that the royal figure seated on a high base is Sita's father King Janaka, and that the scene is of his court (Fig. 139). Like his daughter above, he holds a lotus flower (or a piece of jewellery in the shape of a lotus) while in front of him is a decorated casket. Behind him are royal servants with fans and flywhisks and another important member of the court seated on a plinth (lower than that of the king, however) who may be King Dasaratha, Rama's father. To the right, is a row of archers in princely costumes, probably the defeated contestants, sitting in pairs. Note that they are the only figures holding bows amongst the multitude of warriors. As in the one above, parasols protect all the figures of this register.

In the third register is depicted a compact row of seated high-ranking warriors. One of them at the centre holds a ceremonial crook, while all the others hold swords. Curiously, although the warriors to the left and right are seated facing inwards, all their swords point to the right. The register below, the fourth, is sculpted with another densely packed row of warriors of high rank holding swords or maces. There is no apparent hierarchy amongst them based on costume and armament. Because the ones to the right of the viewer hold their swords with their left arm and the ones to the left with their right arm, they have a kind of symmetry.

The comparatively tall lowest register again illustrates a court scene. Several soldiers, without headgear but wearing simple chignons, seem to be involved in many activities: some are carrying a cartwheel, others are attending horses (Fig. 140), surrounded by others carrying parasols (some closed) and flywhisks. Some young soldiers stand with their sword or mace at rest on their shoulder (Fig. 141) and some kneel on the ground. Their horses are arranged in groups of four.

FIG. 136 The *Svyamvara* of Sita. N. 10

FIG. 137 Sita and her attendants. N. 10

FIG. 138 A brahmin and a prince. N. 10

FIG. 139 King Janaka. N. 10

FIG. 140 Soldiers and squires. N. 10

FIG. 141 Young soldiers. N. 10

FIG. 142 Rama aiming at the target. Baphuon temple.

One such group at the centre of the panel is, because of their location, the most important, and probably destined to pull a royal cart or chariot. In the background tall widely spaced trees and vines probably denoted a garden.

The textual source for this relief is in Book I of the *Ramayana* (*Bala Kanda*, chapters 66-67).

Old King Janaka, sovereign of Mithila, is in possession of a massive and divine ancestral bow which no king or minister on earth could wield. As the price for the hand of his beautiful daughter Sita, he sets the task of drawing the bow. For this purpose, a competition is organised: the svayamvara,[32] *to which the princes of all the neighbouring states are invited (possibly also Ravana).*

Rama, who is in town with his brother Lakshmana and the great Sage Vishvamitra, is summoned by King Janaka to 'behold' the mighty ancestral bow.[33] *Ornate with flowers and sandalwood, the bow is brought in, with great effort, by 500 men and is displayed in front of*

FIG. 143 Rama aiming at the target. N. 10

the royal crowd. Rama calmly raises it, and without effort, affixes the bowstring, fits an arrow and draws it back, but in doing so, he breaks it in the middle with the sound of thunder. Everybody is astounded, and thrown to the ground by the reverberations. When calm is restored, the king gives Sita in marriage to Rama and the wedding is arranged. He also orders the royal counsellors to leave at once for Ayodhya on swift chariots, to bring back King Dasaratha, Rama's father.

By comparing the text with the narrative relief, a few anomalies become apparent concerning the bow, the target and – as a consequence – the main personage.[34]

In this relief, the competition target is a bird perched on a wheel on a tall pole (Fig. 143). Such a target is not described in Valmiki's *Ramayana* where instead there feathres a row of seven sugar-palm trees, nor does it occur in another *svayamvara* episode, that of Draupadi narrated in the *Mahabharata,* where the main protagonist is Arjuna. The bird on the target may be related, albeit tentatively, to a story narrated in the *Ramaker* where Rama displays accurate archery skill in slaying the demon Kakanasura who had transformed himself into a big crow. Thus one may assume that the relief represents the episode of Sita's *svayamvara* of Valmiki's *Ramayana* up to the moment when Rama breaks the bow, but that the sculptors used the *Ramaker* as a source of some of the details or, perhaps, even for the whole story.

With regard to the layout of the relief, the irregular arrangement and ordering of the weapons held by the various personages contribute to the disruption of the symmetry so skilfully used in most other reliefs. In the top register, offset to the left of the viewer, the figure of an over-sized Rama, with flexed legs and outstretched right arm, aiming at the target creates, is a well-defined pyramidal composition.

It is interesting to analyse the temporal sequence of events as depicted in the panel. In the *Ramayana* the chronological sequence starts with Rama being invited to stretch the bow, then lifting and breaking the bow, being offered Sita in marriage, and finally the arrangements for collecting Rama's father, Dasaratha. This sequence is well depicted in the relief. At the top Rama performs the archery test, Sita waits to be given in marriage to him and royal personages witness the event. In the middle of the relief are various dignitaries and soldiers attending the *svayamvara/* wedding ceremony. At the base of the relief, below rows of soldiers, are people in the process of harnessing horses to be attached to the chariot that has the task of collecting Rama's father (as described in the text). In this way, a temporal sequence becomes evident, in a typical case of ellipsic narrative.

N. 11 – Krishna and the *Gopis*

An image of Krishna seated on a mountain peak under a branching tree forms the apex of the pyramidal composition of this relief (Fig. 144), depicted in two pseudo-registers above the western window of the southern arm of the pavilion.

The god is richly attired with crown and jewellery, and is seated on a throne with a serene expression, open eyes and a gently smiling mouth (Fig. 145). He has the barest suggestion of a moustache and a thin beard. His four hands hold his attributes: the discus, the conch, a small spherical object like a pearl between the thumb and the forefinger, and a small conical, pear-shaped container in the hand on his lap. To the left is a male figure in royal attire, seated in the ceremonial position (*lalitasana*) on a throne lower than that of Krishna. One arm is raised to the chest, in a position of veneration; possibly he is a king or Balarama. At the sides, and below these two, are several women in the traditional costume of Khmer court ladies with high pointed crowns; they carry offerings to Krishna – lotus buds and flower branches; some of them seem to be moving at a dancing pace. In the forest surrounding the scene wild animals are depicted; including the peaceful association of a lion, a lioness and a gazelle (Fig. 147).

On the panel to the right of the window are sculpted three pseudo-registers featuring dancing girls, some very young, wearing the characteristic three-pointed crown (Fig. 146). A mountain planted sparsely with trees forms the background.

Although previous authors have recognised that this panel must refer to a story of Krishna, they have not identified which one in particular. It is here proposed that the image represents Krishna with the *gopis* enacting the *Rasalila*, a circular dance. This opinion is based on the fact that in the *Puranas* and *Harivamsa* there is only one occasion in which Krishna is surrounded by women in dynamic movement, either dancing or manifesting their excitement towards their Lord: the event when Krishna's sport with the *gopis* culminates with the dancing of the *Rasalila*. The story as found in the *Bhagavata Purana* (X, chapters 29-33) is related as follows:

FIG. 144 Krishna and the *Gopis*. N. 11

One night (chapter 29), Krishna decides to enact his long promised play with the gopis. When the moon is high in the sky, he plays the flute, setting their passion aflame. In agitation, they hurry to him, their lover, forgetting all their duties. Though obstructed by husbands, parents and relatives, they cannot be stopped as their minds are given to Krishna.

Seeing this multitude of women assemble near him, Krishna attempts to dissuade them from staying out at night when they should be at home with their families, observing their duties. However, giving in to their pleas of disappointment, Krishna proceeds in his love-sports, firstly in the forest and then in the Yamuna river's cool waters. On seeing that the women start to feel proud of their beauty and develop a sense of self-importance, Krishna suddenly disappears with the view of purifying them through suffering and making them worthy of his grace. The gopis, initially deeply distressed and feverish, recover and start to search for him (chapter 30), and when they realise the futility of their behaviour, begin to sing a prayer for Krishna's return (chapter 31). To their surprise, the Lord appears (chapter 32) in their very midst, making them ecstatic with joy.

Under the autumnal moon, he speaks to them about the selfishness of mortals' love and foolishness of accomplishing the objects of desire. In appreciation of their constant devotion, he inaugurates the sport of the Rasa, dancing with them the Rasakrida[35] (chapter 33). But the women fail to form a circle because each one is rooted on the spot for fear of leaving Krishna's side; so, Krishna takes each one by the hand and completes the circle of the dancing, assuming as many forms as there are gopis, enjoying himself dancing. The women's wreaths and ornaments become loose and fall; they are too involved in dancing to re-adjust their dishevelled locks of hair, garments and brassieres. Krishna is fatigued from over-dancing, and moves towards the Yamuna to enter its cool waters in the company of the exhilarated gopis, before disappearing again into the night.

There can be no doubt that this relief refers to some story of Krishna while he was still with the cowherds and their wives, the gopis, because of the presence of cattle in the lower left register. The group of gopis in a state of excitement can also only be found in one of the above episodes of Krishna's life. However, it is difficult to decide which particular part of the narrative is being illustrated.

FIG. 145 Krishna (detail).

Moreover, Krishna is represented in a very formal way, enthroned as Vishnu, in a hieratic attitude, observing or giving a sermon, flanked by his brother Balarama.

In the iconography of Angkor Wat and the best known Khmer temples, Krishna is never depicted playing the flute or dancing, as he should be if illustrating the text of this occasion: instead, he is almost always either sitting in hieratic pose or slaying an enemy. Perhaps the Khmers were not interested in the sensual aspect of the god, but only in his metaphysical essence and therefore emphasised the allegorical meaning of the story (see page 159). This conventional presentation would explain the presence, in this relief, of his brother Balarama, whose attendance at the Rasalila is not mentioned in the original text. Both have attained late youth and Krishna is at the centre of his cult and therefore identified with Vishnu.

Fig. 146 Dancing girls. N. 11

Fig. 147 A lion, a lioness and a gazelle mingle peacefully. N. 11

FIG. 148 Rama killing Kabandha. N. 12

The episode of the *Rasalila* happens shortly after the *gopas* have announced Krishna's divinity (chapter 28): Krishna being the embodiment in every *yuga* of the son of the Lord of Wealth, therefore called Vasudeva, and the equal-to and part-of Vishnu. Indra also names him 'Govinda' (chapter 25). This may explain why, in this relief, Krishna is illustrated in the form of Vishnu and not as the cowherd. His representation in Vishnu's form may also help in diminishing the story's sexual connotation. Krishna moves between two levels of existence, the human and the divine. What seems a miracle to men is simply a display of his divine nature. Paradoxically, it is through tricks and miracles that the god Krishna continuously reveals the ultimate unity of existence.

The figures who surround Krishna make gestures towards him, guiding the gaze of the viewer towards that focal point. As in the relief of Shiva appearing in the Pine Forest (S. 4), the women's garments are in disarray to indicate their excitement for their god – their fervent devotion, before organising themselves into a circular pattern required for the *Rasalila*. They seem to be moving towards Krishna, in small groups, as elements of a series of frames arranged in a temporal sequence. The layout converges towards Krishna immobile under the tree, the centre of symmetry and the top of the pyramidal composition. The narrative continues uninterrupted on the wall beside the window, the elements being the same, and not separated into distinct registers.

The event here depicted is very likely a prelude to the *Rasalila*. In Hindu tradition, the *rasa* is an allegory of the individual soul crying out to the Supreme Soul. Since it is enacted by Krishna's *Yoga-maya* (Lord of Yoga; *Bhagavata Purana*, Book X, chapter 29.1), it implies that the surrender of the individual to the Supreme Soul is possible only with the help of yogic powers and through Krishna. By putting the *bhakti* of the *gopis* to test the faithfulness of their love for him, the story of Krishna is an allegory of the devotion needed by the god's worshippers. As a result, this panel may be read as an allegory of the duty of women to be chaste.

N. 12 – Rama killing Kabandha

The usual flat-shaped pediment over the lintel of the southern door delimits a narrative in a single register. At the centre is the large hideous face of the ogre Kabandha protruding from a body with two large robust arms. The body itself seems to emerge from the ground at the level of the shoulders. The face has two large eyes, a nose like a short tusk, a very large mouth touching the ears, with massive teeth and a pendulous tongue. The ears are pointed and the entire head is covered with thick bristles or scales which, at the top, are grouped in a large chignon. His two arms grasp

Rama and Lakshmana by their waists, pulling them towards his mouth to devour them.

Rama and Lakshmana – almost identical – are both holding their swords high to release terrible blows on the monster's arms. With their other hands they grab the monster by the ribbon which keeps his hair together in a tuft; one each of the two brothers' legs is actually within the monster's mouth. The text stipulates that Rama is on the monster's right, enabling him to cut off his right arm. At either side are two seated figures, kneeling in profile with arms upraised in prayer. They are ascetics, judging from the small goatee and high chignon, probably belonging to the nearby hermitage of Matanga. The scene is set in a dense forest. Indeed, there is a fruit-tree behind Rama, and a branching tree just behind Kabandha's head that looks as if it is part of him. In the foreground, small animals graze in the forest.

The story of Rama and Lakshmana's encounter with Kabandha occurs towards the end of the 3rd book of the *Ramayana* (*Aranya Kanda*, chapters 69-71 of Shastri's edition, and in Pollock's translation,[36] chapters 65-69).

One day, in their search for Sita, Rama and Lakshmana enter the thick woodlands of the Krauncha forest to reach the hermitage of Matanga. There they meet a gigantic monster, the huge rakshasa *Kabandha. He has the unique hideous features of being without head or neck, his face set in his belly, covered with bristling hairs. His single terrible eye with thick lids opens on his chest, and the mouth has fangs and lips, which he licks.*

The dreadful ogre grabs Rama and Lakshmana with his huge arms, holding them with all his strength. In distress, the two brothers insult him, making him angry, but at the right moment they cut the rakshasa's *arms off at the shoulders with their swords: Rama cuts the right arm and Lakshmana the left. Mortally wounded, Kabandha asks the brothers who they are. On hearing the answer, he rejoices realising that they are his salvation. He is, in fact, the* danava *[celestial being] Danu who, having received from Brahma the boon of longevity, one day challenged Indra to a fight. The great god, however, hurled his powerful mace at Kabandha thrusting his thighs and head into his body. Indra also extended Kabandha's arms over four miles and placed a mouth with sharp teeth in his belly. Later, after disturbing and frightening a great* rishi, *Kabandha was told that he would regain his original beautiful form when Rama severed both his arms.*

Thereafter, he had been wandering in the forest waiting for Rama. Having revealed his story, Kabandha tells Rama that if he would put an end to his life and cremate him performing thus a consecration by fire, in a pact of friendship Kabandha will tell them who is acquainted with Ravana. The two brothers proceed to conduct the ogre's ceremonial cremation. When Kabandha, freed from his horrible body, is rising to the sky, he tells them that the only person who can help them is the mighty Sugriva, king of the monkey tribe, who had been exiled by his brother Valin, and was currently wandering on Mount Rishyamuka. They must hurry to him and conclude an alliance that will lead to Sita's liberation. Then, Kabandha re-enters the celestial realms.

Doubts have been raised as to the identity of the *rakshasa* depicted in the relief because the description given in the original text does not agree with what is shown in the relief. Mannikka (1996: 182 and 319) believes that the monster is not Kabandha, but Viradha (the demon who abducted Sita; see N. 6), and that Coedès in 1911 may have taken the giant head of Viradha for the stomach of Kabandha.

A detailed inspection of the monster in the relief reveals that he does not have the features described in the text for Kabandha, but nor does he have those of Viradha. The latter is described in the text as having, besides a huge mouth and pointed ears – featured in the relief – sunken eyes and a deformed belly. Therefore, the particulars of both monsters are not represented literally in either relief (compare with N. 6). If the depiction of the monster's heads is not, therefore, a dependable criterion to define who is who, one has to refer to the action taking place. According to the text, Rama and Lakshmana used their swords to sever the arms of Kabandha, while they 'broke' the arms of Viradha after having transfixed him with bundles of arrows. In the relief under discussion, Rama and Lakshmana are depicted holding swords, not bows and arrows; on the con- trary, in the relief representing Viradha (N. 6), the two brothers are seen energetically pulling the strings of their mighty bows. Moreover, here the monster seems about to eat one leg each of the two heroes, which relates to what is said in the text (Pollock, 65-66). Kabandha did warn them he was tormented by hunger, and because they had entered his domain, they were his rightful prey. In conclusion, it is Kabandha who is represented here.

FIG. 149 The fight between Valin and Sugriva.

Interpretation of the Reliefs of the Corner Pavilions

The reliefs in the corner pavilions acquire their true function within the temple's sacred purpose when considered within the context of all of Angkor Wat's reliefs and its architectural configuration. Whether taken individually or in thematic association, these reliefs reflect the Khmer vision of reality – the way they conceived the world – and emphasise certain principles and concepts relevant at that time. In Table 6 and 7 on pages 172-173, the relief's symbolism is outlined; frequently, each relief may have multiple meanings, derived from the complex symbolism of the original stories found in the sacred texts.

The Thematic Choice

A variety of themes from the Epics and *Puranas* were selected for the two pavilions, and each of these themes often had a multiplicity of symbolic meanings (for examples see entries in tables 4.1.a and 4.1.b). Furthermore, in each relief at least part of the symbolism parallels or complements that of other themes or themes around them (for example S. 1 and N. 1, or S. 1 and S. 2, S. 5, S. 7, S. 11 and S. 12). However, perhaps one of the reasons why the reliefs of the corner pavilion have been relatively neglected since Coedès' study, is due to the difficulty of weaving all these symbolic conjunctions and parallels into a cohesive narrative programme. Presented here is a systematic review of the themes present in the western corner pavilions and of their symbolism in an attempt to put them together into a kind of narrative order.

Thematic choice from the Ramayana
With regard to the selection of themes exclusively dealing with the *Ramayana*, it is evident that no episodes from the first two-thirds of the *Bala Kanda* and of the entire *Uttara Kanda* (respectively the first and last books of the *Ramayana*) have been represented in the reliefs. The reasons for this exclusion are quite clear: the core of the *Bala Kanda* consists of elaborate accounts of the origin of the *Ramayana* and of poetry and of no major epic events. The *Uttara*

Kanda is a heterogeneous collection of myths and legends of some important figures of the epic not mentioned in it before. Furthermore it incorporates the final years of Rama's life as a ruler of Ayodhya, his horse's sacrifice; the appearance of the twin brothers Kusa and Lavo – who were in fact Rama's sons, Sita's return to her mother – the Earth, and finally the return of Rama, his brothers and friends to the heavens and Vishnu.

The *Bala* and *Uttara Kanda* were later, XII century additions (Goldman 1984, I: 15) to the Valmiki text and therefore would not necessarily have penetrated to contemporary Khmer culture. Even if they had, given the conservative nature of religious imagery in general in Southeast Asia it is not to be expected that they would be immediately assimilated into the sculptural repertoire. Significantly, these parts of the *Ramayana* have also been excluded from the local version of the epic, the *Ramaker*, perhaps because they lack dramatic events that could produce the strong visual effects of the main core of the *Ramayana*. Certainly, as has been mentioned before, the Khmers had a preference for visual representa-tions of the conflicts between gods and the forces of evil or for colossal battles like the one of Kurukshetra and Lanka. On a lighter note they enjoyed the acrobatic and humorous adventures of monkeys, although only a few of the prodigious adventures of Hanuman are represented in Angkor Wat, as he is seldom individually recognisable. From the life of Sita, they favoured only three episodes: her *svayamvara* (N. 10), where she is the reward of the contest (not a participant in the action), her captivity (represented by Sita languishing under the *ashoka* tree; N. 8) and her ordeal by fire (N. 5). The important story of Ravana abducting Sita is not depicted in the corner pavilions; it is, however, illustrated in a small exterior half pediment of the western door of the southwestern corner pavilion and also of the eastern door of the northeastern corner pavilion (diametrically opposite). Instead, preference has been given to Viradha's attempt to kidnap her in the corner pavilion (N. 6), and this is also found in half pediments from other locations in the temple.

The emphasis is instead on Rama's role in all the events in which he participates. As a heroic god, he is depicted following Indian iconographic canons (Rao, 1997 reprint, I: 189), holding the arrow (*bana*) with the right hand and the bow (*dhanus*) in the left. He wears the *kirta mukuta*, as a son of a king, and is fully adorned. Lakshmana should be at Rama's left, and of smaller size, not to surpass in height the shoulder or the ear of Rama. However, the figure of Rama or Lakshmana standing at ease with the body in three curves (at the neck, shoulders and hip), is not shown a pose compulsory in India but unknown in contemporary Angkorean art.

Thematic choice from the Puranas

The thematic choices of Puranic myths and Krishna legends are more difficult to assess, due to the large repertoire. When comparing the selection in Angkor Wat with that in the Baphuon, for instance, the absence of stories of Krishna's childhood is noticeable. From this period of his life only the episode of him dragging the heavy mortar (S. 6) is represented, while his dramatic escapes from the murderous Kamsa are avoided. Instead, stories dealing with the adolescent Krishna predominate: Krishna receiving the offering destined for Indra (S. 12), Krishna lifting Mount Govardhana (S. 2), and that of Krishna and the *gopis* (N. 11). These themes of youthfulness may refer to the young age of Suryavarman when he was crowned king ('at the end of his studies'). As in many other Khmer temples, stories of Krishna's adulthood after the killing of Kamsa are missing, perhaps because they refer to the period of life when Krishna, as a king, had to face political and social realities.

Shaivite thematic choice

In ancient Indian mythology, Shiva myths and legends are relatively few compared with those dealing with Vishnu, and this is reflected in Khmer art. Nevertheless, several important Shaivite stories are included amongst the predominantly Vaishnava imagery at Angkor Wat, and this in spite of the fact that the temple was dedicated to Vishnu. However, those depicted on wall panels are confined to the southwestern corner pavilion. The events depicted are his mysterious apparition in the Pine Forest (S. 4), his squashing the hideous Ravana under the weight of Mount Kailasa (S. 5), reducing Kama to ashes (S. 7),

and of histrs betrothal? (or receiving homage?; S. 11). These are important representations from his iconographical repertoire, but do not include the equally important themes of the god dancing the *tandava* (although this does appear on the pediment over the southern door of the Cruciform Pavilion), the destruction of the Daksha sacrifice, intimate events with Parvati, or any story dealing with his son Ganesha. The latter is a deity almost entirely ignored in Angkor Wat except in the XVI century relief of the 'Victory of Krishna over the *asura* Bana' (LP. 6).

Narrative Programme of the Corner Pavillions

As we have seen, mythic material becomes relevant through the use of extended analogies, which were often the product of ethical and religious conventions. This art of allusion, depending as it did on an intimate familiarity with the myths and legends of the Epics and *Puranas*, almost certainly affected the thematic choice for the reliefs of the western corner pavilions. However, when looking at how the themes in each group of twelve panels are arranged on the walls of the cross-shaped corner pavilions, we can see the difficulty inherent in attempting to resolve the narrative programme – if there is any – by organising the panels according to a temporal sequence, or by their thematic or allegorical content. Indeed, it is all too easy to over-interpret in the zeal to discover a structure or a rule.

Thematic programme by textual combinations

A first approach would be simply to combine the stories narrated in the panels of each corner pavilion, and then compare and contrast them with other panels or combinations of panels in the other pavilion. The reliefs from the southwestern pavilion refer mainly to Puranic texts, with only two events out of twelve being from the *Ramayana*. In contrast, in the northwestern pavilion the themes from the *Ramayana* dominate (8 out of 12). Amongst the Puranic themes of the southwestern pavilion, the number of Shaivite stories is relatively high (4 out of 10); there are no Shaivite events in the northwestern pavilion, nor in the temple's other panels. Finally, the Puranic and Ramayanic themes are not shown according to a temporal sequence, whether one visits the corner pavilions in either clock- or counter-clock-wise directions. The images taken from different texts are apparently organised in a manner seemingly devoid of a thematic order.

Pairing by thematic symbolism

Pairing the reliefs by their themes may reveal a narrative programme, but the possibilities of pairing one with another (*see fig. 9*) are complicated by the multiplicity of symbolic meanings of each panel. For instance, the panel of Krishna and the *gopis* (N. 11), symbolic of the surrender of the individual to the Supreme Soul and of the need for devotion, is charged with such a specific meaning that its pairing with any other panel is problematic. Perhaps there could be, in fact, an iconographic analogy with the relief of Shiva in the Pine Forest (S. 4; SW corner pavilion). In both reliefs small groups of agitated women appear joyously reacting to the god's apparition. There is, however, a difference in their allegorical meaning. In the episode of the Pine Forest we are dealing with renunciation of the worshipper in order to become acceptable to Shiva, and with immediate liberation through devotion. In the story of Krishna and the *gopis*, the allegory lies in the need of love for the god, and of total union with Krishna through *bhakti*.

Some associations appear simple and obvious. The panel portraying the 'Invitation for Vishnu to descend' (N. 1) may be paired with that of Akrura's vision (N. 4), as both refer to the divine revelation of Krishna. In the southwestern corner pavilion, the panel of Ravana shaking Mount Kailasa (S. 5) and Shiva reducing Kama to ashes (S. 7), may both allegorically refer to victorious spirituality and the triumph of asceticism. There are pairings that are blatant, being events that are a prelude to later and very significant developments in each god's mythology. Other instances of this can be found in the pairing of the panel depicting the alliance of Rama and Vibhishana (N. 9) with that showing the alliance of Rama and Sugriva (N. 3); or the panel of the killing of Kabandha (N. 12) and the killing of Marica (S. 3).

Mannikka (1996: 182) has put forward a theory of allegorical meanings for the reliefs of the corner pavilions based on combining the themes of the western corner pavilions according to the pattern of the swastika and the lotus flower. However, to sustain such configurations, Mannikka sugsests the existence of a statue of Vishnu or a *linga* at the centre of each pavilion. This is quite unlikely because there are no holes in the floor marking the base of a pedestal on which such a statue could be placed (as clearly visible on the floor at the centre of the Cruciform Pavilion). Moreover, there has been no reason to doubt that the floor slabs of the western pavilions are not the original ones.

Ultimately, however, a meaningful system of pairing and combining in the reliefs remains questionable. A system of references not only requires the interpretation of one panel in terms defined by another, but also the possibility of defining a narrative connection through analogy. This is not an easy task because of the thematic shifting from one panel to another and the viewer may attempt in vain to identify hypothetical relationships. For example, in the southwestern corner pavilion, combining our observation of the relief of 'Krishna lifting Mount Govardhana' (S. 2) with that of 'Shiva in the Pine Forest' (S. 4) could lead us to compare Shiva's exhibition of sexuality towards the sages' wives in order to teach their husbands a lesson, with Krishna's exhibition of miraculous strength, displayed in order to protect his cowherd friends. Similarly, by comparing the relief of 'Shiva reducing Kama to ashes' (S. 7) with that of 'The death of Valin' (S. 8), one may ascertain that, in both stories, the villain is punished by the gods, and that there were sound reasons for their tragic death. Kama's sacrifice was necessary for Shiva to unite with Parvati and procreate, and Valin's death was vital to Rama in order to gain Sugriva's alliance and his army, which will allow him to destroy Ravana and regain his wife.

If the Khmers did intend a concrete set of such combinations, they must have been based on principles, probably of a cosmological nature, of which we do not have any documentation. Otherwise, they may have intentionally used these mythological stories as metaphors for events in the life of Suryavarman II without following a narrative order. For instance, in the case of the pairing of the Churning of the Ocean of Milk (S. 1) and of Krishna lifting Mount Govardhana (S. 2), the allegory of divine intervention and the right to rule are combined with the king's concern and protection for his people.

From what has been discussed above, it is clear that the stories depicted in the panels of the corner pavilions are not arranged according to the narrative sequence found in the original texts (*Ramayana*, *Harivamsa* and *Purana*). If the original intention for the arrangement of the episodes is out of our reach, the fact remains that, through the visual representation of myths and legends from texts that were more meaningful at the time of the building of the temple, the Khmer charged the corner pavilions with intense metaphysical and allegorical paradigms.

Narrative programme of the pediments over the doors
In the corner pavilions, the reliefs in the flat pediments over the pavilion's doors deal exclusively with Vishnu and his *avatars* of Krishna and Rama. In the southwestern pavilion, three scenes narrate events of Krishna's life: 'Krishna as a Young Boy Dragging a Heavy Mortar' (S. 6), 'The Murder of ? Pralamba' (S. 9), and 'Krishna Receiving the Offerings Destined for Indra' (S. 12); only one story comes from the *Ramayana* ('Rama Killing Marica', S. 3). In contrast, all the pediments over the lintels of the northwestern pavilion are devoted to *Ramayana* stories, with the two panels dealing with the theme of alliance (Rama with Sugriva, N. 3, and Rama with Vibhishana, N. 9) facing each other. In their peripheral placement, high above the doors' lintels, the reliefs appear to constitute a semi-independent narrative cycle of the *Ramayana*. Starting from 'Rama killing Kabandha' (N. 12),

'Viradha's Attempt to Abduct Sita' (N. 6), and then 'Rama's alliance with Sugriva' (N. 3), ending with 'Rama's Alliance with Vibhishana' (N. 9). As in the case of the Large Panels, however, this narrative prgramme eludes any path of circumambulation. This is even more the case among the pediments of the south western corner pavilion, where three pediments over the doors tell stories of Krishna' youth (S. 6, S. 9, S. 12), while the fourth is about 'Rama Killing Marica' (S. 3).

Narrative relationship between the wall panel and the window side panel relief
Another important element of the narrative technique lies in the relationship between the narrative of the main wall relief above the window and that of the relief sculpted on the panel beside the window. The elements sculpted in the side panel are either the same as those depicted in the wall panel above, or related to them in narrative continuity. However, no major events are represented; the participating personages are simply subsidiary elements of the main event narrated above. Although in some reliefs they are active participants (moving, dancing, playing drums, etc.), in general, they quietly witness the action above (sitting, watching). Although they are not essential to the action, they serve to elaborate the story; they are 'catalysts' insofar as they increase the density of the narrative.[37]

TABLE 6 SW CORNER PAVILION RELIEFS *(PEDIMENTS OVER A DOOR ARE IN ITALICS)*

No.	STORY'S TITLE	TEXT	DEITY	SYMBOLISM
S.1	The Churning of The Ocean of Milk	*Ramayana Mahabharata Bhagavata Purana*	Vishnu	- Creation - Dharma's re-establishment - Divine intervention - Future benefits - Obedience to god's instructions - Symbolism of the mountain (Mount Mandara)
S.2	Krishna Lifting Mount Govardhana	*Bhagavata Purana*	Krishna/ Vishnu	- Protection of subjects - Destruction of enemy - Benevolent punishment - Symbolism of the mountain
S.3	*Rama Killing Marica*	*Ramayana*	Rama/ Vishnu	- Victory over deception - Punishment
S.4	Shiva in the Pine Forest	*Linga Purana*	Shiva	-Victory over the senses - Triumph over temptations
S.5	Ravana Shaking Mount Kailasa	*Ramayana*	Shiva	- Triumph of spirituality - Victory over enemy - Symbolism of the mountain
S.6	*Krishnu as a Young Boy Dragging a Heavy Mortar*	*Bhagavata Purana*	Krishna/ Vishnu	- Accomplishment of karma
S.7	Shiva Reducing Kama to Ashes	*Shiva Purana Saura Purana*	Shiva	- Victory over love/lust - Symbolism of the mountain
S.8	The Death of Valin	*Ramayana*	Rama/ Vishnu	- Victory over usurper - Accomplishment of karma
S.9	*The Murder of Pralamba & The Dousing of Fire*	*Bhagavata Purana*	Krishna/ Vishnu	- Divine intervention - Protection of subject
S.10	Dvaravati Water Festival	*Harivamsa*	?Krishna/ Vishnu	- Celebration of royalty
S.11	Shiva Receiving Homage or ? The Betrothal of Shiva and Parvati	*Vamana Purana*	Shiva	- Loyalty, importance of *tapas* - Symbolism of the mountain
S.12	*Krishna Receiving the Offerings Destined for Indra*	*Bhagavata Purana*	Krishna/ Vishnu	- Victory of new ideology - Symbolism of the mountain - Subjects' obedience

TABLE 7 NW CORNER PAVILION RELIEFS

No.	STORY'S TITLE	TEXT	DEITY	SYMBOLISM
N.1	Invitation for Vishnu to Descend	*Vishnu Purana*	Vishnu	- Dharma's re-establishment - Divine duty - Revelation of divinity
N.2	Krishna bringing back Mount Maniparvata	*Bhagavata Purana*	Krishna/Vishnu	- Restoration of order - Victory over chaos - Symbolism of the mountain
N.3	*Rama's Alliance with Sugriva*	*Ramayana*	Rama/Vishnu	- Alliance, diplomacy, strategy
N.4	Akrura's Vision	*Bhagavata Purana*	Krishna/Vishnu	- Devotion - Revelation of divinity
N.5	Sita's Ordeal by Fire	*Ramayana*	Rama/Vishnu	- Sacrifice - Purity
N.6	*Viradha's Attempt to Abduct Sita*	*Ramayana*	Rama/Vishnu	- Violence & its punishment
N.7	Rama on the Pushpaka Chariot	*Ramayana*	Rama/Vishnu	- Triumph over evil and adversity, karma
N.8	Sita meeting Hanuman	*Ramayana*	Rama/Vishnu	- Loyalty, hope
N.9	*Rama's Alliance with Vibhishana*	*Ramayana*	Rama/Vishnu	- Alliance, diplomacy, strategy
N.10	The Svayamvara of Sita	*Ramayana*	Rama/Vishnu	- Test of strength - Initiation, competition
N.11	Krishna and the *Gopis*	*Bhagavata Purana*	Krishna/Vishnu	- Victory over the senses - Devotion - Need of penance - Symbolism of the mountain
N.12	*Rama killing Kabandha*	*Ramayana*	Rama/Vishnu	- Destruction of evil

Overleaf: FIG. 150 The Cruciform Pavilion looking south.

Chapter 4

The Cruciform Pavilion

The Cruciform Pavilion, the 'Preau cruciforme' of the French scholars, is a covered courtyard that was almost certainly used for rituals and ceremonies (Fig. 152). Composed of three double-pillared corridors connecting the 3rd and the 2nd enclosures, it is bisected by a fourth corridor to create an enclosed cruciform pavilion (Fig. 150). Over the pillars is a marvellous frieze of dancing *apsaras* (Fig. 153). Each arm of this pavilion has a distinct gateway composed of a large central doorway flanked by two narrower ones (*see plan page 270-71*). Each central doorway has a large horizontal pediment decorated with reliefs, while the lateral doorways half pediments, are also sculpted with reliefs.

Western Gateway

CRU.1 – The Churning of the Ocean of Milk

This relief of the Churning of the Ocean of Milk on the pediment over the central doorway is in a very poor state of preservation, with the figures being barely recognisable (Fig. 151). Furthermore, being a pedimental rather than a wall relief, its composition

FIG. 151 Detail od the Churning of the Ocean of Milk. CRU1

is not as richly conceived as those of either the Large Panel in the 3rd enclosure or that in the south-western corner pavilion. The *devas* and *asuras* are symmetrically aligned on either side of the churning pole, with their legs in a leftward motion. As with the Large Panel, the *asuras* are depicted in the southern portion of the relief (to the left of the observer) and the *devas* in the northern part.[1]

Vishnu in his four-armed form (*Caturbhuja*) is at the centre, holding the snake Vasuki with his lower hands, while the upper two hold the sword and the discus. One of his feet is placed on his incarnation as the tortoise Kurma, who is represented in a flattened state due to the pediment's constricted horizontal space. For the same reason, the churning pole – Mount Mandara – has been shortened. Discernible at its top is a small flying figure similar to that seen in the Large Panel. Half of his body, however, lies outside the composition proper, on the frame. The Ocean is represented as a single undulating line with fish scattered along it. It does not seem that any of the products of the churning have been represented.

For a full discussion of the symbolism of this relief, we can refer to the discussion in relation to the Large Panel and the southwestern corner pavilion relief. Like those, it represents an act of creation, and the re-establishment of order over chaos, and its ushering in of a period of peace and prosperity.

CRU.1R (right) – Krishna as a Young Boy Dragging a Heavy Mortar

To the right of the central pediment is the half pediment depicting this episode from Krishna's childhood (*Bhagavata Purana*, X, chapters 9-10; Fig. 154). This relief differs from the one seen in the southwestern corner pavilion (S. 6) in the characterisation of the two brothers freed by Krishna's uprooting of the two arjuna trees with the mortar. In this

FIG. 152 View of the Cruciform Pavilion from the Central Tower.

FIG. 153 View of the frieze with dancing *apsaras*.

relief, Nalakubara and Manigriva are almost identical twins with youthful hairstyles, simple *sampot*, no jewellery. They point the index fingers of their right hands in the direction of the figure of Krishna while their left hands are raised to their chests in reverence. One of the trees is shown uprooted, and the eroded figure kneeling at the back with a high chignon may be Yashoda, Krishna's foster mother. As in the depiction in the southwestern corner pavilion, the young Krishna wears around his neck a distinctive large charm in the shape of an elaborate ring.

CRU.1L (left) – Krishna Killing the Horse Kesin

In this half pediment, the composition is divided in two registers. In the upper one, Krishna is depicted with the three-pointed hairstyle of the *gopas*, grabbing the front legs of a saddled horse with his right hand, while the left is raised to the eroded mouth of the animal (Fig. 163). Behind Krishna are two crowned figures sitting with their hands in the *anjali mudra*. The lower register is filled with identical crowned figures.

The relief illustrates an episode from the *Bhagavata Purana* (X, chapter 37, 1-8) of one of the many attempts by Kamsa to have his 'nephew' Krishna killed.

Kamsa orders the asura Kesin to kill Krishna. Kesin assumes the form of a terrible horse and assaults Krishna with his mouth gaping and his legs kicking. Krishna grabs the demon by the legs and hurls it into the distance. The animal recovers and charges Krishna again with his mouth open. Krishna then thrusts his left arm into the mouth of Kesin, and as his arm expands, Kesin is choked to death.

Representations of this episode are common on the pediments of Angkor Wat, one of the best being on a half pediment of the eastern door of the southern library of the 2nd enclosure. If the animal represented in this relief is not a horse but a mule, the subject could then be the killing by Balarama, Krishna's brother, of the asura Dhenuka who had transformed himself into an ass (*Bhagavata Purana*, X, chapter 15, 29-34).[2]

FIG. 154 Krishna dragging a heavy mortar. CRU1L

Southern Gateway

CRU.2 – Vishnu Sleeping on Ananta (Vishnu Anantashayin)

This relief illustrates another popular theme of Vaishnava creation (Fig. 156). When Vishnu sleeps on the serpent Ananta who floats upon the shoreless Ocean of Eternity, his actively dreaming mind produces the template of the universe with its three elemental forms (earth, atmosphere and sky), as well as Brahma the architect of creation.[3] In this image, the four-armed Vishnu is depicted reclining on his right side over two coils of Ananta, who in his turn floats on the undulating line of the ocean. The slender and youthful god has a serene and meditative expression (Fig. 155), and holds in one of his right hands the *chakra*, while the other seems to support his head. Of his left hands, one holds the sword or mace and the other is not visible due to erosion. His crown terminates in a cylindrical extension, and he wears conical earrings, necklace, bracelets and a richly decorated *sampot*.

His head is protected by the hood of Ananta's multiple heads (possibly seven in number). His legs are supported by a figure either of Lakshmi or Bhumidevi (his principal consorts) who wears a three-pointed crown and sits close to Ananta's tail. This figure is found in most Khmer reliefs illustrating this story. The upper area of the central part of the composition is eroded, and therefore it is impossible to tell whether or not there is an image of Brahma on a lotus rising out of Vishnu's umbilicus, Brahma's birth being associated with this episode. At

FIG.155. Vishnu sleeping on Ananta. Detail. CRU.2

either end of the scene is a *rishi* with raised arms, in the attitude of offering. These figures kneel on solid earth with trees.

CRU.2R (right)

This half pediment is totally eroded, and therefore un readable.

CRU.2L (left)

This half pediment is very badly preserved and its story cannot be identified. In the upper register, the lower part of the body of Krishna or Vishnu can just be discerned, and the two figures at either side suggest the god is involved in some kind of conflict Fig. 162). In the lower register is a row of adorants.

Eastern Gateway

CRU.3 Krishna Killing Kamsa

Krishna is depicted between two large trees at the centre of the relief in the form of the Vishnu *Caturbhuja*, holding in his lower hands two figures, while the upper hands hold the wheel (*chakra*) and possibly the conch. With his left lower hand, he is grabbing by the hair his infamous enemy Kamsa, who wears a large necklace and circular earrings (Fig. 158). With his left foot, Vishnu seems to be crushing the stomach of Kamsa, who he has thrown to the ground. With his right hand, Vishnu appears to be hitting a figure with all the characteristics of a *rishi*, who clasps Vishnu's right leg from a prostrate position (Fig. 159). He has a pointed beard and his hair is in a topknot. He wears conical earrings, but no other jewellery, and his sampot. At both sides of this scene are seated crowned personages with hands joined in the *anjali mudra*. Amongst them, to the left, is a larger figure, possibly Balarama, further distinguished from the others by a ceremonial fan and various parasols.

This event is narrated in the *Bhagavata Purana* (X, chapter 44, 28-37).

Krishna and Balarama were asked by the perfidious Kamsa to prove themselves in a wrestling competition. Since the two had not yet been invested as kshatriya*, they could not use arms and only had recourse to this type of physical confrontation. Their first opponents were*

FIG. 156 Vishnu sleeping on Ananta. CRU2

FIG. 157 Vishnu defeating two royal *asuras*. CRU4

FIG. 158 Krishna killing Kamsa. Detail CRU.3

FIG. 159 Krishna killing Kamsa. Detail of the rajahotar?. CRU3

Canura and Mustika, of immense size and power, and determined to follow Kamsa's order to kill the youths. Instead Krishna and Balarama manage to overcome them and all the other wrestlers in front of the people of the city of Mathura. On seeing this, the irate Kamsa commands his soldiers to expel Krishna and Balarama from the city, confiscate the wealth of the gopas, and kill all of Krishna's relatives and allies. Krishna flares into a rage and with vehemence springs on Kamsa, knocking off his crown, grabbing him by the hair and throwing him to the ground before crushing the hapless demon king with his weight.

In so far as Krishna is shown slaying Kamsa by throwing him to the ground and crushing the demon under his weight, this relief has rendered a straightforward account of the text. In other reliefs of the same story, Krishna is instead depicted in the process of killing Kamsa with a sword. An unusual feature of this relief, however, is the *rishi*, and his identity is uncertain. He may have been the royal guru (*rajahotar*) in the service of Kamsa, which would explain why he appears to want to stop Krishna from slaying the demon. However, no mention is made of such a character in the *Purana*.

It has also been suggested (Bhandari 1995: 42 and Roveda 1997: 42) that the relief may represent the myth of Vishnu *Trivikrama* (Vishnu Making Three Steps). Indeed, the pose of the figure could indicate the taking of large steps. However, according to Indian epigraphy (Rao 1914, I: 164), Vishnu should be represented either as a young *brahmacharin* (a brahmin boy student) or as a deformed dwarf. His left foot must be raised very high, at least over the right knee when he strides over the Three Worlds (earth/water, sky and heaven). He must also have four or eight arms holding his usual attributes. The Indian tradition also requires the presence of a *kalpaka* tree behind Vishnu, as well as Indra holding a parasol over the god, and Brahma holding with one hand the foot of Vishnu, while washing it with water flowing from a jar held in his other hand. The *asura* Bali should be shown adorned with ornaments and carrying a golden vessel for ceremonial libation, in proof of his gift.

Khmer representations of Vishnu Trivikrama certainly do diverge from the Indian version in several details. Vishnu is shown with a foot raised over a lotus or a small platform, and the distinction between earth/water and the other Three Worlds is effected by the depiction of aquatic animals near the ground where the god is walking, often including a crocodile. These features are clearly visible in the half pediment of monument 'Y' of Prah Pithu (Roveda 1997: 164), in the Eastern Gopura I of Banteay Samre, and in a lintel from the temple of Suan Taeng (Buriram province) in northeastern Thailand (Smitthi & Veraprasert 1990: 143). However none of these Khmer features of the *Trivikrama* are visible in this relief, nor the ones required by the Indian tradition. The episode here depicted, therefore, is more likely to represent Krishna killing Kamsa.

CRU.3R (right)

This half pediment is in an extremely poor state of preservation, but in the upper register one can just make out the figure of a large man with two arms stretched out, each holding a smaller man by the hair. Once again, this may be a depiction of Krishna slaying his enemies, or, alternatively, of a giant *asura* (?Pralamba) being attacked by Krishna and Balarama, or even by Rama and Lakshmana. The lower register shows a row five figures without crowns, each seated within a niche – a highly unusual image amongst the Angkor Wat reliefs.

C.3L (left)

This pediment is completely eroded.

Northern Gateway

CRU.4. Vishnu Defeating two Royal Asuras (CRU 2/25)

The interpretation of the episode depicted in this relief (Fig. 157) is difficult because there are no textual references to a specific episode in Vaishnava mythology of either Vishnu or Krishna fighting two evil royal personages at the same time.

When comparing the two monstrous figures the god is fighting with figures from other reliefs, one can observe that the multi-headed and multi-armed one to the left of Vishnu is none other than Kalanemi as depicted in the Large Panel of the 'Battle of the *Devas* and *Asuras*'. Furthermore, the multi-armed figure to the right is identical to Bana from the

'The Victory of Krishna over the *Asura* Bana' and on the pediment of the south-facing gateway of the 3rd enclosure's southern *gopura*. Assuming these identities for the two royal *asuras*, one possible conclusion is that it represents no particular story, but is instead emblematic of Vishnu's supremacy over even the most powerful of the *asuras's* kings. According to the *Puranas*, Bana, son of Bali, is the primordial enemy of the gods, and Kalanemi is the grandson of Hiranyakasipu, said to have taken the semblance of Kamsa and of Kaliya. In the *Ramayana*, instead, Kalanemi is the *rakshasa* uncle of Ravana.[4]

According to Hindu mythology, the *asura* or *rakshasa* can be reborn several times under different aspects. In Puranic legends, the two doorkeepers of Vishnu, Jaya and Vijaya, having incurred the displeasure of their master (Rao, reprint 1997, I: 147), were cursed by him and condemned to be *asura* forever. They were reborn in several different aspects, of which one was that of the two brothers Hiranyaksha and Hiranyakasipu. The latter afflicted and insulted the gods to the point where Vishnu was asked to intervene in the gods' defence. In the ensuing struggle, Vishnu as the lion Narasimha first kills Hiranyaksha, and then tears Hiranyakasipu to pieces.

Jaya and Vijaya were also reborn as Madhu and Kaitabha. However, in the story of 'The Creation of Brahma' we are told that these two entities were in fact produced from Vishnu's ears when he awakened and created Brahma. They were so proud of themselves that they attacked Brahma lying on the lotus, with the intention of killing him. Brahma woke Vishnu from his sleep, and the subsequent battle lasted for thousands of years until Vishnu finally killed the two *rakshasas* (*Harivamsa*, I, 52). In the relief under consideration, the presence of Chandra (Fig. 164) and Surya depicted on either side of Vishnu seems to confirm an attribution to the Creation myth, and that the two figures could be those of Madhu and Kaitabha. However, there is no precedence for these two demons appearing in the guise of crowned, multiple-armed *asura*.

Given the uncertainty of the evidence, this event must remain unidentified. One last striking element in this relief are the large, flower-like objects with tails sculpted to the left of Vishnu (Fig. 164). They may represent the flowers that celestials usually shower on beloved heroes as a sign of appreciation.

Alternatively they may be the symbols of the righeous power of the god, or of the heat generated by *tapas*.

CRU.4R (right) – Krishna Killing Arishta.
In the *Harivamsa* we are told that Arishta, son of Bali, is ordered to attack Krishna and to do so he takes the form of a savage bull (Fig. 160). Below is the version told in the *Bhagavata Purana* (X, chapter 36, 1-14).

Arishta as a huge bull shook the earth with his hoofs, rushing around wildly, turning up mounds of earth with the ends of his horns, terrorising the people and animals of Vraja (the pastoral district where Krishna passed his childhood). The cowherds called Krishna for protection and he challenged the demon. Arishta dashed at Krishna in fury, furrowing the earth with his hoofs and dispersing the clouds with his upraised tail. With his horns pointed towards Krishna, blood-shot eyes full of fury, he charged Krishna like thunder. The powerful god, having caught Arishta by the horns, threw him in the air. The demon did not die, but sprang to his feet. He charged Krishna again. Krishna, seized the demon once more by the horns, this time hurling him to the ground, crushing him with one foot, and wringing his body as one would wring and twist a cloth. Krishna then pulled out one of the horns and with it stabbed the demon to death.

This story is also sculpted in other half-pediments of the temple, but in none other is it so vividly represented.

CRU.4L (left) – Krishna Subduing the Naga *Kaliya*
This much-loved episode (Fig. 161) is also sculpted in many other sites of the temple, and was taken from the *Bhagavata Purana* (X, 15-17).

Close to the river Kalindi there was a lake that was the abode of the naga *Kaliya. This demon polluted the river's water with his venom, distressing the local cowherds and their cattle. One day, in order to subdue the serpent, the youthful Krishna jumped into the lake and after a strenuous fight, that he seemed initially to be losing, he re-emerged and, standing on the* naga's *heads, began a wild dance to make Kaliya powerless. The wives of the naga pleaded with Krishna singing various hymns describing him as the all-transcendaut one, omniscient creator of the universe. Kaliya also*

Fig. 160 Krishna killing Arishta. CRU.4R

Fig. 161 Krishna subduing the *naga* Kaliya. CRU.4L

submitted to the god. Pleased with this, Krishna spared Kaliya's life and ordered him to leave the river and go with his kinsmen to the ocean.

Apart from the theme of subduing evil, the subject of this episode is also Krishna's awareness of his role as protector. During the struggle with Kaliya, he realised that the women and children of his own village 'had no refuge other than him' and that they were full of devotion for him. Kaliya is the only demon who is not killed by Krishna – just banished, which hints that he may have to be dealt with again, perhaps as Kamsa. If Kaliya was polluting the river, Kamsa was polluting his entire kingdom.

General Comments

It is evident that in the Cruciform Pavilion, all the reliefs still readable deal with one of two main topics: creation of order and prosperity or the destruction of evil. The exclusive representation of episodes from the *Harivamsa* and the *Purana*, and the apparent absence of those from the *Ramayana*, indicate the highlighting of the divinity of Vishnu and Krishna rather than the exploits of Rama, the most human of Vishnu's *avatara*. One is tempted to hypothesise that perhaps, for the Khmer, the more mundane and

sentimental story of Rama and Sita would not conform to the possibly ritual nature of this pavilion.

The relief of the Churning at the western doorway faces that of 'Krishna killing Kamsa' above the eastern doorway, while that of Vishnu on Ananta above the southern doorway faces that of Vishnu/Krishna slaying two royal *asuras* to the north. Thus each relief of creation is opposed by one of evil's destruction. Another interesting feature is that while all the readable half pediments feature episodes from the life of Krishna, the four main pediments feature two acts of creation by Vishnu opposite two acts of destroying evil by Vishnu/Krishna. This emphasis on Vishnu and Krishna in the reliefs becomes more marked as one approaches the central sanctuary at the heart of the temple.

The parallelism between the myth of Brahma's creation (Vishnu *Anantashayin*) and that of the Churning has previously been discussed (*see page 48*). What is perhaps most significant when considering the reliefs of the Cruciform Pavilion, however, is that while Vishnu *Anantashayin* represents the most primal act of creation, the Churning, in fact, places greater emphasis on re-creation, or the re-establishment of order after chaos. As discussed in the case of the Churning in the 3rd enclosure's Large Panels (LP. 4), this act of re-establishment could have been meant to parallel Suryavarman's own accession to the throne.

FIG. 162 Krishna fighting an *asura*. CRU.2L

Fig. 164 The moon. Detail of Vishnu defeating two royal *asuras* . CRU.4

Table 8 CRUCIFORM PAVILION (CRU)

No.	TITLE	TEXT	DEITY	SYMBOLISM
CRU. 1	The Churning of the Ocean of Milk	*Ramayana Mahabharata Bhagavata Purana*	Vishnu	- Beginning of all events - *Dharma's* re-establishment - Divine intervention - Future benefits - Obedience to god's instructions - Symbolism of the mountain
CRU. 1R	Krishna as aYoung Boy Dragging a Heavy Mortar	*Bhagavata Purana*	Krishna	- Accomplishment of karma
CRU. 1L	Krishna Killing Kesin	*Bhagavata Purana*	Krishna	- Victory over evil forces
CRU. 2	Vishnu on Ananta	*Vishnu Purana*	Vishnu	- *Dharma's* re-establishment - Divine duty - Revelation of divinity
CRU. 3	Krishna Killing Kamsa	*Bhagavata Purana*	Krishna	- Victory over evil forces
CRU. 4	Vishnu Defeating two Royal *Asura*	?	Vishnu	- Victory over evil forces - Divine strebgth
CRU. 4R	Krishna Killing Arista	*Bhagavata Purana*	Krishna	- Victory over evil forces
CRU. 4L	Krishna Subduing The *Naga* Kaliya	*Bhagavata Purana*	Krishna	- Victory over evil forces

186

FIG. 163 Krishna killing Kesin. CRU.1L

OVERLEAF: FIG. 165 Looking east from the western *Gopura* IV of Angkor Wat in the rainy season. (V. Roveda)

Chapter 5

Reliefs from other Sites

In such a rich and complex architectural structure as that of Angkor Wat there are hundreds of pediments (double and single) and half pediments over doors, porches and stepped roofs, all carved with reliefs. Regrettably, most of them are in a poor state of preservation and others are completely ruined. Some of the best pediments with narrative reliefs are presented below, following a visiting path from the Western *Gopura* (4th enclosure) to the central shrine (1st enclosure) of the temple. It is important to call the attention of the reader to the fact that two types of pediments have been distinguished here. The first is of the 'decorative' type, with the depiction of a single personage sitting or standing on a *kala*'s face, placed at the centre of a triangular foliage composition, usually with small figures within the leaves' scrolls. The second type is that of a truly 'narrative' pediment with sculptural representations of scenes taken from Sanskrit texts.

Reliefs of the *Gopuras* of the 4th Enclosure

Four entrance pavilions, or *gopuras*, provide access to the enormous grounds surrounding the temple complex. Linked together by a perimeter wall, they form the 4th enclosure of Angkor Wat. It is thought that during the XII century the vast expanse of space between Enclosure IV and Enclosure III contained not only the royal palace and government buildings, but also functioned generally as a city. As all these buildings would have been made from wood or other such perishable substances, no traces of their construction have been found above ground.

As already discussed, the temple complex is oriented to the west – the direction of Vishnu – making the Western *Gopura* the main entrance to Angkor Wat, a fact emphasised by its grand architecture

which overshadows that of the enclosure's other three *gopura*. Positioned at the end of the *naga* causeway (Figs. 167 and 168) over the moats, the Western *Gopura* is almost 235 metres in length, which is exactly that of the 3rd enclosure's western face. It is composed of a central pavilion forming the main entrance to the complex, flanked by two lateral pavilions (Fig. 166); all three structures are topped with towers. Leading from this trinity to the north and south are long galleries covered with corbelled vaulting connecting the central entrance complex with two large gateways without towers. These are commonly known as the Elephants Doors, since they were meant to accommodate the passage of these animals, as well as of carts. The long galleries were windowless on their eastern face, but formed an open terrace on the west with two parallel rows of pillars.

The exceptional magnificence of Angkor Wat's Western *Gopura*, was meant to induce in the visitor a separation from earthly affairs as they entered into a divine realm. It reflects a 'rite of passage' from a profane to a sacred environment. In particular, the Western *Gopura* demarcates a place where the devotee could prepare himself for the religious experience of the shrine and experience of the divine (*darshana*: 'seeing'). As Mannikka suggested (1996: 70), the high standard of the inner and outer decoration of the Western *Gopura* attests to the ritual and spiritual importance that the Khmers must have placed on this type of passage.

Over three of the axial doorways are the most beautiful lintels of Angkor Wat. On the portico's lintel is sculpted an elaborate mythological scene (Fig. 175) of a battle between *devas* and *asuras* with the participants on war chariots or elephants, sometimes sculpted as part of the decorative elements of the garland (Fig. 173). On the lintel over the grand doorway leading into the central pavilion is

FIG. 166 The northern end of the Western *Gopura*. (V. Roveda)

FIG. 167 The main entrance of the Western *Gopura*. (V. Roveda)

FIG. 168 The seven-headed *naga* of the balustrade. (V. Roveda)

FIG. 169 The portico of the main entrance. (V. Roveda)

a beautiful depiction of Vishnu *Anantashayin* with a lotus-bearing Brahma rising from the reclining Vishnu's umbilicus (Figs. 174 and 179). At the god's side, Lakshmi (Shri Devi) extends her arm to touch her husband's hand, but the portion of the relief depic-ting her holding Vishnu's foot has eroded away; other deities attend Vishnu's awakening (Fig. 180). As this is the first relief that a visitor to the temple would see, it is appropriate that it should take the theme of Creation.

The door pillars are also richly decorated, with festoons surrounding celestial figures, including the god Vishnu, unusually depicted holding a rosary in one of his four hands (Fig. 171). Even more extraordinary is the lace-like sculpting of deities of the Hindu pantheon in recesses to the side of the main door (Fig. 172).

The relief on the lintel above the doorway of the central pavilion leading onto the *naga* cause-way has the most intricate carving to be found in all of Angkor Wat (Fig. 176). Vishnu and Lakshmi appear again, but this time seated side-by-side on a plinth sup-ported by a lion (Fig. 170), and flanked by two pairs of attendant deities also seated on 'lion thrones'. Behind Vishnu rises a pole, at the top of which stands a dancing figure, which is possibly meant to be a standard such as those seen in the reliefs of the 3rd enclosure (Large Panels 2, 5 and 7). To the right of it is a large figure with a single crowned head and ten arms, riding a chariot pulled by a lion supporting the identification of Ravana. He brandishes a sword at the four-armed (*Caturbhuja*) Vishnu standing on the shoulders of Garuda. Other images of deities on elephants (Fig. 173) and of Vishnu on Garuda appear in clusters over the lintel. This and the previous elaborate lintel are placed in diametrical opposition; the one facing west displays an image with the theme of Creation, while the one facing East depicts an image of the supremacy of Vishnu over the forces of evil. In

FIG. 170 Detail of Fig. 176.

FIG. 171 Detail of pillar decoration from the western entrance of the Western *Gopura*. (V. Roveda)

FIG. 172 Detail of the decoration at the sides of the main entrance of the Western *Gopura*. (V. Roveda)

FIG. 173 Detail of Fig. 176.

FIG. 174 The lintel of the western entrance of the Western *Gopura*.

FIG. 175 The lintel of the western portico of the Western *Gopura*.

FIG. 176 The lintel of the eastern door of the Western *Gopura*.

FIG. 177 Medalion decoration on the wall of the southern Elephant Door. (V. Roveda)

FIG. 178 Frieze of the wall of the southern Elephant door. (V. Roveda)

this way they encapsulate most of the essential Pancharatra's myths.

Almost all of the door jambs of the Western *Gopura's* inner three pavilions are covered with what the French scholars have termed 'tapestry' reliefs, which will be discussed in more detail in a section below. The eastern walls of the long galleries are not decorated with narrative reliefs, but carry a continuous frieze of dancing *apsaras* (each 40-50 cm in height) wearing the three-pointed crown and a long flapping sarong. The walls of the Elephant Doors have some of the most refined and delicate tapestry reliefs (Fig. 177) and refined floral moulding to be found in Angkor Wat (Fig. 178). On the eastern side, all the walls of the Western *Gopura* are decorated by a continuous frieze of guardians brandishing a club or a sword, mostly standing on the backs of their mounts (horses, lions, dragons, etc.), and flanked by two Garuda-like animals (Fig. 181). The entire composition is framed by a multi-lobed foliate scroll, which is part of a larger theme of foliate scrolls emerging from a *kala* mouth. Many large *apsaras/devatas* are also sculpted all along the inner wall, and are probably the most elegantly conceived of the entire temple.

The pediments of this imposing building are all very badly preserved. The ones of a narrative type are incomplete and difficult to read, while those of a decorative type depict the usual small *deva* seated on the *kala's* head. In the pediment over the central porch, which is the first pediment the visitor sees entering Angkor Wat, eroded elements of the Battle of Lanka taken from the *Ramayana* can be seen (Fig. 169). The north-facing pediment of the northern 'Elephant door' has a fragmentary pediment displaying at the top the curious figure of Vishnu hanging on the trunk of a tree terminating with three bushy branches (Fig. 166).

The Northern, Eastern and Southern *Gopuras* of Enclosure IV also each have a central shrine/portal flanked by two lateral shrines/portals, but these groupings are only about 60 metres in length, and all are in poor condition. Their interiors are unfinished, bare of decoration. However, their exterior pediments carry important reliefs.

At the Southern *Gopura* only a few half pediments with battle scenes, and the western pediment with a relief of Krishna on Garuda's shoulders, have survived the ravages of time.

At the Northern *Gopura* most reliefs are fragmentary; the scenes of Krishna/Vishnu fighting various demons are barely recognisable. However, the west-facing pediment has a relatively well-preserved depiction of Krishna lifting Mount Govardhana over a register of naturalistically-sculpted cows and their herders (Fig. 183). The pediment originally over the northern entrance has been re-assembled on the ground in front of the *gopura*, and, like the scene on the western pediment of the Southern *Gopura*, shows Krishna on the shoulders of Garuda.

FIG. 179 Vishnu on Ananta. Detail of Fig.174.

FIG. 180 Detail of Fig.174.

FIG. 181 Frieze of the east-facing wall of the Western *Gopura*. (V. Roveda)

FIG. 182 Yama on his buffalo. Eastern *gopura* of the 4th enclosure. (V. Roveda)

FIG. 183 Krishna lifting Mount Govardhana. Northern *gopura* of the 4th enclosure. (V. Roveda)

FIG. 184 The fight between Valin and Sugriva. Eastern *gopura* of the 4th enclosure. (V. Roveda)

The Eastern *Gopura* could be accessed by an earthen levee over the moat. It is most likely that at the time of the construction of the temple, there was no wall at the sides of the Eastern *Gopura* to allow the entrance of carts and animals, and the building materials needed for the temple and the city. Today, one can drive through a breach in a wall that was probably built later. The best-preserved narrative reliefs of this *gopura* are to be found on its southern pediment and half pediment. The former has a depiction of Yama on a buffalo (facing south; his direction and that of the underworld, Fig. 182), and the latter a depiction of Sugriva fighting Valin (Fig. 184).

The reliefs of the 'Libraries'

The courtyards of the 4th, 3rd, and 2nd enclosures each contain a pair of free-standing pavilions in their western sectors. Because these structures have large windows and a clerestory just under the roof line, the first archaeologists believed they were libraries, but it is far from clear whether this was in fact their function, and if not, then what was. They could indeed have been repositories for sacred manuscripts or equally for ritual objects, images and offerings. There are no libraries within the 1st enclosure – the central shrine – presumably because this is the sanctum sanctorum, being the space of the gods and the peak of Mount Meru.

Libraries of the 4th courtyard
The library to the north is in a very poor state of repair and fragments of its narrative reliefs are scattered about on the ground. The more intact southern library has some interesting reliefs. On the north face is a heavily restored pediment of Garuda carrying a mountain peak on which stands Krishna (Fig. 185). This relief is flanked by a half pediment with a representation of Krishna lifting Mount Govardhana (Fig. 186). On another half pediment, on the southern side of the monument, is a depiction of Rama's monkey allies engaging Kumbhakarna in fierce battle (Fig. 187).

Libraries of the 3rd courtyard
Here, the libraries – which have the unique feature of being built on a very high base – are isolated in a courtyard not easily accessed by the galleries of either the 3rd or 2nd enclosure. Their function is thus particularly difficult to ascertain. Conceivably they were originally designed to be part of the 2nd enclosure's system of galleries as their bases raise them to the same level as the latter. The pediments and half pediments of the eastern and western portals of each pavilion are richly decorated.

On the northern library, the reliefs are damaged and eroded to such an extent that the episodes of the *Ramayana* and the adventures of Krishna they depict can only just be identified as coming from either one or the other of these story cycles; Once again, the southern library is in a better state of preservation, and the western pediment bears an image of Varuna riding a goose and holding a noose in his left hand (Fig. 188); compare this image with the drawing on page 131. He is surrounded by three rows of male attendants or worshippers. Below, the pediment over the porch has fragments of a male figure riding a horse (Fig. 189). This, most likely, is a depiction of Kubera, and he is surrounded by three rows of smaller human figures in an agitated state and holding swords. The pediment over the eastern door of the library displays a crowned figure riding an ass or a horse; if it is the former, he could be identified with Yama. The half pediment to the north is a magnificent illustration of Viradha amongst his jubilant *rakshasas*, tightly grasping Sita whom he has just kidnapped, while below Rama and Lakshmana are about to loose their lethal arrows at him (Fig. 190). On the opposite side, the southern half pediment depicts Krishna in the process of killing the horse Kesin sent by Kamsa to kill him (Fig. 191).

Libraries of the 2nd courtyard
The libraries of the courtyard of the 2nd enclosure are the temple's smallest structures, dwarfed by both the massive and towering central shrine of the 1st enclosure as well as by the gallery walls of both enclosures. A slightly raised cruciform walkway connects them to the 2nd and 1st enclosures. Although richly decorated, the libraries are in a poor state of preservation, and their reliefs cannot be identified.

Fig. 185 Krishna on Garuda. Southern library of the 4th enclosure. (V. Roveda)

Fig. 186 Krishna lifting Mount Govardhana. Southern library of the fourth enclosure. (V. Roveda)

Fig. 187 Kumbhakarna assaulted by monkeys. Southern library of the 4th enclosure. (V. Roveda)

Fig. 188 Varuna on his goose. Southern library of the 3rd enclosure. (V. Roveda)

Fig. 189 Kubera on a horse. Southern library of the 3rd enclosure. (V. Roveda)

Fig. 190 Viradha's attempt to abduct Sita. Southern library of the 3rd enclosure. (V. Roveda)

Fig. 191 Krishna killing Kesin. Southern library of the 3rd enclosure. (V. Roveda)

FIG. 192 The king (?) on an elephant (detail of Fig. 193).

The Pediment Reliefs of the 3rd and 2nd Enclosures

Pediments of the 3rd enclosure

Each of the eight galleries of this enclosure has a *gopura*, and the corner pavilions each have four portals. All these architectural elements are provided with pediments and some also with half pediments. In addition, there are pediments along the telescopic roofs of the galleries. The ensuing complex arrangement of pediments of a 'decorative' and 'narrative' type seems to follow simple rules:

1 - The pediments of the corner pavilions and those along the roofs of the galleries which are facing the inside of the temple or the gallery's roof are of a decorative type, while only those of the corner pavilions facing outside are of a narrative type.

2 – The pediments of the *gopura* are all of the narrative type.

The western *gopura* is the most important architectural feature of the 3rd enclosure as it is the main entrance to the temple proper as well as to the Cruciform Pavilion. Over its central, exterior portal is a west-facing pediment (Figs. 192 and 193) depicting a king seated on a howdah under parasols and fly-whisks and a standard with an image of Garuda. Below are rows of marching soldiers holding swords. Whether the royal figure is human or divine (perhaps Indra), this pediment is almost certainly a reference to Suryavarman II's prowess, of his heroism in war, and of his triumphant return from battle. The design and

iconography are particularly redolent of the king's image leading his army from his howdah in the Historic Procession (LP. 2). An argument against its parallel identification as Indra fighting one of his many *asura* enemies from the back of his elephant Airavata is that the elephant should have three heads, although this is not always the case in Khmer iconography (see the image of the deity in N. 1).

On a west-facing pediment over the central gateway of the southern *gopura* is featured a battle scene (Fig. 194) in which all the protagonists are female with the exception of an eroded male warrior to the right. The woman-warriors, holding a weapon with their raised arms, are led by a crowned princess? riding a horse-driven chariot. She holds bow and arrows and she is facing a single man depicted in the fighting posture. Bhandari (1995: 22) has suggested that this may be an illustration related to the legend of Prince Kaundinya. The latter was an illustrious brahmin who came to the land of Cambodia from across the sea armed with a sacred javelin. On arrival, he planted the javelin in the ground to mark the place where he would build the capital of his kingdom. He married the princess Soma, a mermaid or *nagi*, and started a royal dynasty. The dowry her *naga* king father provided was to drink all the waters covering the land of the Khmer, transforming the muddy soil into fertile land. *Nagas* and water are two fundamental elements of some of the earliest Khmer myths, predating those imported from India.

In the Chinese version of this story (Thierry, 1997: 39), when Wen Tian (Kaundinya) arrives at the shores of the land of the Khmer, the queen of the country, Liu Ye (Willow Leaf) attacks his merchant ship in order to pillage it. An arrow shot by the Indian prince, however, pierces her little boat. She submits to him, and becomes his wife. The legend adds that because his wife was naked, like all her people, the prince took a piece of fabric from his cargo, folded it in half and made a hole in it for her head. Regrettably, no details that could confirm the above legends are depicted in this relief which seems to illustrate an idealised battle between Kaundinya and Soma with her army.

On a south-facing pediment of the southern *gopura* is an interesting relief divided into four pseudo-registers (Fig. 195). The lowest of these depicts the image of the crowned Aniruddha lying on the

FIG. 193 The triple pediment of the western *gopura* of the 3rd enclosure. (V. Roveda)

FIG. 194 Kaundinya's legend. Southern *gopura* (eastern extension) of the 3rd enclosure. (V. Roveda)

FIG. 195 Aniruddha bound by Bana's *naga*. Central door of the southern *gopura* of the 3rd enclosure. (V. Roveda)

ground, bound by the coils of five snakes, and surrounded by *rakshasas* in warlike attitude, who also crowd the register above. In the third register from the bottom, Aniruddha is shown on foot fighting the multi-armed Bana on his war chariot, in an episode preceding his capture by Bana. More *rakshasas* are depicted in the topmost register. The events of this relief prefigure those to be found in the Large Panel of the enclosure's northern gallery (LP. 6) in which Krishna fights Bana and rescues his grandson. They are part of the myth narrated in the *Baghavata Purana* (Book X, chapter 55) that refers to Bana's discovery of Aniruddha with his daughter Usha. The *rakshasa* king sends some guards to seize Aniruddha, but the valiant youth slays them with an iron club and is only captured when Bana uses his magic powers to transform his arrows into snakes which bind the young hero.

On the roof of the central portal of the eastern *gopura* is a south-facing pediment in which the figure of a god, or a king, with his consort on his left thigh, is depicted sitting on a high plinth covered by a canopy, or within a small pavilion or temple (Fig. 197). Below him are three rows of female adorants, or courtiers, holding lotus buds and wearing the traditional three-pointed crown. If he was meant to represent Vishnu or the adult Krishna, he would have been represented with four arms, as in almost all other depictions in the temple. He is, therefore, more likely to be Rama with Sita after his accession to the throne in Ayodhya.

Over the central portal of the northern *gopura* is an east-facing pediment decorated with Krishna /Vishnu mounted on Garuda fighting the five-headed and ten-armed *asura* Bana (Fig. 198). A pediment on the roof of the NW corner pavilion has a relief with the depiction of Rama, with his bow, seated with Hanuman at the centre of a composition of vegetal scrolls commonly seen in the 'decorative' pediments at Angkor Wat (Fig. 196).

Over the southern portal of the Cruciform Pavilion leading onto the courtyard is a pediment of Shiva dancing (the *tandava*?) over a *kala* head. The triangular composition is made up of foliage scrolls of which the four at the base contain human and animal figures (Fig. 199). One cannot help noticing that the

FIG. 196 Rama and Hanuman (or Sugriva). Northwestern corner pavilion of the 3rd enclosure. (V. Roveda)

FIG. 197 A royal ceremony. Central door of the eastern *gopura* of the 3rd enclosure. (V. Roveda)

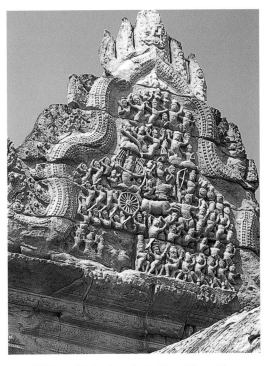

FIG. 198 Krishna fighting Bana. Central door of the northern *gopura* of the 3rd enclosure. (V. Roveda)

FIG. 199 Shiva dancing. Southern door of the Cruciform Pavilion. (V. Roveda)

FIG. 200 Viradha's attempt to kidnap Sita. Northern corner pavilion of the 3rd enclosure. (V. Roveda)

unusual southern positioning of an image of Shiva in the temple conforms to the others in the southwestern corner pavilion (S. 5, S. 7 and S. 11).

Among the half pediments on the *gopuras* of the 3rd enclosure are reliefs covering a great variety of themes. In general, they bear no relation to the pediments they flank. For example, the east-facing pediment of the northeastern corner pavilion which carries an eroded scene with Krishna is flanked to the south by a half pediment with Viradha's attempt to abduct Sita, and Rama and Lakshmana on the point of piercing Viradha with arrows (Fig. 200). To the north, the pediment is flanked by a half pediment depicting Rama and Lakshmana at rest in the forest amongst monkeys.

Regrettably, a great number of half pediments of the 3rd enclosure are either eroded or missing. Amongst the readable ones worthy of note are the successful abduction of Sita by Ravana which is depicted in the half pediment of the southwestern corner pavilion (Fig. 201). The two half pediments flanking the pediment of the southern *gopura* show Krishna/Vishnu slaying *rakshasas* grasped by the hair (Fig.

202). Another over the northern lateral portal also depicts Krishna/Vishnu fighting against *rakshasas*, one of whom is sculpted fighting upside-down. Over the northern doorway, the southern half pediment displays another scene of Rama and Lakshmana resting in the forest (Fig. 203), while its northern partner illustrates Hanuman during his scouting mission to Lanka, in the process of disturbing Ravana regally seated in his palace. The narrative simplicity of the half pediment of the northern doorway is striking. In the upper register of the relief, Krishna is depicted lifting Mount Govardhana (Fig. 204), flanked by Balarama and the cowherds. In the lower register are more cowherds with their animals. Time and weather have eroded the relief, and the details have disappeared.

Pediments of the 2nd enclosure

Most of the pediments facing into the 2nd enclosure are totally eroded or in poor condition, as are the architectural elements to which they belong (*gopura* and corner towers) having been built with poor quality sandstone. Amongst the few that are still read-

FIG. 201 Ravana's abduction of Sita. Southwestern corner pavilion of the 3rd enclosure. (V. Roveda)

FIG. 202 Krishna/Visnu slaying *rakshasa*. Southern *gopura* of the 3rd enclosure.

FIG. 203 Rama and Lakshmana in the forest. Northern *gopura* of the 3rd enclosure.

FIG. 204 Krishna lifting Mount Govardhana. Northeastern corner pavilion of the 3rd enclosure. (V. Roveda)

able, the most interesting is one over the southern doorway of the southwestern corner pavilion. At the centre, Rama and Lakshmana are represented lying on the floor bound together by snakes with cobra's hoods (*nagapasa*) (Fig. 205). These are Indrajit's arrows transformed into snakes, which he shot at the two heroes during the battle of Lanka (*Ramayana, Yudda Kanda*, chapters 45-50). Garuda eventually frees them. At the northwestern corner pavilion are illustrated some further battle scenes with heroic figures on chariots, but they come from unidentified sources.

Contrary to the outside facing pediments, all those facing into the 2nd enclosure's courtyard are well preserved and seem to be devoted to battle scenes from the *Mahabharata* and the *Ramayana*. For example, on the southern *gopura* is an episode from the battle of Lanka dealing with the grave injuries suffered by Lakshmana from the magic weapons of Ravana (Figs. 207 and 208) and not from those of his son Indrajit as has been previously suggested by many authors. This assault takes place not in chapters 73-74 of Book VI of the *Ramayana* (*Yudda Kanda*), but instead in chapters 101-102, when all of the generals, brothers and sons of Ravana have been killed, and both armies have suffered horren- dous casualties.

Ravana himself enters the battlefield and fights vigorously with Rama using magic weapons which are in turn neutralised by Rama's supernatural weapons. At a certain moment Lakshmana with a single arrow cuts off the head of Ravana's charioteer and Vibhishana with his mace kills the beautiful horses. The infuriated Ravana launches a spear at Vibhishana. The valiant Lakshmana places himself in its path, shielding Vibhishana. The spear 'nails' Lakshmana to the ground. Rama rushes to his aid and with his powerful hands gets hold of the spear, snaps it and draws it out from his brother's body. He then swears to Hanuman and the other allies that "either Ravana or Rama will cease to exist". Ravana then runs away, and Rama (chapter 102) instructs Sushena to send Hanuman to Mount Mahodaya to collect the magic herbs to restore Lakshmana to life. At once Hanuman flies to the mountain, but cannot recognise the herbs needed. He, therefore, uproots the entire peak and carries it back to Lanka. Sushena then chooses the right herbs, crushes and gives them to Lakshmana who instantly recovers to everyone's amazement.[1]

This story is depicted in a masterly way in the pediment. At the centre, Rama is about to pull out the spear from Lakshmana's body using both hands, holding his brother's body in place with one foot. Lakshmana, of smaller size, lies in the arms of a powerful monkey, possibly Sushena. To the left of Rama, Vibhishana kneels on the ground. The central figure towering over the scene is mysterious as no other human or divine personage is mentioned in the *Ramayana* as attending the scene. The best explanation is that he may be Vishnu overlooking the event to make sure of its success. The scene in the upper part of the pediment is easily recognisable: Hanuman and another monkey are carrying large rocky pieces of the sacred mountain with the magic herbs. The lower register shows grieving monkeys crying and pointing up to the unfortunate Lakshmana.

Over this pediment is another, badly eroded one depicting another event from the battle of Lanka, that of Kumbharkarna's death (*Yudda Kanda*, chapters 65-67). The giant *rakshasa* is being attacked by hordes of monkeys who bite his legs and head. To his right is Rama, flanked by Lakshmana and Vibhishana (Fig. 209).

In a north-facing pediment over the southeastern lateral portal of the enclosure gallery is a depiction of the Death of Valin (Fig. 210). The dying monkey king is shown in the arms of a partly eroded image of his wife Tara. To the right stands Rama, of whom only the head is preserved. The actual fight between Valin and Sugriva is sculpted in the top part of the pediment, but is in a poor state of preservation. Surprisingly, the same scene is illustrated again on an east-facing pediment over the northern lateral portal of the western *gopura* (Fig. 211). Here a large monkey figure, hardly comparable to the frail image of Tara in Khmer iconography, supports the dying Valin. According to the *Ramayana* (*Kishkindha Kanda*, chapters 16-25), it should be his wife Tara who embraces him during his long agony. This figure, however, could be Valin's son Angada, borrowed from a local version of the event. Above this scene is one of Rama and Lakshmana watching the fight between Valin and Sugriva, of which only the lower part is preserved. Altogether, this relief seems to be in a different sculptural style, missing the plastic and naturalistic manner of the previous one, and may be therefore, a later reworking.

FIG. 205 Rama and Lakshmana bound by Indrajit's *naga*. Southern door of the southwestern corner pavilion of the 2nd enclosure. (V. Roveda)

FIG. 206 Krishna and Balarama entering the realm of the dead. Northeastern subsidiary door of the courtyard of the 2nd level. (V. Roveda)

An unusually sinister scene is illustrated in the pediment over the eastern lateral portal of the northern enclosure gallery. It depicts a *rakshasa* king with fangs enthroned over three compact rows of *rakshasas*, interrupted at the base by the energetic appearance of two human figures wearing crowns (Fig. 206). Seven offering vessels with pointed lids are depicted on the ground in front of the *rakshasa* king. Tentatively, this relief might be interpreted as the event narrated in the *Baghavata Purana* (Book 10, chapter 85, 32-58) in which Krishna and Balarama enter the realm of the dead.

One day, after Vishnu's speech "pregnant with philosophical significance", his wife Devaki – mother of Krishna and Balarama is surprised to discover that the two had brought back from the realm of the dead the sons of their preceptor Sandipani. She expresses thus the desire to have brought back to life her sons who had been murdered at birth by Kamsa, who were the elder brothers of Krishna and Balarama. So instructed, Krishna and Balarama, resorting to their Yogamaya power, enter the world of the dead (Sutala), where Bali governed with his army. The rakshasa *receives them with joy and respect, overcoming his usual hostility to the* deva *through his devotion to Krishna, and agrees to release Devaki's six children. Krishna and Balarama bring them back to life and present them to Devaki. Nourished by mother's milk and affection, the children "regain their self-knowledge". She then blesses Krishna and Balarama for their miraculous exploit.*

The heroic size of Krishna and Balarama contrasts with that of the *rakshasas* of which the one depicted at the centre of the bottom row holds a club (or a stick of command [*danda*]) and could represent Yama. The small figures crawling on the ground seem to have the features of *rakshasas* and therefore cannot be Devaki's children. Perhaps the seven containers with pointed lids contain the souls of Devaki's six children and of Sandipani's sons.

All the pediments over the roofs and facing the galleries are of the decorative type, as are those of the 3rd enclosure. In the pediment over the southern *gopura*, facing east, the personage at the centre of the foliage scroll is that of Indra on Airavata.

The pediment reliefs of the 1st Enclosure and Main Shrine

The towering central shrine of the temple was meant to be the abode of Vishnu and as such represented the five peaks of Mount Meru, comprising the four towers of this 1st enclosure as well as that of the central shrine. The central tower is at the intersection of the north-south and east-west axis, and is the point through which passes the vertical pole of the universe. This is represented by a well extending some 25 metres below the shrine's floor, at about the same ground level of the 2nd enclosure. A colossal statue of Vishnu would have stood in the shrine, and Claude Jacques believes that the eight-armed image now worshipped as the Buddhist Avalokiteshvara in the southern lateral shrine/portal of the Western *Gopura* was that image (1997: 156 and 182).

Mannikka (1996: 81) has suggested that the central tower is symbolic of the Churning of the Ocean of Milk. It could have been so if the image of Vishnu inside the shrine was placed over the well representing the axis/churning post, at the bottom of which would be the turtle Kurma. Moreover, the stone lotus capping the roof of the central tower is equated with the lotus seat of Brahma over the central axis of Mandara, or to the top of the lotus stalk itself. We have already discussed that the Churning imagery so far encountered could have been analogous to the beginning of Suryavarman II's reign and a new time-cycle, the *Krita Yuga*, of eternal righteousness.

Buddhist monks walled the shrine's four doors up in the XIV or XV century and the new wall was decorated with large images of Buddha. Over each original doorway are lintels with reliefs featuring Vishnu with four deities at both sides. In the south-facing doorway, Vishnu is depicted sleeping on Ananta.

The entire decoration of this sanctum sanctorum of the temple is quite extraordinary. The outer walls of the galleries are sculpted with a tapestry of large medallions featuring dancing figures; the balusters of the windows are beautifully chiselled as if they had been turned on a lathe (Fig. 212). The inner walls of the galleries are ornamented with delicate tapestry-type reliefs composed of interlacing thin ribbons, while those on the door jambs are of

FIG. 207 Detail of Fig. 208.

FIG. 208 Rama extracting Ravana's spear from the chest of Lakshmana.
Northern face of the southern *gopura* of the 2nd enclosure. (V. Roveda)

Fig. 209 Kumbhakarna attacked by monkeys. Pediment above that of Fig.208. (V. Roveda)

Fig. 210 The death of Valin. Southeastern subsidiary door of the courtyard of the 2nd level. (V. Roveda)

Fig. 211 The death of Valin. Northern door of the western *gopura* of the 2nd enclosure. (V. Roveda)

the floral type, with the exception of the door jambs of the main doors of the central sanctuary, which, like the outer walls, have medallions with mythological figures (location P2 of Coedès; see page 223). Most of the pillars along the four corridors leading from the galleries to the central shrine carry reliefs of *devatas*; the ones around the central shrine are slightly smaller in size than the ones on the outer walls and of a greater refinement. They are probably the last to be sculpted at Angkor Wat (Fig. 213).

The four double-pillared roofed corridors of the 1st enclosure leading to the central tower divide its courtyard into four components. A small porch interrupts the centre of each corridor and leads on either side into one of the sunken courtyards. These porches must originally have been decorated with a small lintel and a pediment bearing reliefs. However, of the latter, only a few are still in place after the renovations carried out in later centuries by kings and devotees who restored damaged parts or added missing elements. One can see how columns and pillars taken from other sites of the temple have been used to support lintels and pediments. For example, the reconstructed north-facing pediment over the porch of the western corridor includes a stone fragment with flames enveloping the upper part of Sita's body, together with two *apsara* gracefully holding flower garlands, probably part of the representation of 'Sita's ordeal by fire' (Fig. 214). Amongst the small lintels of the same connecting corridors, the one facing east in the northern corridor represents Krishna on Garuda in a position of confrontation with Indra on Airavata. If the reading is correct, it may be dealing with the episode of Krishna's combat with Indra for possession of the Parijata tree.[2]

Pediments and half pediments of the main shrine and 1st enclosure

The architectural complexity of the central tower gives rise to a wealth of stepped pediments and half pediments richly decorated with reliefs. In general, the farther away from ground level, the more they become deeply carved and simpler in composition, emphasising the main figure. Each face of the central tower has graduated stepped pediments of which only the lowest ones are still readable, while the upper ones

are in total, or almost complete ruin. Three of the four lower pediments refer to stories of Krishna/Vishnu's victory over demonic personages, and the fourth represents Hanuman.

– Central tower, southern face. In the lowest of the double pediment, Krishna/Vishnu is depicted holding two *rakshasas*, one by the hair and the other by the leg (Fig. 215). They may be Canura and Mushtika, the two powerful wrestlers sent by Kamsa to kill him. Alternatively the demons are Madhu and Kaitabha who were secreted from Vishnu's ears when he awoke and created Brahma, and who were later killed by the god for their arrogance before he slew Kamsa. The pediment overlying the one just described is in poor condition. However the image of Krishna/Vishnu is clearly depicted striding over a large human figure in the act of running away, perhaps Kamsa.

– Central tower, eastern face. The lower pediment illustrates the story of Krishna (with four arms) triumphant over a *rakshasa* who is held by the hair, most likely Kamsa (Fig. 217). However, the use of a sword to kill Kamsa is unknown in the *Harivamsa* and *Purana*, and may have been drawn from local versions of the event or be simply a case of artistic license. An interesting detail is the circular object with a tail to the right of Krishna's torso, which is meant to represent the blazing nature of his power or one of the flowers showered from the sky by the gods. The higher pediment is totally eroded.

– Central tower, northern face. In the lower pediment, Hanuman is shown holding two demons in his raised arms; below him are shown several heads of a horrific *rakshasa* which are in three superimposed layers (Fig. 216). He probably represents Ravana or Trishiras, one of his sons killed by the monkey hero during the battle of Lanka (Book VI [*Yudda Kanda*], chapter 70). The higher pediment carries the remains of what was once a magnificent representation of Krishna on Garuda moving towards the West.

– Central tower, western face. Of the two large superimposed pediments (Fig. 218), the lowest pediment depicting Krishna lifting Mount Govardhana (Fig. 219), was probably considered the most significant

FIG. 212 Inner window of the Central Tower. (V. Roveda)

FIG. 213 Gallery with *devatas*. Central Tower. (V. Roveda)

FIG. 214 Sita's ordeal by fire. Northeastern courtyard of the 1st enclosure. (V. Roveda)

FIG. 215 Krishna killing Canura and Mushtika. Central Tower, south face. (V. Roveda)

FIG. 216 Hanuman at Lanka. Central Tower, north face. (V. Roveda)

FIG. 217 Krishna killing Kamsa. Central Tower, east face.

FIG. 218 The Central Tower seen from the north-west. (V. Roveda)

FIG 219 Krishna lifting Mount Govardhana. Central Tower, west face. (V. Roveda)

given its western position. Curiously, Krishna is sculpted standing on a tall tapering plinth, so as not to be masked by the frame of the pediment below. Overlying this pediment is another probably depicting a specific moment of the Vishnu *Trivikrama* event, just before Vishnu took the famous three steps to re-conquer the three worlds stolen by the demon Bali (Dimmit & van Buitenen 1978: 80). Here, Vishnu is slaying the *asuras* who attacked him immediately after his transformation from the dwarf Vamana into the gigantic shape of Vishnu. To the left of the god are visible two attendants still holding the jars with the hospitality gifts.

All the tower's higher pediments are in a very bad state of preservation, and only sparse fragments of the scene's protagonists are visible. Each of these pediments is, of course, flanked by half pediments. Of those on the south face, to the left of the main pediments, one still shows the eroded figure of the boy Krishna crawling on the ground between two trees (Fig. 222). His large pendant seems to be the same as he is wearing in the relief of the same subject in the southwestern corner pavilion ('Krishna as a Young

Boy dragging a Mortar', S. 6, page 103). The half pediment below displays Krishna fighting an enemy over rows of worshippers, some of whom appear to be bald (monks?) (Fig. 223).

A few episodes from the *Ramayana* are depicted in the remaining half pediments of the main shrine. The ferocious fight amongst the monkeys and a royal figure depicted in the half pediment to the left of the western pediment may refer to the defeat of Kumbhakarna in the battle of Lanka. The half pediment to the left of the main eastern pediment (Fig. 221) illustrates Rama and Lakshmana resting in the forest together with Hanuman in royal attire and some chattering monkeys in the lower register. In the half pediment to the right of the northern pediment is again depicted the ever-popular death of Valin (Fig. 220). Despite the limited space, all the protagonists are fully illustrated. Rama can be seen at the centre, hiding behind a tree, in the process of releasing the lethal arrow in the direction of Valin who is entangled in a fight with Sugriva in the top part of the composition. In the lower register, Valin is seen dying in the arms of his beloved Tara, surrounded by grieving monkeys.

Fig. 220 The death of Valin. Central Tower, north face.

Fig. 221 Rama and Lakshmana in the forest. Central Tower, north face.

Fig. 222 Krishna dragging a heavy mortar. Central Tower, south face (V. Roveda)

Fig. 223 Krishna fighting an *asura*. Central Tower, south face. (V. Roveda)

216

The four *gopuras* of the 1st enclosure have exterior-facing porticoes surmounted by pedimental reliefs but no carved lintels. Furthermore, they also have roofs ornate with pediments of the decorative type. Noticeable is the one facing west over the northern *gopura* (Fig. 224) which features Kubera sculpted amidst ornamental elements, including several mongooses, the animal associated with him in Hindu iconography. The galleries that connect the *gopura* with the main shrine have doorways descending into the small square courtyards surmounted by small pediments, one depicting Sita's ordeal (*see Fig. 214*) and another Indra on Airavata preceded by Krishna on Garuda.

In the 1st enclosure there are also four towered corner pavilions with doorways giving onto the courtyard of the 2nd enclosure in an almost identical arrangement to those of the 2nd enclosure which give on to the courtyard of the 3rd enclosure. These doorways have carved lintels and pediments, and are accessed by steep stairways, as are the porticoes of the *gopura*. Some of the pediments are still in good condition. On the one from the southwest corner-tower facing west, one can still see Krishna subduing the *naga* Kaliya (Fig. 225). The pediment over the southeast tower facing west depicts Vishnu (?) seated amongst acolytes (arranged in a tightly interlocking layout, Fig. 228), while most of the remaining pediments seem to represent battle scenes between Krishna and his enemies (Figs. 226 and 227), while *Ramayana* stories are apparently absent.

Based on the reliefs that have survived, it would seem that the primary, pedimental reliefs of the 1st enclosure and its magnificent central tower, are devoted to the exploits of Vishnu and Krishna, while Rama's stories occupy a subsidiary position in the half pediments.

Themes and arrangement of the pediment reliefs
As a high percentage of the pedimental reliefs have been destroyed, and the majority of the survivors are either badly eroded or fragmentary, any interpretation of their combined iconography is perhaps the most conjectural of any which can be applied to the reliefs of Angkor Wat. For instance, unless one is certain of the episode a relief is drawn from, it is difficult to say if a figure with ten arms represents Bana, Kalanemi or Ravana; the latter being identifiable only if the figure has five heads which have not broken off or eroded away. Some of the *rakshasa* figures are indistinguishable from monkeys with a hair tuft (especially in half pediments); and a heroic figure with a bow is not necessarily Rama, particularly if appearing in a large battle scene without participating monkeys.

FIG. 224 Kubera surrounded by mongooses. Central Tower, northern gallery, facing west. (V. Roveda)

Fig. 225 Krishna subduing the *naga* Kaliya. Southwestern corner pavilion of the 1st enclosure. (V. Roveda)

Fig. 226 Battle scene with Krishna. Northeastern corner pavilion of the 1st enclosure. (V. Roveda)

Identifying the many battle scenes is in itself problematic, as Hindu mythology contains so many of them, including the battle of Kurukshetra, of Krishna against Paundraka, of Indra against Ravana, and of Rama and allies against Ravana's hordes.

It seems highly probable that the pedimental reliefs were originally intended to be part of an iconographic programme, although, bearing in mind the great architectural complexity and the enormous dimensions of Angkor Wat, that programme may not have been that strictly dictated by the Brahmans and the *shastras*. However, given what has survived, only the most general considerations can be formulated. The first is that among the pediments and half pediments in the *gopura* portals providing entry to the 3rd and 2nd enclosures (as opposed to those which provide access to their inner courtyards) themes of divine events were sculpted mainly to the west and east, while episodes from the *Ramayana*, instead, appear to be concentrated to the north and south. Among these could be events related (directly or analogously) to the life of Suryavarman II, but they are intercalated throughout the pediments without an easily understandable programme. As already noted, all the reliefs dealing with Shiva in Angkor Wat are in southern locations, contrary to the general rule that Shiva's images should be placed on the northeast side of the temple.

The Lintel Reliefs

Although there are hundreds of lintels in Angkor Wat, only a few carry narrative reliefs. The decorative function they perform at older Khmer sites has been largely replaced at Angkor by the imposing pediments they support. In the 3rd enclosure, none of the doorways with porches have sculpted lintels. The best to be found in the temple are those of the Western *Gopura*, and they have been described above (see Figs. 174-76). In the 3rd enclosure, the doors giving exterior access to the corner pavilions have an imposing lintel structure, as do those of the corner towers of the 2nd and 1st enclosures. In addition, the doorways of the 2nd enclosure's northern and southern *gopuras* that give on to its interior courtyard also have lintels. All of these are decorated with large, elongated foliage elements that are not connected into the usual undulating horizontal garland – apparently, characteristic of a style initiated during Angkor Wat's construction. Above the *kala* at the lintel's centre there is usually a small mythological figure or group (Fig. 229). In the case of those in the 1st enclosure, this group is usually a god with a sword seated on the *kala* flanked by small *simha*, a god standing over the raised arms of a *simha*, a god standing on the back of a horse, or of Vishnu/Krishna standing on Garuda. Particularly noteworthy is the image of Indra seated on Airavata

FIG. 227 A battle scene with Krishna. Eastern *gopura* of the 1st enclosure. (V. Roveda)

FIG. 228 Vishnu (?) and acolytes. Southeastern corner pavilion of the 1st enclosure. (V. Roveda)

on the lintel of the doorway of the 2nd enclosure's southern *gopura* giving onto the interior courtyard.

The Pilaster Reliefs

Most of the temple's doorways have richly decorated pilasters, which, at their base, have a small narrative relief. This is particularly true of some of the pilasters of the Cruciform Pavilion, and at doorways in the galleries leading into the corner pavilions and *gopuras* of the 3rd enclosure. It seems that the sculpting of narrative reliefs at the base of pilasters was first introduced either at Beng Mealea or at Angkor Wat, which thereafter established a tradition for Angkorean temples.

Located at the base of the fish-bone layout of the floral decoration covering most of the pilaster's surface, the narrative scenes usually inhabit a small triangular area forcing the sculptor to narrate the scene exclusively through the figures of its protagonists. Any subsidiary elements are stylised in such a way that they evanesce into the floral trellis above. Amongst the best examples are:

– The deity Preah Thorani. Cruciform Pavilion, northern gallery (Fig. 230).
– A monkey *dvarapala*. Cruciform Pavilion, western doorway (Fig. 231).
– Krishna lifting Mount Govardhana. Central eastern *gopura* of the 3rd enclosure, eastern side (Fig. 232).
– Krishna and Balarama; western *gopura* of the 2nd enclosure, eastern side (Fig. 233).
– Krishna/Vishnu ripping apart the chest of Hiranyakasipu, central western *gopura* of the 2nd enclosure, eastern side (Fig. 234).
– Krishna knocking down Chanura and Mushtika, eastern gallery of the 3rd enclosure (Fig. 235).
– Brahma (or Varuna) on *hamsas*; Cruciform Pavilion, northern gallery (Fig. 236).
– The Churning of the Ocean of Milk, northern gallery (Fig. 237).
– Shiva as an ascetic. Pillar at the beginning of the 3rd enclosure gallery with the large panel LP. 6 (Fig. 238).
– Shiva dancing between Vishnu and Brahma, attended by Ganesha (exceptional appearance at Angkor Wat). Western end of the gallery with the large panel LP. 4 (Fig. 239).

– Viradha's attempt to kidnap Sita. Eastern *gopura* of the 3rd enclosure, western door (Fig. 240).
– Krishna lifting Mount Govardhana, eastern end of the gallery with the large panel LP. 2 (Fig. 241).

Other commonly treated subjects include: 'Krishna Subduing the *naga* Kaliya', 'Vishnu Standing on Garuda', 'Indra on Airavata' and the ubiquitous god seated holding a sword or an axe. (Rama-of-the axe?).

Ornamental Reliefs

Besides the reliefs mentioned above, most of the architectural elements of the temple, such as false doors, pilasters, colonettes, plinths, cornices, etc, are decorated with patterns of foliage or flowers, more or less stylised, that repeat over large surfaces. Furthermore, the exterior walls of the temple's galleries, *gopuras*, pavilions and towers are decorated with over 2,000 images of *devatas*[3] and *apsaras*, some standing alone or in small groups, others dancing.

The depiction of the *devatas* at Angkor Wat raises the question of whether the Khmers wanted to represent concepts of the *Lakshmi Tantra* – assuming that this text was known at that time (it was compiled between the IX and XII centuries). In fact, the *Lakshmi Tantra* not only glorifies Lakshmi as the *shakti* of Vishnu-Narayana, but also women in general as beings created in the cherished form of Lakshmi, and it advocates their worship. In addition, it alludes to the particular path to liberation and power of the left-handed Tantras that requires a female partner.

The considerable amount of *devatas* and *apsaras* reliefs is likely due to two, perhaps combined, reasons. First and foremost, these celestial women were believed to live in the skies attending to the needs of the gods and therefore their presence on the walls of the temple has the function of transforming it into a celestial palace, the house of the gods. The second reason lies in the inborn auspiciousness of women, which is then transferred to the monument upon which they are portrayed (Dehejia 1997: 6). The classic Indian text codifying artistic representations, the *Shilpa Shastra*, asserts the potency of women's fertility and equates it

FIG. 229 Lintel of the northeastern Corner Pavilion of the 2nd Enclosure. (V. Roveda)

FIG. 230 The deity Preah Thorani. Cruciform Pavilion, northern gallery.

FIG. 231 A monkey *dvarapala*. Crudiform Pavilion, western doorway.

FIG. 232 Krishna lifting Mount Govardhana. Central eastern *gopura* of the 3rd enclosure, eastern side. (V. Roveda)

FIG. 233 Krishna and Balarama. Western *gopura* of the 2nd enclosure, eastern side. (V. Roveda)

FIG. 234 Krishna/Vishnu ripping apart the chest of Hiranyakashipu, central western *gopura* of the 2nd enclosure, eastern side. (V. Roveda)

FIG. 235 Krishna knocking down Chanura and Mushtika, eastern gallery of the 3rd enclosure. (V. Roveda)

FIG. 236 Brahma (or Varuna) on *hamsas*; Cruciform Pavilion, northern gallery.

FIG. 237 The Churning of the Ocean of Milk, northern gallery.

FIG. 238 Shiva as an ascetic. Pillar at the beginning of the 3rd enclosure gallery with the large panel LP. 6.

FIG. 239 Shiva dancing between Vishnu and Brahma, attended by Ganesha. Western end of the gallery with the large panel LP. 4.

FIG. 240 Viradha's attempt to kidnap Sita. Eastern *gopura* of the 3rd enclosure, western door. (V. Roveda)

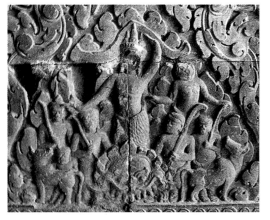

FIG. 241 Krishna lifting Mount Govardhana, eastern end of the gallery with the long panel LP. 2.

with growth, abundance and prosperity. A sacred or temporal monument (ie. royal palace, temple) could only, therefore, become auspicious if adorned with representations of women.

The sacredness attached to this conception overturns the present Western view that these women are the object of the gaze and that man is the bearer of 'the gaze', with all the concomitant implications of power over what is gazed upon. *Devatas* were sculpted by male artists to enhance the sacredness and auspiciousness of the monument and not simply for the viewing pleasure of men, even if the female forms express sensuality. The *Shilpa Prakasa*, another X century text providing guidelines for temple architects and sculptors, unequivocally states that figures of women are indispensable to temple wall decoration (Dehejia: *ibidem*), and lists 16 types best employed, instructing the sculptor on how exactly these figures should be carved within the confines of an upright rectangle. It further dictates their poses: they could be relaxed and indolent, looking into a mirror, smelling a lotus, adorning themselves with flowers, or garlanding themselves with twigs, adjusting their anklets, or holding their flywhisks.

The similarly abundant reliefs of *rishis* strengthen the identification of the temple with their abode, Mount Meru. All these celestial and ascetic images converge to elevate the temple from an earthly structure into a super-terrestrial one.

The 'Tapestry' Reliefs

Although the 'tapestry' reliefs may seem of little significance in comparison with the large narrative reliefs from the 3rd enclosure's corner pavilions and galleries, they have several elements that make them unique. They are composed of a thick mesh of medallions, each containing a single image that often serves as reference to a specific myth or legend. They present, therefore, the essential iconographic elements of each story's protagonist, and can be used to help identify or confirm characters and stories in reliefs from other sites of the temple. In many instances, this image is then combined horizontally and/or vertically with others to compose a short story. Thus each image, or unit, is like a word, which combined in a logical way creates a phrase, and

the way in which the combination takes place res-pects certain rules – a syntax. When combined horizontally and vertically, they become a unique mental and visual exercise like a crossword. Furthermore, since they are reliefs of the narrative and not the decorative type, they also function as contributors to the sacred discourse of Angkor Wat.

Design of the tapestry reliefs

In 1913, George Coedès called to attention these shallow-carved reliefs in the shape of a trellis of medallions. The medallions range in diameter from 12-20 centimetres, and are interlaced with each other. In some instances, the trellises covered entire walls as well as the door jambs (Fig. 245) and pilasters, simulating 'tapestry' decoration ('decor en tapisserie'). As is the case with almost all the sculptural reliefs at Angkor – excepting the Large Panels – no inscriptions are associated with these reliefs. Their appearance at Angkor Wat marks the first introduction of this type of carving, which can also be found at Bayon and in temples like Ta Nei, Ta Som and others. At Banteay Kdei it was executed on the ceiling of half-galleries in imitation of wood coffered decoration with rosace carvings, and later, in the temples of Vat Nokor, Ta Prohm of Bati, on the blinds of the false windows.

The designs of the tapestry reliefs must have been produced through the use of stencils (Roveda 2001; Fig. 243). These were possibly made with paper or thin copper sheets, and their design transferred to the stone by rubbing them with black ink, thus creating an image for the sculptors to follow. In this way, the carving could proceed quickly, especially in the wall areas and door jambs using standardised patterns. The use of stencils is proven by some of the medallions having been sculpted upside-down (Fig. 243), as on the eastern jamb of the external door of the northern portal of the central shrine (2P of Coedès)! The use of stencils here raises the possibility of their use on other, larger reliefs, supporting the assumption that the Large Panels of the northeastern quadrant of the 3rd enclosure – sculpted in the XVI century – were based on XII century drawings. It seems, however, that the depth of carving on the tapestry medallions depended on the individual sculptor. Moreover,

FIG. 242 Detail of the large pendant worn by *devatas*. Northern outer wall of the southern gallery of the second enclosure. (V. Roveda)

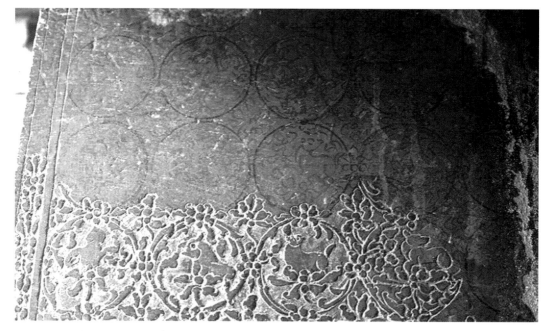

FIG.243 Traces of stencils in black ink (upper part pf the photograph) and of the medallions sculpted following the outlines. (V. Roveda)

sometimes the composition is 'moderate' (as in P91), and the story is easily readable; other times it is 'excessive', as in the story of the *Bhikshatanamurti* (83P). In this case, the figures are scattered on the thin background foliage, and the circular border of the medallions has almost completely disappeared.

There is a considerable variety in the themes represented by the figures in the reliefs. The following subjects are the most commonly found: a man with a bow or a spear running after an animal; an un-armed man running; a princely man holding his sword or axe; or more identifiable figures such as Vishnu, Krishna, Rama and Balarama, Brahma, Indra and Airavata. Also depicted are pairs of *rishi* and cowherds, the latter sometimes close to their animals. Horses, lions, deer, foxes, mongooses, rabbits, boars, squirrels, rats, dogs, birds – including parrots and phoenixes – can also feature, either fleeing, charging or more statically posed. A miraculous flower or a lotus is also often depicted with a figure seated on or popping out of its blossom. The medallions of the so-called Elephant Doors of the Western *Gopura* are larger and typically feature a man fighting a large monster, the latter being something like a cross between a bird and a dragon. It is interesting to notice that the bodies of these animals merge

FIG.244 Detail of the relief depicring Shiva appearing in the Pine Forest, with the god sculpted upside-down. (V. Roveda). See also Fig. 248.

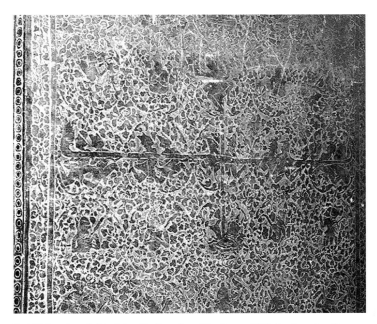

Fig.245 Tapestry relief depicting the Churning of the Ocean of Milk. Southwestern Corner Pavilion. (V. Roveda)

into the trellis of the medallion above, in a transformation process typically evidenced by the so-called *gana*. The latter are peculiar elements of Khmer iconography, where a human figure with the head of a crowned elephant transforms his trunk into the horse on which he is riding!

The vast majority of the tapestry reliefs do not combine into a narrative; the same image, or pairs of images (a man on a lotus flower or simply a lotus flower), repeating themselves in the medallions all along a particular surface. On the walls surrounding the baluster windows, the tapestry reliefs are always composed of pairs of birds – parrots or phoenixes – in a circular movement holding each other's beaks. However those that do combine to tell stories can either be short, humorous anecdotes (a man pursuing an animal which can be perceived also as an animal chasing the man), or well-known myths. The best preserved and the most commonly-illustrated are the legends of Vishnu and Krishna from the *Puranas* and *Harivamsa*. They include an overwhelming number of representations of the episode of 'Krishna Lifting Mount Govardhana (symbolic as it is of divine protection) and of Vishnu/Krishna fighting on the shoulders of Garuda. In descending order of frequency follow illustrations from the *Ramayana*

('Rama Killing Marica', 'Rama Killing Valin' and the duel between Valin and Sugriva, 'The Alliance between Rama and Vibhishana', 'The Battle of Lanka'). A few are dedicated to Sita, her abduction, her captivity in Lanka, the meeting with Hanuman and Trijata, the exchanging of jewels with Hanuman and her ordeal by fire. The ever popular 'Churning of the Ocean of Milk' appears five times, the favourite Shaivite story of Arjuna and the *kirata* a few times, and one tapestry relief seems to narrate the story of Shiva *Bhikshatanamurti*. Often the same topic recurs at a different site of the temple, emphasising its popularity and significance.

The plan on page 268-269 shows the location of the most important tapestry reliefs with reference to the publication of Coedès, 1913 of whose ink rubbings still serve as the best illustrations. The numbers and letters in brackets refer to Coedès' plates, some of which are reproduced here, and serve as co-ordinates for locating the figures sculpted.

The Churning of the Ocean of Milk (Coedès, plate I, Fig. 246)
This scene appears (Coedès P60) on the southern jamb of the eastern door of the northwestern corner pavilion exiting into the gallery with the Large Panel

A   B   C   D   E

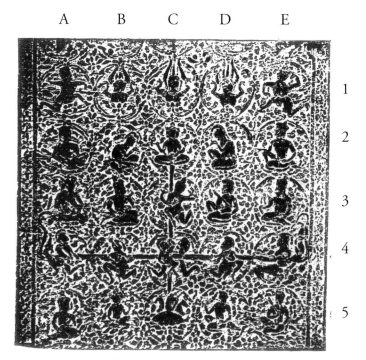

Fig. 246 The Churning of the Ocean of Milk.

of the 'Battle of the *Devas* and *Asuras*' (LP. 7). Another example appears on the eastern jamb of the doorway leading into the southwestern corner pavilion from the gallery with the Large Panel of 'The Battle of Kurukshetra' (LP. 1; Coedès 82P). A poorly preserved example is also on the eastern door jamb of the southern door exiting the southwestern corner pavilion (Coedès 80P); in these last two instances the relief faces west.

In the first location (60P), one can see Vasuki (horizontal 4); the pivot made by Mt. Mandara (C 2-5); Vishnu (C3); Brahma (C2) flanked by two worshippers, the *devas* and *asuras* (horizontal 4); and the turtle Kurma (C5) behind whom appear the heads of the goddess Shri (Lakshmi) and the horse Ucchaihshravas. There is another, roughly sketched head, which is possibly that of the elephant Airavata. At the top is the usual row of *apsaras* (horizontal 1), some of which (l B, C, D) are represented frontally, flying in horizontal position, with legs higher than their bodies, emphasising their full bosoms. Medallions with seated worshippers and/or royal personages fill the rest of the composition. In this relief, the reading follows a cruciform

pattern created by Vasuki and the vertical post of Mount Mandara. Once recognised, this composition stands out from the remaining unspecified decoration of the wall.

Arjuna and the Kirata (Coedès, plate II; Fig. 247)
This scene is sculpted on the southern jamb of the highest central stepped doorway of the Cruci-form Pavilion (Coedès P35). The action is sculpted in rows 2 and 3, where Arjuna (B3) and Shiva, as a *kirata* (D3), are depicted with the disputed boar at the centre (C3) between the two. They are flanked by *rishis* recognisable by their high chignons. In the row above, Arjuna and Shiva face each other in hand-to-hand combat (B2 and C2), surrounded again by *rishis*. This episode, taken from the *Mahabharata* (*Vanaparvan, Kairataparvan*) has been illustrated several times and in many Khmer temples (Bapuon, Wat San Kev and Bayon).

Below this event is a row of five dancing *apsaras* (4 A, B, C, D, E) with the three-pointed crowns. Below them is another row with a dancing Shiva (C5) with many arms (*Natakeshvara*), flanked – to the left of the viewer – by Vishnu (B5) and – to the right – by the multi-headed Brahma (D5) followed by Ganesha (E5). At the top of the relief is a row of *rishis*, of which the one at the centre (C1) is seated in meditation, while the others are active. Ascetic 1A is represented upside-down, probably in some form of yoga position, unless the sculptor used the stencil upside-down!

Shiva in the Pine Forest (Coedès, plate III; Fig. 248). This scene is located on the eastern jamb of the doorway leading from the western *gopura* into the gallery with the Large Panel of 'The Battle of Kurukshetra' (Coedès 83P). Although Coedès interpreted this relief as the story of Ravana transforming himself into a lizard in order to penetrate Indra's harem, he was aware that this was highly hypothetical due to the absence of female figures. On the basis of several iconographic elements and their relation to the panel of the southwestern corner pavilion (S. 4), there is no doubt that this is Shiva *Bhikshatanamurti* appearing in the Pine Forest.

At the centre of the upper row is an ascetic seated in meditation or making penance (C1). He is identified as Shiva by the presence of surrounding worshippers (l A, B, D). He is seated in meditation and in the medallion below him appears a figure within the frame of a door that has a crocodile over the lintel (C2). The scantily dressed figure is Shiva *Bhikshatanamurti* and is represented upside down. Coedès interpreted this peculiarity as an attempt to illustrate a less important image of the ascetic Shiva appearing in a physical-sensual form. The need to represent Shiva upside down to explain that the god is acting as the erotic-Shiva and not as the ascetic-Shiva is unconvincing. Shiva seems to be surrounded – on the same row (B2 and D2) and on the row below (3A, B, C, D) – by the wives of the brahmins joyfully dancing; we know from the original text that they were scantily dressed and with disorderly hair, mesmerised by the beautiful appearance of Shiva. This may have induced Coedès to interpret them not as women but as fighting men. In row 4 are quieter figures, probably the brahmins themselves, and below, at the centre, are two unidentified personages one of which (C5) seems to be playing a musical instrument (*vina* or sitar), surrounded by working ascetics (5A, B?, D, E). The remaining underlying rows (6, 7, 8) depict forest animals active-

ly hunted by the ascetics. Some ascetics are involved in pastoral activities like grazing (B6) or milking a cow (C6); below, one can see a hunter (E8) ambushing a sleeping animal (D8).

Multiple composition (Coedès, plates IV and V; Fig.s 249 and 250)
This is sculpted on the Western *Gopura's* southern lateral entrance (Coedès P91). Coedès recognised that this wall composition (illustrated in two plates) is one of the most interesting of its type at Angkor Wat, being composed of seven distinct episodes, in which the sculptors demonstrated great mastery in combining the needs of the story with those of the decoration.

1 - Unspecified scene (rows 1-3). High in the relief is a scene of a brahmin (B3) and of several other figures paying homage to celestial beings and gods, including *kinnaras* (A1), a *naga* (B1) and Garuda (C1) – all badly preserved. Also present is Shiva (C2) dancing between Vishnu (D2) and Brahma (B 2), and Ganesha (A2).

2 – 'The Churning of the Ocean of Milk' (rows 4-6). These rows show Vishnu holding a stylised short pole in C5 bearing a seated Brahma (C4) and standing over the turtle Kurma (C6) behind whom one can clearly see the heads of Shri Lakshmi and of Ucchaihshravas peering out. The *devas* and *asuras* pulling the invisible Vasuki are depicted in row 5. The cruciform shape created by the Mandara post and the pulling action which highlighted the story in the reliefs of Coedès's Plate I, is here missing or fused with the foliage defining the medallions, making the story's interpretation more difficult.

3 – 'Krishna lifting Mt. Govardhana' (rows 7-9). All the medallions depict squatting, frightened cowherds and shepherds with their animals, and isolated animals, with the exception of C7 in which Krishna is shown with his left arm lifting Mount Govardhana to create shelter for his *gopas* from the torrential rain sent by Indra.

4 – 'Rama Killing Valin' (rows 10-13). The two monkey brothers Valin and Sugriva are shown fiercely fighting each other in C l0 and C11. Below, close

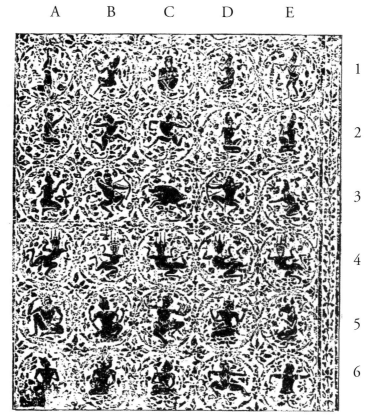

A B C D E

1

2

3

4

5

6

FIG. 247 Arjuna and the *kirata*.

to Lakshmana (D11), Rama (C11) is about to release, from his stretched bow, the fatal arrow by aiming at Valin in the medallion above. The dying Valin is shown below, recumbent in the arms of his affectionate spouse Tara (Dl2). In some medallions, agitated monkeys express their grief (F11 and A12) while others are crouched in dismay (C12). The most moving is the one in E12 who extends his arm out from the medallion to touch the feet of the dying king. Valin's many wives are depicted in row B12, F12 and in all of row 13, wearing the three-pointed crowns.

5 – 'Alliance Between Rama and Vibhishana' (row 14). In the left half of this row sit Rama (C14) and Lakshmana (B14), holding their bows, according to their traditional iconography. Rāma is facing Vibhishana (D14), who is seated with his left arm on his chest, another common iconographic gesture. He is followed by his generals, clearly

depicted as monkeys with tails, wearing crowns (E14).

6 – 'The Battle of Lanka' (rows 15-17). The main protagonists are Hanuman (C15) and Ravana (C16). Hanuman is distinguishable by his crown amongst the somersaulting and jumping monkeys of row 15, while Ravana is recognisable by the ten arms on each side of his body. Ravana is being assaulted from above by Hanuman and by other monkeys all around him. Rama is not shown.

7 – 'Hanuman Exchanges Jewels with Sita' (rows 17-18). Hanuman is represented twice in this row: first as a small monkey (C17) on the *ashoka* tree, and later squatting or sleeping in the branches (D17). Below is Sita (D18) seated in the *ashoka* grove, in the traditional pose holding her head with one arm, surrounded by Ravana's *rakshini* of whom the benevolent Trijata is represented with a human face (B and E18).

A   B   C   D   E

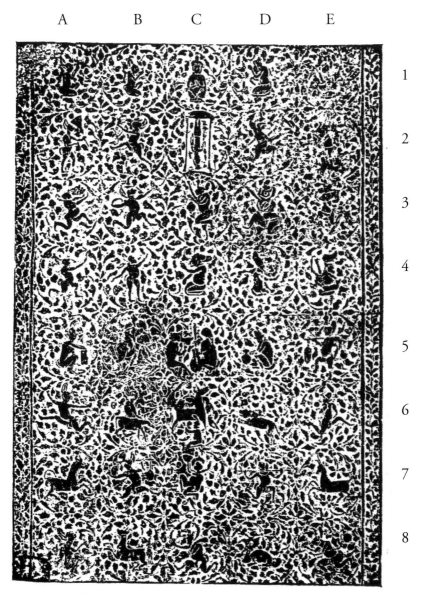

1

2

3

4

5

6

7

8

FIG. 248 Shiva in the Pine Forest.

'Alliance between Rama and Vibhishana' (Coedès, plate VI; Fig. 251)

This relief is displayed in the southern jamb of the lateral southern entrance of the 3rd enclosure's western *gopura* (Coedès P84; is this necessaing. Rama (C2) and Lakshmana (D2), holding their bows, are seated facing Vibhishana (B2), who is squatting close to a monkey (B1), possibly Hanuman. The latter is also represented in the row below (A3) where the badly preserved scene seems to show another moment of the same meeting.

'The Battle of Lanka' (Coedès, plate VII; Fig. 252)

Located in the western jamb of the lateral southern entrance of the 3rd enclosure's western *gopura* (Coedès P85), Lakshmana is depicted in medallion C3 immobilised by Indrajit's spear in the midst of fighting monkeys of rows 1-3. He is surrounded by

A   B   C   D   E   F

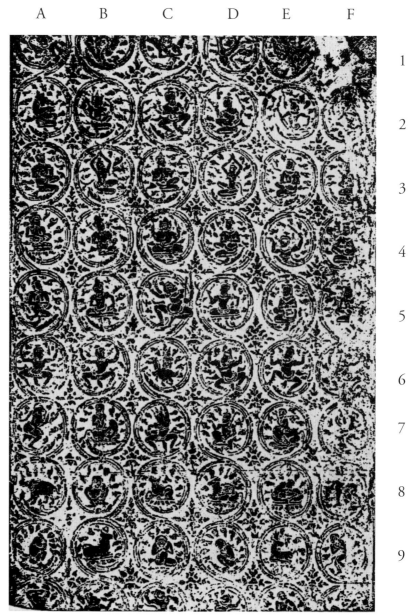

1
2
3
4
5
6
7
8
9

FIG. 249 Multiple composition.

friends (B4) and monkeys (A4) in distress. It is not clear if the large figure in medallion D4 is Vibhishana or Sushena bringing aid to the wounded man. Hanuman may be the figure sketched in medallion E4, flying to the Himalayas to collect the magic herbs. Below this scene, is a row of monkeys curiously represented standing (row 5) in mourning.

The fiercely fighting monkeys, of which Hanuman is the most illustrious, are depicted with one leg and one arm raised very high, almost in an acrobatic position. This pose is also used for the Hanuman standards carried by Khmer soldiers in several reliefs, and particularly in that of the Historic Procession (LP. 2).

Ramayana multiple composition (Coedès, plate VIII; Fig253)

This sequence is located on the eastern jamb of the interior doorway of the northern portal of the central shrine (Coedès P2).

1 – 'The Fight of Valin and Sugriva' (rows 1 and 3). In the top row of the composition, from left to right, is Lakshmana standing holding his bow (Al), followed by Rama in the flexed position of the archer ready to shoot (B1). To the right of Rama are the two monkey brothers, probably with Valin first, since he is presenting his back to Rama (C1), and then Sugriva (Dl). The last figure of this row is unidentified, as are all the other monkeys of the underlying row (A-E2); two of which (B2 and C2) have an arm raised pointing in the direction of the fight between Valin and Sugriva. Row 3, questionably belonging to this story, seems also to contain gesticulating monkeys.

2 – 'The Killing of Marica' (row 4). The medallions of the row twice represent Rama following the appearance and disappearance of Marica in the bushes (B4, C4 and E4, D4). In the E4 medallion Rama is in the act of releasing his lethal arrow at Marica (D4) who seems to be turning his head away.

3 – 'Viradha's Attempt to Abduct Sita' (row 5). Viradha grabbing Sita is clearly shown at the centre (C5) between Rama and Lakshmana (B5 and D5) who are about to kill him; the medallions at both ends are not identifiable (A5 and E5).

4 – 'The Battle of Lanka' (rows 6-9). The medallions of this door jamb depict a multitude of fighting figures, most of whom are agitated monkeys, one of powerful build (C7) being either Nila, Sugriva's general, or the ubiquitous Hanuman. The other figures are strange beings, most likely the *rakshasas*. Rama and Lakshmana (A8 and B8) are sculpted at the moment of releasing arrows against Ravana (D8), who is shown large and with many arms. In this relief several medallions contain figures of which only a torso is shown, as if they are emerging from a flower. It is not that the personages have lower bodies with multiple locomotion extensions, as Coedès initially believed.

Ramayana multiple composition (Coedès, plate IX; Fig. 254 and P2).

On the opposite door jamb of the above sequence is another also drawn from the *Ramayana* (Coedès P2). Apart from the main protagonists of the stories, all the personages seem to be emerging from flowers.

1 – 'Sita's Ordeal by Fire' (rows 1-3). The setting has gardens with trees in which animals are climbing (Dl). Sita is represented in the C2 medallion in the middle of the fire's flames. A small crowned figure kneels near her, probably the god Agni. Rama (B2) and Lakshmana (A2) are observing the ordeal. Another unidentified princely personage is seated under a tree (D2). In the row below (3) are several monkeys with raised arms, greatly agitated; the one in A3 clearly points his arm and finger in the direction of the ordeal. (Compare with the depiction in N.5)

2 – 'The Meeting of Hanuman and Sita Accompanied by Trijata' (rows 4-5). Under an *ashoka* tree, on which a small animal (Hanuman?) has climbed (B4), Sita is seated in the typical attitude (B5) of holding her head with one arm in desperation; then she seems to listen to Hanuman who is kneeling in front of her (C5). The monstrous *rakshinis* of Ravana are all around her, with horrifying faces, some with a beak (D4 and D5), while the one friendly to Sita, the kind Trijata (A5), has a human face and wears the royal three-pointed crown. There are two figures in medallions A4 and C4 pointing their fingers at the scene. Although their arms and fingers are directed towards the upper part of the tree (B4), the tree itself is clearly connected, via its trunk, to the underlying scene (B5).

3 – Unspecified scenes (rows 6-10). It is difficult to read these five rows because one cannot identify the plot; moreover the left part of the doorjamb has eroded away. Noticeable is the figure in medallion B8 in a horizontal position, two royal figures facing each other with bows (B-C9) and Garuda (Bl0).

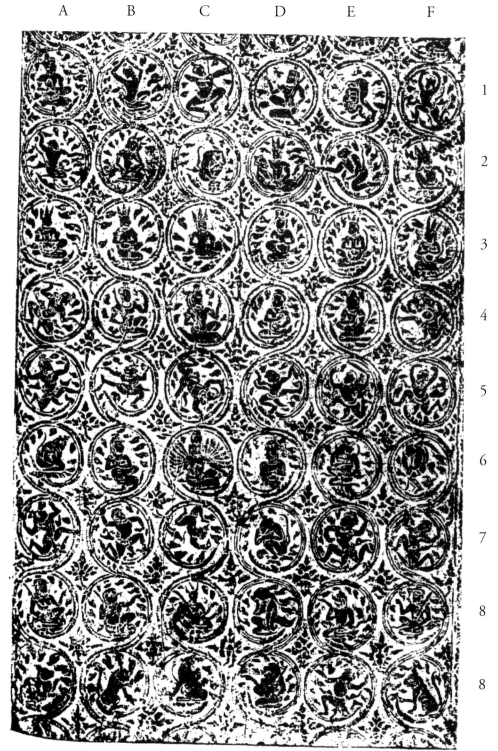

FIG. 250 Ramayana multiple composition.

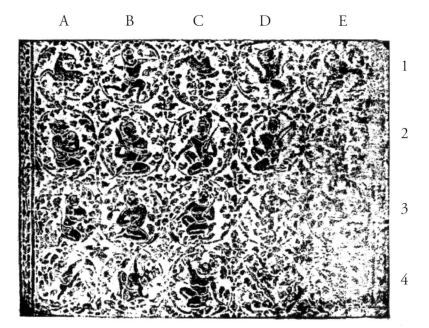

A   B   C   D   E

1

2

3

4

FIG. 251 Alliance between Rama and Vibhishana.

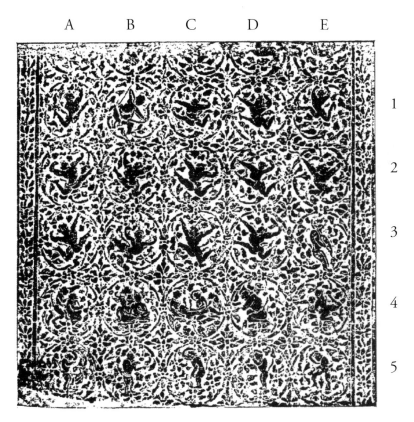

A   B   C   D   E

1

2

3

4

5

FIG. 252 The Battle of Lanka.

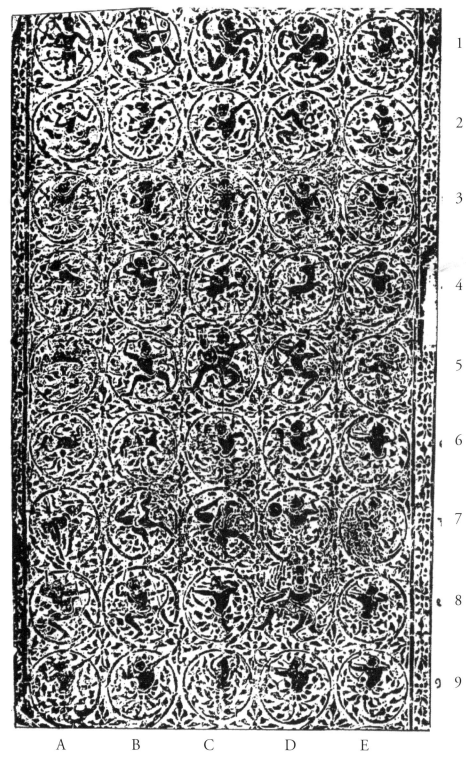

1

2

3

4

5

6

7

8

9

A   B   C   D   E

FIG. 253 *Ramayana* multiple composition.

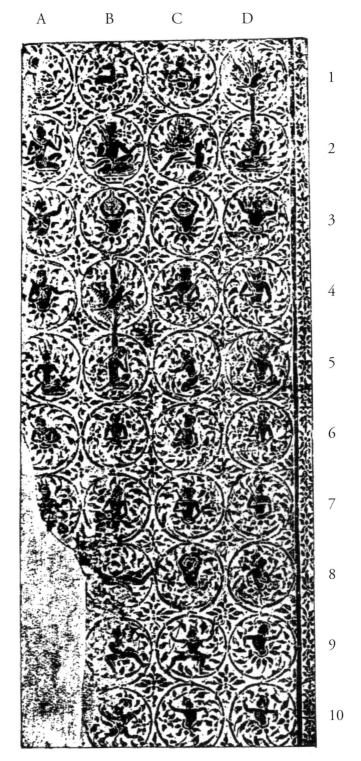

FIG. 254 *Ramayana* multiple composition.

Chapter 6

Interpretation of the Reliefs

The reliefs of Angkor Wat encapsulate a set of visual codes established by the Khmer in the XI and XII centuries; these codes express the aesthetic, social, religious and economic organisation of the time, particularly in relation to how these interacted with the Khmer elite and their exercise of power. Visual language, like verbal language, is a form of communication. The image plays some part in producing its meaning, but so does the reader; the impact is largely determined by the reader's interest and reactions to the events depicted.

Khmer sculptors executed their reliefs based on an iconography which utilises Indian narratives from the classic texts, and which possibly also had developed local idiosyncrasies. Thus the architects of Angkor's decoration were influenced in their conception of the reliefs by visual imagery deriving from textual descriptions. Although these images, especially when sculpted on walls of temples, may have functioned as a replacement for texts in a partly illiterate Khmer society, they did so on the basis of overwriting these texts. The reliefs functioned in the same way as any verbal telling. In a process of intertextuality (the relationship between a text and those demonstrably present in it), the reliefs became new texts, which would in all likelihood have still been interpreted to the public by a priest, and not read directly by the layman.

Visual Narrative Techniques

At Angkor Wat the techniques of visual representation, or visual narration, were employed with a high degree of sophistication. For the first time in Khmer art, the artists had to face large stone surfaces on which to depict stories-long rectangles in the galleries and almost square in the corner pavilions. In the galleries, the challenge was that of sustaining a visual interest in the narrative over exceptionally long panels. They resolved the task through well-spaced layouts, with the figure of the main personage/s acting as the centre around which the other figures revolved. The various figurative elements – like words – were composed in phrases drawn from Hindu stories. When a single register was inadequate for the visual narration of a story, multiple registers were used within the same panel. The linear 'order of telling' an event as a frieze, was used in the Large Panels of the galleries of the 3rd enclosure. In the corner pavilions, the representation of events in a more restricted space often required the adoption of the more complex 'ellipsic method'. Out of a complex and lengthy story, the artists selected a few culminating moments, which would convey the event narrated from the original Hindu texts. Never before in Khmer art had this visual narrative technique been used so efficiently. It was undoubtedly taken as a model for the reliefs of Banteay Chmar and the Bayon.

The layout of narrative elements and method of narration in the corner pavilion reliefs seem largely to follow a monoscenic layout, where the depiction of a single scene/event is preferred. Layouts of the polyscenic type (several scene/events depicted in the same panel) are instead the norm in the Large Panels. Their almost impossibly long extension of the narrative space was purposely created by the ideators/sculptors to allow the narration of multiple scenes. Only in this way was it possible to depict the various 'tableaux' of 'The Heavens and Hells' (LP. 3), and the several army commanders parading with their platoons in 'The Historic Procession' (LP. 2). Even the great battle compositions can be considered representations of a polyscenic type. In 'The Battle of the *Devas* and *Asuras*' (LP. 7), each of the Hindu deities is confronted by an *asura*,

FIG. 255 Girls presenting gifts. Heavens and Hells.

239

FIG. 256 Rama and Lakshmana. Baphuon, western *gopura* of the 2nd enclosure. Compare with Fig. 67. (left) (V. Roveda)

FIG. 257 Vishnu ripping apart Hiranyakasipu. Baphuon, eastern *gopura* of the 2nd enclosure. Compare with Fig. 233. (V. Roveda)

creating separate battle scenes, while 'The Battle of Lanka' (LP. 8), each large monkey figure is similarly involved in combat with a *rakshasa*.

Vidya Dehejia (1997: 81) has questioned whether the several modes of visual narration in Asian art detected by Western scholars are purely a research tool, or whether these modes indeed reflect some ancient ordering. However, it is undeniable that some choices were being made at the time of the relief's creation concerning the manner in which the story's plot and message were to be communicated. And it is reasonable to assume that the Khmers were operating within an artistic tradition that instinctively disregarded time's linear progression, and placed a greater emphasis on spatial ordering. It also seems clear that although the stories narrated in the reliefs are faithfully derived from the Indian texts, their narrative language and sculptural style are uniquely Khmer.

It may be that in Khmer art, as in ancient India, the articulation of temporal succession in visual representations was of little consequence to the artists. This was perhaps because in their cosmology, time was considered without beginning or end and structured by a system of cycles which defy astronomy and the concept of cyclical time. Moreover, one can also speculate whether this conception of time was related to the region's literary tradition where each story itself contained further stories, and each plot contained numerous sub plots. The oral tradition of these tales as well as their dramatisations take great satisfaction in presenting an entanglement of sub-plots. An excellent example of its visual manifestation can be found in the relief of 'Shiva in the Pine Forest' (S. 4) where below the main action of Shiva appearing in the doorway, there is a row of ascetics in meditation. However two groups of them are depicted in the act of running towards two young *gopis*, creating a sub-plot that adds to the already sensual flavour of the main story.

At the present state of our knowledge, a few stories in the reliefs of Angkor Wat remain uninterpreted, either because of a lack of narrative and iconographic clues, or because they are in a very poor state of preservation. The firmly interpreted ones here examined are mythological-temporal allegories constructing a discourse that requires the full attention and participation of the visitor.

Finally, it should be noted that there is a notable homogeneity in the sculptural style of the reliefs that decorate the western corner pavilions as well as six of the large panels of the 3rd enclosure and at other sites of the temple. Subtle differences exist in the depth of the carving and some slight stylistic variation - almost certainly due to different workshops, or teams of sculptors. In general, all the narrative reliefs of the temple appear to be contemporaneous with its construction, apart from, as mentioned above, the panels in the northeastern quadrant sculpted much later in the XVI century. These last also differ in sculptural style and iconographic details from the earlier ones. It is also highly probable that the reliefs, at least those in protected areas like galleries and pavilions, were painted with colours over a basic coat of white wash; specks of the latter are still observable in reliefs of the corner pavilions and cruciform pavilion.

The Selection of the Themes

When comparing the reliefs of the different parts of Angkor Wat to each other (corner pavilions, large panels, pediments, lintels and door jambs) or those of other Angkorean temples (Banteay Srei, Baphuon, Wat San Kev, Banteay Samré), one notices that the same stories and events have been selected again and again, almost as if following a canonical rule. It may be that this reflects an adherence to Indian texts demanded by the Brahmans, who may have considered such choices essential to the preservation of the classical traditions against an insidious tide of local invention. Alternatively, these could be the stories endlessly repeated by the Khmer bards, and which particularly excited the people's imagination. Another possibility is that they instead suited the designs and fancies of the political elite.

As mentioned in the Introduction, the inscription of Sdok Kok Thom identifies the famous Divakarapandita as the *rajahotar* at the time of Suryavarman II's accession. For the purpose of this book, it has been assumed that he and the other brahmins selected the themes of the reliefs of Angkor Wat. Their choices may have been dictated by the need to fulfil several principles, but foremost among these was to create a most sacred monument to Vishnu, and one which would accrue merit for Suryavarman II, and reflect his supreme importance.

It is also possible that the themes of the temple's reliefs may have been drawn from Khmer manuals dealing with architectural (*vastushastras*) and sculptural canons. In these presumed manuals there may have already been a selection of themes from the Indian epics, and even different forms of narrative, with certain incidents and characters being emphasised at the expense of others. Some may have stressed theological concepts (creation and divinity) others the prowess of the heroes (battle and combat scenes), or romantic affairs (abduction and love stories). In other instances, they may have praised secular values (royal establis ment, life at court) or spiritual ones (penance and asceticism).

Fig. 258 Hanuman assaulting Ravana. Baphuon, eastern *gopura* of the 2nd enclosure. Compare with Fig. 68. (V. Roveda)

Fig. 259 Bishma on a bed of arrows. Baphuon, eastern *gopura* of the 2nd enclosure. Compare with Fig. 9. (V. Roveda)

FIG. 260 Krishna killing Kamsa. Banteay Srei, northern library, west face. Compare with Fig. 216. (V. Roveda)

FIG. 261 Ravana or Virada kidnapping Sita. Banteay Srei, western lintel of central shrine. Compare with Figs. 199 or 200. (V. Roveda)

The criteria of choosing the themes to be illustrated are difficult to detect, particularly when considering the innumerable possibilities that were excluded. A very general observation is that events related to the amorous encounters of Krishna or Rama have been largely excluded, as well as those related to Krishna's pastoral life. This would seem to suggest that the Khmer preferred scenes of action over contemplative ones; it is obvious that these would not enhance the heroic image of Suryavarman II. In relation to the *Ramayana*, it is surprising to notice the absence of any representation of the episode in which Rama killed Shuparnakha, Ravana's sister, the incident which triggered all that was to follow; from Ravana's vengeance and his abduction of Sita to the great battle of Lanka. The event of Sita's abduction is relegated to a half pediment, and the ensuing stories of Jatayu and Sampati, the royal vulture friends of Rama who witnessed Sita's abduction are not sculpted. These last were well illustrated in the reliefs of the Baphuon temple.

The thematic choice for the long galleries was comparatively simple, involving as it does only five mythic battles, one event on the theme of Creation and the 'Historic Procession' and 'Heavens and Hells'. These long galleries could have been subdivided into a series of panels drawn from Hindu mythology in a variety of ways, but it was resolved to create eight uninterrupted panels depicting epic battles and processions on the walls surrounding the courtyard of the 3rd enclosure. Convesely, In the two western corner pavilions, the walls are a patchwork of smaller scenes sculpted on entire walls, with others over the windows, and still others in small pediments over the doors. One can speculate that the original thematic programme for the corner pavilions may have included reliefs for the two eastern corner pavilions, thus adding twenty-four more panels, and completing the 'message' of the 3rd enclosure.

Earlier models

The reliefs of earlier temples, like Banteay Srei (967?AD), and Baphuon (c.1060 AD) may shed some light on the choice of themes for the Angkor reliefs, and may even have served to inspire their choice. The author has challanged the accepted date of Banteay Srei and believes that some of its elements are younger, in particular the narrative reliefs of the libraries (Roveda 2000: in press).

The temple of Baphuon supplies a greater variety of mythological themes than that of Angkor Wat due to its decorative programme of considerably smaller panels (at the most 60 cm long and 40 cm high) on the *gopura* of the 2nd enclosure. Here one finds a rich repertoire of stories dealing with Krishna's early childhood (the exchange of children, the massacre of innocent children, the desolation of Vasudeva and Yashoda), none of which is represented at Angkor Wat. However, Baphuon shares with Angkor such scenes as Krishna subduing the *naga* Kaliya and slaying the bull-monster Arishta, and perhaps also the elephant Kuvalayapida. Vishnu is depicted in human form rather than in his incarnation as *Narasimha,* when ripping apart the chest of Hiranyakasipu (Fig. 257). At Baphuon there is also a great variety of stories from the *Ramayana,* with many not found at Angkor. These include scenes of Rama and Lakshmana (Fig. 256), Rama and Hanuman in the battle of Lanka confronting all sorts of *rakshasa,* on foot or on chariots (Fig. 258). A panel also depicts Rama and Lakshmana as prisoners of the magic arrows of Indrajit. In another panel,

Garuda (or a flying Hanuman, with a simian tail!) rescues and frees them. The cycle of adventures of Kumbhakarna is illustrated in a few panels. Other panels tell of Rama's alliance with Sugriva; of Sita as prisoner of Ravana seated under the *ashoka* tree (with one arm sustaining her reclined head in a gesture of great desolation), and exchanging jewels with Hanuman; and probably of Sita's ordeal by fire (with Sita holding her arms above her head). A fragment of a pillar illustrates an archer aiming at a bird on a pole similar to that of the *svayamvara* of Sita found in Angkor Wat's northern Corner Pavilion (N. 1; see Fig. 133) At Baphuon there are also several Shaivite stories which deal with the life of ascetics. The most famous is illustrated in a series of three stacked panels narrating the story of Arjuna and the *kirata,* and is concluded in a separate fourth panel depicting Shiva rewarding Arjuna with magic weapons. Battle scenes from the *Mahabharata* are also depicted, the most striking representing Bhishma dying on a bed of arrows (Fig. 259). Other panels depict scenes from Khmer daily life, a theme that will be abundantly resumed at Bayon, but is conspicuously absent from Angkor Wat.

The small pediments and lintels of Banteay Srei reflect a Khmer preference for Puranic stories, such as that of 'Ravana Shaking Mount Kailasa' (Fig. 262), the rain of Indra that precedes 'Krishna Lifting Mount Govardhana', and Krishna killing various

FIG. 262 Ravana shaking Mount Kailasa. Banteay Srei, southern libary, east face. Compare with Fig. 91. (V. Roveda)

FIG. 263 Shiva and Kama. Banteay Srey. southern library, west face. Compare with Fig. 94. (V. Roveda)

enemies including his arch-enemy Kamsa (Fig. 260). Several images of Krishna – or Vishnu – killing various monsters while holding them by the hair, or splitting them in two, also appear there, together with the popular story of 'Shiva Reducing Kama to Ashes' (Fig. 263). Shiva is also represented dancing, and with Uma (Parvati) on his bull Nandin, or as a *kirata* competing with Arjuna over the killing of the boar. The *Ramayana* repertoire of Banteay Srei includes Ravana's and Viradha's abduction of Sita (Fig. 261), the ferocious hand-to-hand combat of Sugriva and Valin, and the return of Rama, Sita and Lakshmana to Ayodhya on the Pushpaka chariot. From the *Mahabharata*, preference is given to the combat between Bhima and Duryodhana rather than to dense scenes.

The reappearance at Angkor Wat of themes present at older temples – although in different form and style – seems to support the hypothesis that Khmer temple-planners and sculptors may have used sculpture manuals or *shastras* illustrating the themes to be executed in their sacred monuments. They may also have simply followed the thematic examples given by these earlier temples themselves. A relationship with the latter is undeniable, as is a continuity of iconographic models right down to the small details in the depiction of the individual subjects. For example, at Baphuon (southern *gopura* of the 2nd gallery) and at Angkor Wat (pediment of the southwest corner of the 1st enclosure) Krishna subdues Kaliya while seated astride the *naga*, and in the attitude of splitting the monster's head in two. This does not reflect the original text or Indian iconography where the god simply subdues Kaliya by stamping on the monster's head with his feet. Similarly, the posture of Sita as prisoner sustaining with one arm her reclined head in a gesture of great desolation is also identical in both temples.

Some images in the pediments of Banteay Srei may have been literally copied at Angkor Wat. The Banteay Srei Ravana (in the act of shaking Mount Kailasa) is the same that in Angkor's southwestern corner pavilion (S. 5), and all the elements of the pediment in which Sugriva and Valin are fighting at Banteay Srei reappear in the same corner pavilion (S. 8). At Angkor Wat, however, the dying Valin is placed below the scene of combat and Rama releasing his fatal arrow. In the Banteay

Srei pediment, as well as in one lintel, the legs of the fighting Valin and Sugriva are depicted characteristically intertwined, casting the model for this combat which will recur in Angkor Wat and many later temples. Equally, the image of Krishna killing Kamsa on the south-facing pediment of Angkor Wat's main shrine is reminiscent of the Banteay Srei pediment: in both Krishna grabs his enemy by the hair, and holds a double-bladed axe in his right hand. Also common to both the pediments is Krishna with the hairstyle of a *gopa*: the only difference is that, in Angkor Wat, instead of a single-tuft of hair, he has three.

Thematic pattern and the mandala

The study of the sculptural reliefs of the temple – and in particular of those in the corner pavilions – is the foundation for any proposals on a pattern of thematic distribution or narrative programme. Given the fragmentary and damaged state of the pedimental reliefs, in addition to the fact that not all the pediments, half-pediments, tapestry and lintel and door jamb reliefs were completed in the XII century, makes any proposals virtually impossible to formulate. It may even be possible that some of these were later additions.

One proposal has been that the arrangement of the reliefs may have been intended to follow the architectural plan of the temple that was possibly based on a *mandala* pattern. In particular, Mannikka (1996: 55) assumes that for Angkor Wat it is the diagram of the *Vastupurusamandala*, since the latter takes into account constellations and planetary gods (*deva* and *nakshatra*) which she has taken as the key elements for her research into the astronomical and numerical symbolism of the temple. In the Indian architectural tradition (Kramrisch 1991), the *mandala* is based on the square and presents different designs according to the number of squares in the grid. The *mandala* with 49 squares seems to have the closest parallel with Angkor Wat, while in India it is the one with 64 equal squares which has an especially sacred significance, although the one with 81 elements is also common. In both cases, it is imperative for the *Vastupurusamandala* to be square, the perfect square being sacred in the hierarchy of Indian architectural symbolism, and much more meaningful than the circle. At Angkor Wat, only the 1st enclosure is square, all the others being rectangular. When drawing diagonal and orthogonal lines along the cardinal and sub-cardinal points starting from the centre of the temple, no meaningful thematic arrangement becomes visible. And this applies also to each of the western corner pavilions. The problem is that, although the *Vastupurusamandala* may have been applied to Angkor Wat for astronomical and astrological purposes, in itself it does not refer to myths and legends from the *Puranas* and the *Ramayana*. It is thus of little assistance to the research into the thematic distribution of the panels. Perhaps, other mandala diagrams should be considered. Indeed, if the plan of the temple were based on a mandala, it would very likely be one unknown to us.

The Symbolism of the Reliefs

In the process of examining Angkor Wat's vast programme of reliefs, critical interpretations of the symbolism of each of the narrative reliefs have been put forward. Based on these, some generalisations can be drawn.

The concept of the dharma and sacrifice
Sacrifice is a form of offering involving a special action and ritual. In Hindu belief, sacrifices are required by the gods to mantain order in the cosmos and on earth. Vishnu has to sacrifice himself by taking the form of an *avatara* (human incarnation) and descend on earth to re-establish the dharma (universal order) that makes life possible.

The initial golden age established by the gods was not a state of balance. In fact, the *asuras*, after being defeated by the gods, were relegated to the hells, but could not accept such inferiority. They decided to spread on earth where they appear as animals, evil beings and more frequently as princes. As a result, the brahmins are oppressed as well as all living creatures who – as a result – go to complain with Brahma, or other gods, calling for an intervention. The *avatara* re-establishes order, makes sure that the good supersedes the bad, guarantees the victory of the *devas* over the *asuras*, and, at the same time, repays the gods for what was taken from them. In so doing, he brings a new golden age, a new *Yuga* – his intervention corresponding thus to the point of passage from one cosmic age to another, from one *Yuga* to the next.

The theme of sacrifice permeates the reliefs of Angkor Wat. On a grand scale, it is evident in all the battle scenes that decorate the galleries of the 3rd enclosure. For instance, 'The Battle of Kurukshetra' (symbolic of a phase of destruction) took place when the dharma was brought to a crisis by the fratricidal intents of the Kauravas; the ensuing bloody combat was the sacrifice needed for the restoration. This may have been the reason why the Khmers represented this event in such a prominent way, at the entrance of the temple, despite its being considered generally of an inauspiceous character in Hindu ideology, and even of ill omen in Southeast Asia. The other Large Panels illustrating 'The Victory of Vishnu over the *Asuras*', 'The victory of Krishna over the *Asura* Bana', The Battle of the *Devas* and *Asuras*' and 'The Battle of Lanka', all emphasise the concept of war as sacrificial combat for the restoration of the dharma. Even the participation of Vishnu in the 'Churning of the Ocean of Milk' can be seen as a sacrifice necessary for the production of the *amrita* which would lead to the final "law and order" of the dharma.

Amongst the reliefs of the Corner Pavilions of the western galleries of the 3rd enclosure, the relief of 'The Death of Valin' (S. 8) is another enlightening example of sacrificial symbolism. Here, Valin – though noble in character – is the sacrificial victim who has to die in order to redress the dharmic imbalance caused by his actions of banishing his brother and taking his wife. At first glance, the viewer may feel compassion for the figure of the dying Valin, represented with great mastery lying in agony on the ground, his chest pierced by Rama's arrow, and lovingly attended by his wife Tara. The sense of loss inherent in any tragic death is strongly present in the image and demands our sympathy for the heroic character. However, our understanding changes if we consider that Rama's lethal arrow is the element freeing Valin from his bad kharma. Rama killing him in an ambush is not anymore a treacherous acttion but a necessary sacrificial act.

Two more panels of the Corner Pavilions, that of 'Rama's Alliance with Sugriva' (N. 3) and 'Rama's alliance with Vibhishana' (N. 9) display actions which were essential to defeat Ravana and re-establish the dharma, no matter how ruthless or cruel events these may be.

The maintenance of the dharma requires the presence of a good king whose punishing power commands respect, but who submits to the rules of the brahmins, who are the guardians of the dharma (Biardeau 1976: 11). Just as an *avatara* is needed to resolve a cosmic crisis, a king is important for the enforcement of order on earth. In total contrast, an earthly king who is intoxicated by his power and hopes to gain the celestial kingdom for himself, is identical to a king of the *asuras* such as Ravana, or at the very least like Valin. An evil king who, having rejected his human origins, takes advantage of the power of a boon received from a god or of the power acquired through *tapas*, and upsets the equilibrium of the dharma, is inevitably the cause of a crisis that triggers the intervention of an *avatara*.

On a symbolic level, any usurping king can then present himself as a necessary interruption to restore the dharma of his kingdom, and even equate himself to an *avatara* of Vishnu, believing his is thereby a divine mission. This was very relevant to Khmer kings, the majority of whom were not the rightful heirs of their predecessors. This may be the case of Suryavarman II depicted in the Large Panel of the 'Historic Procession', where his competence in maintaining the law of dharma on earth is clearly demonstrated by his royal authority. In the following Panel, that of 'Heavens and Hells' the necessity to respect the dharma is visually emphasised by the punishments meted out to those who fail to do so.

Another interesting iconographic feature related to the maintenance of the dharma is that of the ubiqitous figure holding the *danda* (stick of command, sceptre), depicted standing or sitting on the *kala*'s head in the majority of Khmer lintels. The *danda* constitutes the essence of the royal power and the king the pivot of the progress of the Three Worlds (Biardeau 1994: 48). The king superiority lies in the ability to replace disorder with the order of the dharma. The best means for him to achieve this is by enforcing punishment, to bring his subjects to submission. The tool of punishment is the *danda* which become thus the protector of the dharma taught to the king by the brahmins. Similarly, the *danda* is held by various deities both as a symbol of their divine power, or as a tool to exercise their power over humans, commonly.depicted sitting or standing over the head of a *kala* in most of Khmer lintels.

Metaphysical meanings

Three of the themes in the reliefs themselves embody important concepts of the Vaishnava doctrine: 'The Churning of the Ocean of Milk' (S. 1, LP. 4, CRU.1), 'Invitation for Vishnu to Descend' (N. 1) and 'Krishna Receiving the Offerings Destined for Indra' (S. 12). The first refers to the genesis of the universe, to Vishnu creating things (*amrita*, deities, *apsaras*, mythic animals, etc.) and bringing order to the earth – re-establishing the dharma. The second refers to Vishnu's incarnation in human form as Krishna in order to save and redeem humankind. The last relief comments on the futility of offerings made to old and lesser Vedic deities such as Indra, and how they should instead be offered to the Supreme Lord Vishnu, in the form of Krishna. It is a statement of the supremacy of the Vaishnava cult, and also of that of the mountain in XII century Khmer society. Similarly, the repeated representations of Krishna subduing the *naga* Kaliya may refer to the abolishment of *naga* cults. The many representations of 'Krishna lifting Mount Govardhana' symbolise that the new god (Krishna) protects his people in his capacity of divine preserver and restorer (Vishnu).

The panel of 'Invitation for Vishnu to Descend' (N. 1) is a text in itself, containing the fundamental Pancharatra concepts of creation and *avatara*.[1] The stories of Vishnu's descents into his earthly manifestations as Krishna and Rama, with the mission to put an end to evil forces, contains also the concept of the perfect god-hero. This is especially reflected in Rama, he being the ideal towards which ordinary mortals should strive. They are allegories that were very convenient to Khmer kings who associated themselves with these deities and heroes to justify their divine right to rule over the Khmer.

Vishnu incarnates at the end of each *yuga* because, in his own words: "whenever dharma is forgotten, whenever lawlessness prevails, I manifest myself: in every age [*yuga*] I return to deliver the righteous, to destroy the wicked and to establish dharma" (*Baghavad Gita*, 4.7). This brings about another important concept – that of cosmic time. The *yugas* are four in number and make up the world cycle.

First is the *Krita Yuga*, the golden age when there is unity, one god, one veda, one ritual. Secondly the *Tetra Yuga* when righteousness begins to decline by one quarter; thirdly the *Dwapara Yuga*, when righteousness again declines by a further quarter, and the vedas split in four; and finally the *Kali Yuga*, when there is a further decline by one quarter, and disease, despair and conflict dominate. At present we are in the fourth stage which began in 3102 BC. The other important 'teaching' conveyed by this myth, and expressed in so much detail in the relief, is indicated by the astronomical and cosmogonical significance of the deities who, headed by Brahma, visited Vishnu to ask him to 'descend' on earth.

The lotus' symbolisn in the Creation

Narayana is the central figure of the creation. The identity or the form of this absolute being changes according to the various *Puranas* – all being sectarian. In the Vaishnava context of Angkor Wat, the identification with Vishnu of the *Bhagavata Purana* (Book VIII, 7) is followed. Vishnu-Narayana sleeps on the 'single wave' of the Primordial Ocean, the wave representing chaos or the primordial matter. He lies on the snake Shesha that, by the fact of floating at the surface of the Primordial Ocean, is still a symbol of the inform. When Vishnu wakes up and concentrates to create, a lotus comes out from his navel and Brahma appears, with four faces, installed in the heart of the lotus. The surging lotus represents a separation from the level of chaos: the cosmos finds a central point and the support on which to develop. Vishnu's navel represents the female organ that is impregnated through the mediation of the lotus, and the lotus inserted into the navel plays the part of the male element that gives form to the *inform*. The symbolism of the lotus as the seed inside the chaos from which the Universe will develop elucidates the sexual symbolism of the act of creation (Biardeau 1994: 15).

A further symbolic aspect of the lotus is its circular form evoking that of the *chakra*, the Wheel of Time, the Weeel of the Dharma. In this case, Vishnu's navel could be the hub of the wheel, or the axis on which the wheel turns. Vishnu, as a supreme *yogin*, is master of time as well as of the dharma.

The symbolism of kingship

We know from epigraphical and historical data that the role of king served very much as the lynch pin of Khmer society. He united the various fiefdoms of the empire, and exerted his power to maintain them as a strong unity. Suryavarman II had to establish his kingship on several basic concepts. As a Vaishnava king he had to follow the *avatara's* model, and possibly believed himself to be an *avatara*, a human incarnation inspired by his god to perform certain deeds on earth. For a king following the path of Vishnu, the most important duty was that of re-establishing the dharma in Khmer territory, and by his subjects he could also have been perceived to be the preserver and restorer of the dharma.

The kingship's concept must have been associated with local animistic cults, of which unfortunately nothing is known from epigraphy, but that seem to be implied in the *devaraja* cult. Many hypotheses have been put forward by scholars on the meaning of the *devaraja* and its cult instituted by Jayavarman II (r. 802-850). Once seen as a cult in which the king himself turned into a god, it is now believed that the 'god' of this cult was unlikely to have been the Khmer ruler but rather an indigenous divinity elevated to a similar rank of king ('the god who is king') and supreme protector of the Khmer land (Jacques 1990: 62).

Solange Thierry has suggested an interesting parallelism between kingship and the myth of 'The Churning of the Ocean of Milk' (1997). For her, the king, by equating himself with Vishnu, created large basins, *barays*, moats and canals, as if they were the Sea of Milk, thus transforming the muddy and uncultivated land into a 'lake of ambrosia.' His mountain temple, Angkor Wat, was the mythic Mount Mandara used as the axial pivot for the churning. Because of this, it was also the axis of an inexhaustible prosperity. 'With the procreation and the joy of the Universe in mind', the king churned his moats and basins, and from them sprang the irrigated rice fields, and ultimately, and not without laborious effort, the ambrosial rice.

More examples of kingship's symbolism are also to be found in the two images of 'Krishna Lifting Mount Govardhana' and 'Krishna Receiving the Offerings Destined for Indra' illustrated in the same pavilion (S. 2 and S. 12). Krishna's need to lift Mount

Govardhana is symbolic of the god's concern to protect his people from the misadventures caused by another, albeit less powerful, god (Indra). It may also refer to a god protecting those who – abandoning a previous cult – have adopted the Vaishnava belief. The secular parallels are obvious: the king protecting his people from the miseries caused by lesser Khmer kings, and enemies like the Chams and the Dai Viêt. In these stories, the Khmer may have also perceived the equivalence of the king with Krishna, of the secular and the divine ruler. The theme of 'Krishna lifting Mount Govardhana' is most frequently recurs at Angkor Wat. Finally, another example of kingship symbolism can be found in the relief depicting 'The Churning of the Ocean of Milk', constantly used by the Khmer to evoke the beginning of the rule of the new king, bringing prosperity to the Universe.

The concept of usurpation

This concept would have been of some importance to Angkorean kings, considering that the majority of them did not attain sovereignty through paternal lineage. Although Suryavarman II dispossessed and killed his grand uncle, King Dharanindravarman, he did not perceive himself as a usurper because of his matrilineal right to the throne. Therefore, inspired by his brahmins, he may have found some characters of the *Ramayana* quite appropriate to what he saw as his justified, but perhaps a little ambivalent, situation. In particular, we have discussed how episodes like 'The Death of Valin' and 'Rama's Alliance with Sugriva' both deal with the motif of usurpation. A further point is that since Valin was the son of Indra and Sugriva the son of Surya, the shifting of suzerainty from the lunar to the solar dynasty justified Sugriva usurping his half-brother. Suryavarman II may have considered himself as a solar monarch, and compared himself to Rama who had to kill Valin and support Sugriva's project of usurpation to avoid a cosmic crisis. In the second story, the pact of the Rama/Sugriva alliance, it is the usurper Sugriva who is indispensable to Rama for recovering Sita and to putting an end to Ravana.

In the reliefs, however, another perception of usurpation is depicted, that which is encapsulated in the figure of Kamsa in the outstanding reliefs of the Main Tower (east face) of the Cruciform Pavilion (CRU.3). Not only did he usurp the throne of King Ugrasena of whom he pretended to be the illegitimate son, but he was also a liar because he was instead the son of a demon who had seduced Ugrasena's queen. Kamsa was a cousin of Devaki, the mother of Krishna, and therefore he was a cousin, not an uncle of Krishna, as he is often called. Since it was foretold that Krishna would murder him, he persecuted Krishna and tried many times, by different means, to kill him. Eventually Krishna did kill him and re-instated Ugrasena as the king of Mathura. For these reasons, the depiction of Krishna killing Kamsa, putting an end to his tyrannical rule and re-instating a lawful king, is displayed many times in the temple, although in the relatively 'minor' spaces of the pediments.

Perhaps also 'The Battle of Kurukshetra' can be taken as an allegory of the rise to power of Suryavarman, and his bloody battle for gaining the throne, during which he – like Arjuna – had to kill his relative, Dharanindravarman.

Whatever the means of obtaining it, the right to rule clearly underpins the great epics of the *Mahabharata* and the *Ramayana*. The former concerns the legitimacy of the succession to the kingdom of Kurukshetra by the Pandava and ultimately by Arjuna. Although Bhishma was the legitimate heir being the eldest son of king Samtanu, he stood aside in favour of his two younger stepbrothers and renounced having sons of his own that could rival these junior branches. Similarly, the *Ramayana* narrates the adventures and sacrifices Rama had to endure before regaining his right to become king of Mithila.

The notion victory

This notion is developed in many stories depicted throughout the temple. It is particularly evident in the battle scenes of the Large Panels discussed above. In the southwestern Corner Pavilion the emphasis is on the extolling of the Vaishnava ideological victory over the cult of Indra (S. 12), and the many other various evil beings. Stories such as 'Rama Killing Marica', 'Shiva in the Pine Forest' and 'Shiva Reducing Kama to Ashes' also allude to victory over deception, lust and the weakness of the senses. The principles enhanced by these panels do not refer only to the gods, but also, or perhaps specifically, to Suryavarman II. Through these allegories, Suryavarman may have been creating the sacredness of his kingship, claiming similarity to his divine protector.

The notion of strength.

At Angkor, the stories of 'Krishna Lifting Mount Govardhana' and of him subduing the *naga* Kaliya (western pediment of the southwestern corner pavilion of the 2nd enclsure) are amongst the most characteristic demonstrations of the god's great physical power, although this facet of the deity is also represented in his depiction as an infant when he is shown dragging the mortar and easily uprooting two trees (S. 6 and CRU.1R). A comparison of Krishna and Hercules' strength is quite common in modern literature dealing with Krishna, in addition to their sharing great appetites. It is undeniable that the demonstration of spiritual power is key to any religious story, but those representations of Krishna's prowess could be specifically symbolic of the qualities most needed by Khmer kings. Physical strength, in addition to moral fortitude, would have been seen as essential qualities for a ruler frequently involved in disputes with his neighbours and nobility. Quite often in the reliefs Krishna/Vishnu is displayed fighting enemy forces of superior and overwhelming numbers, and in several cases he confronts these hordes alone ('Victory of Vishnu over the *Asuras*'). He always manages to defeat them.

The cult of the mountain

The theme of the mountain is consistently represented in several of the panels of the corner pavilions. In the Churning, Mount Mandara is used to churn the Ocean of Milk. It is the same mountain, referred to by the name of its peak – Mount Maniparvata, which Krishna retrieves when it is dropped into the ocean by the clumsy *devas* and *asuras* while frantically setting up the Churning. In another of Krishna's myths, we are told that the god asks his cowherds to venerate and make offerings to Mount Govardhana rather than to Indra. The latter would seem to be the first of the Puranic stories introducing the sacredness of the mountain. Again it is Mount Govardhana that Krishna uplifts to shelter the cowherds. In depictions of Shiva, he is often shown on Mount Kailasa (his sacred abode). In the corner pavilion relief (S. 5), it

is this mountain that is first shaken by Ravana, and then used by Shiva to crush the demon king. In the Large Panel of 'The Historic Procession' (LP. 2), it is Mount Shivapada that is the sacred place chosen for the assembling of Suryavarman's court, and from where the king and his army will descend in parade.

Besides these famous mountains, visual representations of rocky hills or peaks are common among almost all the narrative reliefs; they are subtle visual examples of mountain symbolism. Some of the best examples are to be found in the panels of 'Shiva in the Pine Forest' (S. 4), 'Shiva Reducing Kama to Ashes' (S. 7), Shiva receiving homage (? S. 11), and 'Krishna and the *Gopis*' (N. 11).

The symbolism of the directional orientation

As mentioned before, in Khmer art and architecture certain divinities are often considered to be symbolic of specific cardinal points, at least with regard to the emplacement of their statues in temples. In the arrangements of the narrative reliefs of Angkor Wat, however, it seems that this tradition was not taken into account. Thus reliefs with Shiva's image are in a southerly location when this deity is firmly identified with the northeast in Indian cosmology. In architecture this orientation was later adopted for the subsidiary Shiva's shrines in the temples of Jayavarman VII, such as Preah Khan and Bayon. At Angkor Wat, only once is, Shiva's image sculpted in the correct position, the northeastern quarter, in the Large Panel of ' The Battle of the *Devas* and *Asuras*' (LP. 7). Here he is the object of veneration on the part of Vishnu, although the scene may have been modified in the XVI century when it was sculpted.

There was, however, an effort to orient the relief of 'The Churning of the Ocean of Milk' along the north-south axis, so that the demons should be placed within the appropriate southern region, while the *devas* inhabit the north. This is evident in the Large Panel LP. 4, and in the southwestern Corner Pavilion (S. 1). The rule seems to have been enforced mainly with this event and only occasionally with other scenes. Although it is respected in the panel of 'The Battle of Lanka' where Rama and his allies are positioned to the north and Ravana's army to the south, in the panel of The Battle of Kurukshetra the Kauravas are to the north while the

Pandavas (the heroes) and Krishna (*deva*) are placed to the south.

The reliefs of 'Krishna Lifting Mount Govardhana' throughout the temple generally face west, the direction of Vishnu. In a sense, therefore, the temple's central tower to the east of these reliefs could be interpreted as allegorically replacing the image of Mount Govardhana in the relief.

The symbolism of Vishnu/Krishna

In the reliefs, the depiction of Vishnu and Krishna with four arms (*Caturbhuja*) is frequent. The inscriptions of Phimeanakas, Preah Vihear and Thvar Kdei (Coedès 1911: 210) indicate the popularity of the *Caturbhuja* cult in Cambodia, but only at Angkor Wat did it find its most pervasive manifestation.

In Khmer iconography, Vishnu is represented not only as himself on his *vahana* Garuda, but also in the form of any one of his *avataras*, most frequently Krishna. Clearly, the reverse munst also be possible, that Krishna can be represented as Vishnu, with his attributes and *vahana*. In several reliefs depicting stories where in the Sanskrit texts Krishna is the protagonist, Vishnu seems to be sculpted instead. For instance, in the panels portraying 'Krishna Bringing Back Mount Maniparvata' (N. 2), 'Krishna and the *gopis*' (N. 11), 'Krishna Receiving the Offerings Destined for Indra' (S. 2) and the relief possibly depicting 'The Murder of Pralamba' and 'The dousing of a fire' (S. 9), either Krishna is represented as Vishnu, with crown and four arms holding the usual attributes, or Krishna is depicted as a *gopa* with his characteristic hairstyle and no crown. In this fashion, Krishna appears also in the reliefs that narrate the story of 'Krishna Lifting Mount Govardhana' (S. 2) and 'Akrura's Vision' (N. 4).

The Khmers may have perceived Krishna as being identical Vishnu, and not simply as a human manifestation. The *Bhagavata Purana* certainly encourages this assumption (1, 3, 27): 'Krishna is Bhagavata himself.' Krishna is therefore looked upon as a full manifestation of Vishnu; he is one with Vishnu himself in a manner that Rama is not. This would explain why Khmer artists represent him interchangeably with images of Vishnu. A good example of this can be seen in the relief where Krishna receives the offerings destined for Indra (S. 12), because in the text Krishna explains that Vishnu is the ultimate recipient

of worship. Furthermore, in the Large Panel of the 'Victory of Krishna over the *asura* Bana' (LP. 7), it is Vishnu who appears 7 times with 8 arms and 15 heads, and six times riding his *vahana* Garuda. In fact, according to the original Indian texts, it should be Krishna in the company of Balarama and Pradyumna.

The depictions of Krishna with four arms may be a Khmer iconic convention, or simply the acknowledgement that Krishna, in being Vishnu's incarnation, was one and identical with him.

Krishna's human aspect

Vishnu's central role as guardian, protector and preserver is ever-present in his image. Moreover, it is through the symbolism of Vishnu that the complete identity of god and universe is made clear. This in turn implies the full identity of god and man, evident in Rama and Krishna. The divine-human duality of Krishna is clear in the stories narrated in the *Purana* and *Harivamsa*, and in the reliefs the human element is often highlighted.

In his early years, Krishna, as a solar god and hero, is an infant prodigy. Like other god-boys such as Arjuna, Karna (a son of Surya) and Rama, he performs wonderful tasks by killing monsters before reaching manhood. Krishna's legends provide a full list of his fantastic actions: he kills the monstress Putana, the ass Dhenuka, the bull-demon Arishta, the horse-demon Kesin, destroys the twin *Arjuna* trees, slays the demon Pralamba, the elephant-demon Kuvalayapida, the demon Canura. He tears the rope with which he was bound (hence the epithet 'Damodara'), fights and subjugates the serpent Kaliya, and lifts a Mount Govardhana with a finger.

When Krishna becomes a youth, his charm takes on a sexual connotation. He wanders the woods at night in an amorous mood, singing and playing the flute to beguile the cowherds' women. The ultimate expression of this is when he becomes the centre of the circular dance *Rasalila*, in the course of which he multiplies his forms to gratify the desire of each woman (*Bhagavata Purana*, Book X, chapters 29-31). Following this episode, the *Brahmavaivarta* (a late *Purana*) tells of Krishna's love-play with the beautiful Radha, and the act of love is described in affectionate detail, from the arousing to the consummation of desire. The role of Krishna as lover of the *gopis* and of Radha expresses his sensual aspect and points out the presence of opposites (carnal/spiritual) in his divinity. It symbolises the unity of these polarities of the god through the metaphor of sex, and the longing of the human soul to experience spiritual unity with the god.

The assertion that Krishna (*Bhagavata Purana*, Book X, chapter 33, verse 26) enjoyed all those nights without losing a single moment of enjoyment…but he controlled all the energy within himself' does not leave any doubt as to his sexual enjoyment. When, in the text, doubts are raised about the propriety of Krishna's conduct of "seducing sensually the wives of others" (chapter 33, verse 28), it is countered that this is the prerogative of 'mighty rulers', and only them. Commoners cannot emulate the acts of God as this is against their precepts (chapter 33, verse 32). Certainly the history of India and Southeast Asia contains many examples where this concept of a 'mighty ruler' would have been used to justify similar actions of earthly kings and princes.

The *Rasalila* and what follows can be considered as young Krishna's initiation; his rite of passage from childhood to adolescence, while the murder of Kamsa marks his entering into manhood, and his becoming the guardian of the Yadava clan. The persistent definition of him as a young pre-pubescent boy in the *Puranas* and *Harivamsa* may reflect an inhibition on the part of the writers to expose the real sexual nature of his acts, and their consequences. Indologists do not seem to see Krishna's sensual aspect in this way. As Goldman has emphasised (1978 and 1984-90), there is a general lack of interest, or even hostility towards a modern vision or a psychoanalytic interpretation of classic Indian texts. Commentators to the *Bhagavata Purana* find it difficult to understand why Krishna, the protector and upholder of morality, inflicted 'outrage on the wives of others', and find all sorts of reasons to deny it. The list of reasons is quite long: that extraordinary persons cannot be judged by ordinary standards, that Krishna's behaviour was an attractive device to introduce ordinary people to spirituality, and that the *Rasalila* was intended for extinguishing carnal desires. After all, Krishna had resorted to the *Yoga-maya* for the purpose of sport with the gopis, since he had already triumphed over sex; the word 'playing' used in the text would not connote sexuality, being the same verb as used for Krishna playing with boys, and so on. Other Indian scholars

believe that, since there is no evident reference to Radha in the *Bhagavata Purana*, she was "extorted by acrobatic feats of grammar and logic" from a line (30.28) of chapter 10. Or that by making the non-existent Radha a married wife of Krishna, the social impropriety of playing the *rasa* with the maid-servants of one's wife would be exonerated, and so on. In general these commentaries agree in regarding the Krishna of the *Rasalila* and Radha as the metaphysical Krishna and not the historical Vasudeva Krishna, and that the author of the *Bhagavata Purana* intended to depict a symbolic event about the metaphysical Krishna and not involve the historical Krishna. The text emphasises that the attachment of the *gopis* may be physical, but any strong feeling, say sexual love, hatred or affection, directed towards the Lord, would lead to *moksha*.

Critics have commented on the impropriety of a devotional text like the *Bhagavata* including such highly erotic episodes and their visual description. Various attempts have been made to overcome these problems. Some authors (Tapasynanda 1981) believe that the whole episode of Krishna and the *gopis* is symbolic, not factual, denying historicity. Many others believe that Krishna was only a boy of 10 or 11 at that time, so that the erotic descriptions of him and the *gopis* are only 'exaggerations', thus accepting historicity and denying any ethical problem. G. V. Tagare (1976) is of the opinion that in this episode the historical Krishna Vasudeva becomes the metaphysical divine Krishna, holder of the *Yoga-maya* divine powers. Krishna moves between two levels of existence, the human and the divine. What seems a miracle to men is simply a display of his divine nature. Paradoxically, it is through tricks and miracles that the god Krishna continuously reveals the ultimate unity of existence.

Significance of Shiva's myths
As mentioned before, Shaivite myths are depicted in the southern corner pavilion of the western side of the temple, the sacred side of Vishnu. Usually Shiva is considered the Lord of the northeastern quarter. Anomalous is also his depiction as dancing god (*Nataraja*) at the centre of the decorative pediment over the exterior southern door of the Cruciform Pavilion.

Curiously three stories – 'Shiva in the Pine Forest' (S. 4), 'Ravana Shaking Mount Kailasa' (S. 5), and

'Shiva Reducing Kama to Ashes' (S. 7) – all show a relationship with the Vaishnava doctrine. In the text, the story of 'Shiva in the Pine Forest' ends with the chaos created by the *linga* of Shiva, and the need for the gods – particularly Vishnu – to intervene to re-establish order. The connection between Shaivism and Vaishnavism is even subtler in the episode of Shiva reducing Kama to ashes. Kama, after having been reduced to ashes by Shiva, was reborn as Pradyumna, son of Krishna and Rukmini. Finally the Ravana who attempts to disturb Shiva's meditation is the same that reappears as a central figure in the *Ramayana*, as the archenemy of Rama, one of Vishnu avatars.

Besides their unusual southwestern location (considering that Shiva was the guardian of the north or north-east) the presence of narrative reliefs of Shaivite myths should not be surprising at Angkor Wat. Shaivite devotionalism,[2] by itself individualistic in its aim of personal union with Shiva, was also practised within the social context of overlordship (Walters 1979: 432) or kingship. The ruler, through strict devotion to the god demanding austerities and strict self-control, would achieve an intimate relationship (*shakti*) with Shiva through which he would gain spiritual and temporal powers. He may even been believed to possess magic powers, and the gifts offered by him to favourite subjects were seen as transmissions of supernatural power capable of benefiting the recipients in the beyond. It may be that these attitudes perpetuated pre-Hindu indigenous ideas of supernatural prowess wielded by great men. Since asceticism and the life of the ascetics had to be taken as a model, kings were portrayed in art and epigraphy as ascetics, as devotees of Shiva. In this context, Shaivite myths and the thousands of ascetics' images sculpted in Khmer temples become understandable. It might be that they could have been used by the ideators of the temple to satisfy the king's need for reaffirming the importance of asceticism, penance and *tapas*, thus avoiding the danger of false asceticism and the weakness of many so-called sages.

The problem of Shaivite themes being sculpted exclusively in a southwesterly location remains unresolved. (*see N. 1*), and that in Khmer architecture, areas designated to Shiva are always to the northeastern (or the northern) part of the temple, like at Preah Khan and Beng Mealea.

It is also worth noticing that Shiva's image is sculpted in the western end of the Large Panel of the Battle of the *Devas* and *Asuras* (LP. 7), for once positioned in the correct northeastern quarter. In here he is the object of veneration on the part of Vishnu, although the scene may have been modified in the XVI century when it was sculpted.

In this context, Shaivite myths and the thousands of ascetices' images sculpted in Khmer temples become understandable. It might be that could have been used by the ideators of the temple to satisfy the king's need for reaffirming the importance of asceticism, penance and *tapas*, thus avoiding the danger of false asceticism and the weakness of many so-called sages.

OPPOSITE: The Central Tower seen from the Northwest. (V. Roveda)

Chapter 7

Conclusions

The Sacredness of Angkor Wat

Today's visitor to Angkor Wat may find the temple quite been bare. The rooms once filled with hundreds of sacred statues of the gods, richly apparelled and adorned with jewels, are now empty. The doors of the shrines have vanished. The cult objects that filled the Preah Pean (Cruciform Pavilion) and the galleries of the 2nd enclosure have been pillaged over the centuries or removed to the Phnom Penh Museum and the Siem Reap Conservation depot. The sacred statue of Vishnu was toppled from its original position of supremacy in the central shrine and probably lost.[1] All the wooden accessory buildings packed in the courtyards at the time of Suryavarman II and the bustling city filling the great space between the 4th and 3rd enclosures, have disappeared. Apart from this, it is conceivable that most of the reliefs would have been painted. Today, therefore, one can only guess at how the great temple looked when it was in use, with all the ceremonial paraphernalia, the flags and lamp standards, the brilliant offerings and a multitude of priests and attendants in fine courtly robes.

Nevertheless the sacredness of Angkor Wat can be unravelled through the reading of its architectural symbolism and the meaning of the narrative reliefs. As with all sacred places, Angkor Wat is invested with elements which involve both the supernatural sphere and the power of temporal ambitions. Defining a specific place as sacred implies that it carries with it a whole range of rules and regulations regarding people's behaviour in relation to it, as well as a set of beliefs bearing on the non-empirical world, often in relation to the spirits of ancestors, as well as of powerful divinities. The concept of the 'sacred' is important because wherever it is attributed, powerful emotions and attitudes come into play. Even if we can accurately define the meaning of the word 'sacred' in our own

language, it is likely that our estimation of what that word meant to different cultures and religions of a different time will be somewhat off the mark. All concepts are necessarily limited by the language in which they are expressed.

The sacred complex at Angkor Wat – set amongst forests, surrounded by moats and canals, with a colossal entrance gateway (Western *Gopura*), four sequences of enclosures with their own *gopuras*, several cloisters and staircases, rooms with hundreds of pillars, and the shrine hardly reachable at the top of a huge stepped mound – could unquestionably recall the dwelling of Hari (Vishnu) in his continent, the Harivarsa. Jean Filliozat (1961: 195) noted that the description of the Harivarsa of the *Kurma Purana*[2] as a marvellous imaginary continent outside India, inhabited by people of different complexion and with a magnificent palace of Hari, had no model in Indian architecture, where monumental pyramidal structures of difficult access are unknown. Thus, Filliozat suggested that a temple outside India must have inspired the grandiose description of the *Kurma Purana*, and the perfect candidate had to be Angkor Wat. The writer/s of the *Purana* may have learned of a construction consecrated to Vishnu outside India. We know, from inscriptions, that several brahmins travelled from India to the country of the Khmers and must have taken back descriptions of Suryavarman II's Vaishnava temple.[3] Therefore, the splendid Angkor Wat could have inspired the Puranic description.[4]

The transformation of Angkor Wat from a Hindu temple into a Buddhist monastery in the XIV-XV century created a dual system of beliefs, possibly in recognition of the site's sacredness which perhaps predates Angkor Wat's construction. This long sacred heritage continued through time, until Angkor Wat had assumed a historical and political significance as well. It is currently the emblem of the country,

FIG. 264 Vishnu, detail, NW corner pavilion, N. 11.

255

appearing on the national flag and on contemporary banknotes, where it simply symbolises modern Cambodia. Even the resident Vietnamese army and the Khmer Rouge showed respect for Angkor Wat.

From the XV century onwards Angkor Wat continued to function as a sacred site, the main regional Buddhist temple and monastery.[5] While the restoration of older images was also considered a pious deed, the best way of gaining merit was the donation of new images, and in large numbers, as mentioned in several inscriptions (the one of 1631 and another of 1701 are particularly instructive; see Giteau 1975: 153). The donors were usually well-off people, high-functionaries, religious dignitaries, or a group of believers. Sometimes, the donations included canonical texts, cult objects, and gifts to the monks, usually made on the occasion of a pilgrimage. It is estimated that during the XVII century some 300 statues were donated, of which about 140 were of precious metals, 36 in stone, and the rest in different materials. In the XVIII century, inscriptions celebrating donations become rarer, even though statues continued to be donated.[6]

The answer to the question of why Angkor Wat, rather than the Buddhist sanctuary of Bayon, became a major Buddhist centre of devotion must include the fact that Angkor Wat was a more suitable 'space' than Bayon. The monument has large courtyards, spacious, airy galleries where the monks could pray, perform their ceremonies, and large 'libraries' to store and assemble the instruments of the cult, and receive the donations from the faithful. Bayon does not have any such facilities. Its narrow winding passages in the central honey-combed mound, may have been too claustrophobic for the faithful. Angkor Wat was a clearly defined, well-structured sacred space, while at Bayon the space was dispersed beyond the temple itself throughout the extensive area of the old city of Angkor Thom.

Narrative Reliefs and the Sacredness of the Temple

When Khmer artists sculpted the walls of Angkor Wat, the conventions for the representation of images required a common visual vocabulary and grammar. Paradigms of size, emplacement, layout, iconographic conventions, combined with the sculptural style of

the reliefs, all contributed to create the 'Khmerness' typical of Angkorean art which is so different from Indian art. Although the text of Angkor Wat is unquestionably sourced in India, its language is unmistakably Khmer.

In the previous pages, it has been demonstrated that an arrangement of the reliefs according to a 'logical' order or a narrative sequence is not evident. Perhaps there was a fundamental underlying cosmological scheme or a *mandala* pattern that eludes us today. However, the author proposes an explanation by which the makers of Angkor Wat may have followed the Vedic tradition in which the content of the narrative is considered to be of secondary importance to the sheer ritual act of reciting. In some Vedic chants, the eulogy of a particular deity often includes spurious elements indicating that the content was not so important, or, at least, neutral. What counted was the actual ritual of reciting of these stories. In India, the sophisticated lyrical metres and descriptions of the *Bhagavata Purana* – the most authoritative Pancharatra text – were often chanted according to a recitation's tradition rather that following the story's narrative. This primacy of rituals may have been adopted by the Khmers when visiting Angkor Wat's galleries and the corner pavilions of the 3rd enclosure, perhaps chanting or reciting *mantras* or of the various sacred texts illustrated in the reliefs. From the ritual narration or reading a new knowledge of the stories was created as well as a new way of thinking about them. It follows that there could not have been a 'logical' and sequential 'order of visiting' as we see today, but simply variable paths that reflect the rituals needed for specific ceremonies and sacrifices and a religious calendrical sequence.

Nevertheless, the fact remains that through the visual representation of myths and legends from the Sanskrit texts, the reliefs were charged with intense metaphysical and allegorical meaning. Altogether, they generate a rich symbolism with a variety and depth of meanings that must be intrinsic to the overall religious and mythological symbolism of the temple expressed in association with its architecture. To this end, Indian texts were used to introduce, or reinforce, values in Khmer culture, in a process of denotation/connotation that must have been specific to the time of Suryavarman II. If the *Purana*, *Harivamsa* and *Mahabharata* were addressing general philosophical, religious, moral and political principles, the *Ramayana* emphasised personal values in the figure of the protagonist – Rama the hero – who could be easily identifiable with that of the king and kingship, the exemplary figure of a king having the right to rule on earth (*chakravartin*) in intimate association with the divine (*devaraja*).

The Khmers used myths as a language to overcome the discrepancy between profane time and sacred time, between the time of wars and strife and the remote time of the myths. Most of the reliefs illustrate - through mythological battles – the deeds of Vishnu and his *avatara* to put an end to the chaos spread by evil forces, to re-establish the *dharma* and thus initiate a new era. Myth is synonymous with eternal return, with the desire to be united with a cosmic beginning in a continual present (Eliade 1958). The myths and rituals were the means by which the Khmers constructed a sense of cosmic harmony, persuading themselves that they lived in that same time. The end of profane time was the beginning of the transformation re-introducing, at a higher level, the sacred.

The climbing of the steps of the first staircase leading to the causeway over the moat, and the long walk along the causeway, are the first act in the initiation that will be completed by passing through the Western *Gopura*. Following this, one enters a sacred space and a surreal world of images. The magnificence of this *gopura* is meant to indicate to the pilgrim that – besides entering the temple/city and abode of Vishnu – he/she is initiated into the mysteries of Vaishnavite beliefs. Its ritualistic importance has never been emphasised enough by previous scholars, neglecting thus the spiritual and religious significance paid to this ritual 'passage'. After this initiation, the pilgrim will be facing an even vaster, richer and more complex sacred space enlightened by narrative and decorative reliefs sculpted – with great refinement – on all available architectural surfaces.

One of the functions of these reliefs was to embellish the temple, the abode of the god, or even to transform Angkor Wat into a heavenly palace. The hundreds of celestial courtesans (*devata* and *apsara*) depicted over the walls of the temple, in the galleries and towers of the four enclosures were part of the temple's cosmic design. Furthermore, the decoration of the monument with tales from Sanskrit texts and scenes from the life of the king was used to add a new dimension to the complex functioning of the temple and for fulfilling its sacredness.

There seems to be a selection of visual themes in the reliefs, from the outside towards the centre of the temple, from complex mythological and epic stories towards single mythic events of great significance. They converge towards *para*-Vasudeva at the center of the temple, the symbolic column of light and the axis of the universe. Equally, this process moves from 'below' (the *gopura* and the galleries of the 3rd and 2nd enclosures) upwards (to the shrine), in a sort of three-dimensional *mandala*. The greatest variety of themes takes place in the 3rd enclosure with its pediments, half pediments, lintels and large panels, illustrating narrative reliefs from the Puranic myths of Vishnu and Shiva and the stories from the *Ramayana* and *Mahabharata*, as well as from historic events. A greatly reduced thematic variety exists in the 2nd enclosure, where the *Ramayana* prevails, while the decoration of the cruciform pavilion that unites these two enclosures is purely Vaishnava in content, probably due to its ceremonial use. When one reaches the 1st enclosure, a change towards prevailing Puranic myths occurs. There are no more pediments depicting Rama's conflicts and adventures traditionally considered to reinforce the concepts of kingship. Instead, the symbolic actions of Vishnu or Krishna, become clearer as if to emphasise the spiritual aspect of the core of the temple, from where they irradiate to the four cardinal directions, over the Khmer kingdom and beyond.

The 1st enclosure, with its magnificent central tower, was the realisation of Mount Meru and the ultimate shrine of Vishnu. The impact that one feels when reaching it is all the greater because one is facing it after emerging from the intimate, shaded surroundings of the cruciform pavilion, or the darkness of a 2nd enclosure gallery. Just the view of its elevation is imposing: from ground level to the top of the main tower is a height of about sixty-five metres.[7] After climbing the high and steep main staircase, in itself an arduous act of 'separation' from the rest of the temple, one reaches the gallery of the 1st enclosure, with its very large windows with stately balusters, and pillared galleries on the inside. The white Cambodian light streams from everywhere, making these the brightest and most sunny corridors of Angkor Wat, demonstrating the masterly use of light's symbolism by the Khmer architects. The elevation is so high, the light so intense, and the decoration so sophisticated that one feels elevated far above the surroundings.

The narrative reliefs that we have examined are texts that are part of the larger context of the temple as a whole, completing its extensive hermeneutic field. This, together with the architectural symbolism of Angkor Wat, creates the image of a universe ruled by the gods. Suryavarman II, as the patron of this immense temple (and city), may have perceived himself not only as the ruler of the Khmer empire, but also as the sovereign of the world of Indian myths and legends reinforced by Vaishnavite and Shaivite devotion, the cult of ancestors and Brahmanical precepts. Even if he may have used the sacredness of the temple as a symbol of his kingship, the foremost meaning of the temple remains that of a religious statement, a declaration of sacredness. Architecture and reliefs come together in the production of a sacred and metaphysical meaning, well beyond that of the highest visual manifestation of devotion towards Vishnu. The construction of this sacredness was the main objective of the temple.

FIG. 265 Vishnu reclining on Ananta. Central sanctuary, southern shrine. (V. Roveda)

Notes

Chapter 1

[1] Coedès 1954, V: 297-305 and 300-311; Finot 1912, 2: 26.

[2] This fact about Divakara's career is inferred from the inscription on the stele of Sdok Kak Thom, numbered K.194 (Coedès & Dupont 1943: 145).

[3] Coedès 1962: 235.

[4] The doctrine of the Pancharatra is drawn primarily from the early Samhitas (Compositions), in particular those from sections of the *Mahabharata* and, most of all, from the *Bhagavata Purana* (Rukmani 1970: 198). It was based on the identification of Krishna Vasudeva with Vishnu, elevated thus from a heroic 'tribal' status to the rank of Supreme God. Essential to the Pancharatra are the dogma of the *avataras*, and the doctrine of the Creation. Pure Creation consists of the emanations (*vyuha*) from Vasudeva (or Vishnu with Lakshmi) to Samkarshana, Pradyumna and Aniruddha where each emanation originates from the previous one, 'like a flame proceeding from another flame'. To this act of creation further belong the 39 *avatars*, 'descents' or 'incarnations' of God, all listed in the *Sattvata Samhita*. The better known are Krishna, Rama, Samkarshana (or Balarama), Parasurama, Narasimha, Pradyumna, Trivikrama, Narayana, Hari and Kalkin. That the Pancharatra was one of the most popular sect is proved by King Yashovarman I (r. 889-900) dedicating to its followers an ashrama at Prasat Komnap.

[5] Atherton Packert C., 1985: 201-224.

[6] Bhattacharya 1961: 97 and 1997: 45.

[7] Sharan 1974 : 239.

[8] In this book, narrative reliefs (simply 'reliefs') are those in which the visual narrative discourse takes place in the single composition depicting the actions or episodes logically referring back to earlier episodes, describing the particular of the present and indicate the direction that the narrative may take in the future. The narrative image is open-ended, leading forward, backward, or to other actions or stories, whether these appear in another relief (panel) or in the viewer's memory (Stansbury-O'Donnell, 1999: 14).

[9] Vidya Dehejia has noted that a *Ramayana* manuscript from Nepal, written on palm-leaf and dateable to 1020 has been found in India. At least from between that time and the introduction of printing in the nineteenth century, the *Ramayana* was regularly copied by hand in all parts of the Subcontinent, and more than two thousand manuscripts are known to exist (Dehejia 1994: 10).

[10] The Valmiki version is believed to be the first literary form of Rama's story, and therefore it has been taken by many scholars as the 'definitive' *Ramayana*, from which all other editions 'divert'. This is questioned by Paula Richman who prefers to consider it just one telling among others, such as the Tamil narrative by Kampan, the Cambodian *Ramaker* and so forth (Richman 1991: 7). In Richman's opinion, a comparison between Valmiki's and Kampan's *Ramayana* would reveal that they are telling the same story, with the difference that Kampan's rendition of some events is shaped by the Tamil *bhakti* tradition emphasising different religious aspects and the relationship between god and devotee. Kampan's Ramayana is not a divergence from Valmiki's, just a different voice within the *Ramayana* tradition.

[11] Goldman 1990: 22.

[12] K.359, Coedès 1929: pl. III.

[13] Jean Przyluski first noticed the variants, pointing out that Khmer sculptors must have known a different local version of the story of Rama's archery contest to obtain Sita in marriage (the *svayamvara*). Around the same time, W. Stutterheim expressed a similar opinion concerning Malay and Javanese reliefs which, since the beginning of the IX century, depicted also stories from a version very different from the *Ramayana* of Valmiki, presumably a local popular version (Przyluski 1923: 319; and Stutterheim 1925). In 1933, Van Stein Callenfels carried this hypothesis forward when he attempted to explain the anomalies of some reliefs from Angkor Wat. Between 1938 and 1972, François Martini provided evidence defending the originality of the Cambodian reliefs and their fidelity to the Indian text by advocating the use of a partial *Ramayana* edition in the Khmer language, edited by S. Karpeles in 1937. However, he did not take into consideration the inevitable influence that visual elements of the famous reliefs of Angkor Wat may have had on the arrangement of certain events in later literary compositions, such as that for the Ramaker.

[14] In particular, in the Tamil tradition, the great monkey Valin intervenes in the Churning. Already in the IX century, a relief from Candi Prambanan (Java) shows the details of fish carrying away in their jaws the stones laid down by the monkeys. These details exist also in the Malay version, and in many others from India (Zieseniss 1963).

[15] Cahiers de l'EFEO, 6, 1936: 24-29

[16] The importance of the concept of flying palaces in Khmer mythology may be explained from an old local legend, probably based on an Indian tale, reported by Henri Marchal (1955: 15). There was a young prince by the name of Preah Ket Mealea, most beautiful and perfect, son of the king of Indrapastha (an old name for Cambodia). His qualities were so outstanding that the god Indra living in his heavenly palace came to earth to abduct him. After a while, the *devatas* (celestial beings like the *apsaras* but living on Mount Meru; called also *tevodas* or *devatas*), complained about his human smell and expressed their dissatisfaction with Indra. The latter had to please the *devatas* and had the prince sent back to earth. To comfort him, Indra had a heavenly palace built by all the celestial people, including the architect of the gods, Preah Pusnuka. The location was decided by the bull Nandin to the East-South-East of the hill of Phnom Bakeng. On this story was based the legendary origin of Angkor Wat.

[17] 1933: 7-21.

[18] 1944: 33.

[19] 1947-50: 527.

[20] The architecture of the temple followed a numeric plan – constructed in pyramidal elevation it carries a total of 109 towers, The central, topmost tower represents the universe's axial pole, while the 108 smaller towers surrounding it represent the cosmic revolutions around the pole. According to ancient Indian astronomy, there are 27 lunar houses in 4 lunar phases, adding up to a total of 108. Moreover, 108 is the basic number of the Great Year, and the sacred number of Indian tradition. Another point that Filliozat stressed was that when viewing any of the temple's four faces, the number of towers within the frame of vision added up to 33, which corresponded to the 33 gods (*Trayastrimsha*) which inhabit Mt. Meru. In general, he interpreted the function of the monument to conform to the Indian ideal of royalty and the exaltation of the merits (panegyric) of Yashovarman (*see the inscription from Sdok Kok Thom, for example*).

[21] *Angkor Wat, Time, Space, and Kingship*. Mannikka's theories have to be taken with some reservation and need further clarification. For example, about the correctness of using the cubit arm of a young king (?16 years old Suryavarman II) as the unit of measurement of the temple's elements; then, the assumption that some measurements have to be taken following paths of circumambulation which include one or three circuits around or along a point where images had presumably been placed by the Khmers, and so on. Furthermore, her database is derived from plans and measurements of the temple published by G. Nafylin in 1969, which may not be accurate enough to justify the magnitude of the statements and conclusions that the author is putting forward. Mannikka (1996: 128) provides an example of the application of numerology to Angkor Wat's reliefs. In the panel of the Historic Procession, the 19 ministers of King Suryavarman II are opposite to the 19 gods under Indra on the northern wall; the 19 leading officers under Rama in the battle of Lanka are fighting the 19 officers of Ravana. In both cases 19 is paired against 19. Numbers can thus organise elements of reliefs into recognisable subsets and create internal relationships.

[22] Maxwell 1997: 19-20.

[23] The importance of the number five intrinsic to the Pancharatra, is demonstrated by a look at the profile along the surface occupied by Angkor Wat which reveals an elevation in five steps. The first level is the one reached when ascending to the Western *Gopura* and that continues along the extensive *naga* causeway. The second level is represented by the large terrace surrounding the temple proper and on which the cruciform naga terrace is built. The third, fourth, and fifth level are composed respectively by the platforms of the third, second and first enclosures.

Chapter 2

[1] This work was reprinted in 1995 by S.D.I. Publications, Bangkok.

[2] 'The Song of the Lord' narrated in the *Bhagavad Gita* was written in metrical form by an unknown poet around 200 BC, and added to the eighteen books of the *Mahabharata* narrating the great battle of Kurukshetra that lasted eighteen days. Similarly the *Gita* is divided in eighteen sections, each of 700 verses.

[3] When this gallery collapsed in 1947, the eastern portion of this relief sustained heavy damage. Although the mural was carefully put together again under the direction of Henri Marchal of the EFEO, there were nevertheless several gaps in the scene of the Hells. Luckily, however, one does have recourse to the photographic record in the monograph on Angkor Wat by Finot, Goloubew and Coedès (1929-32); some inscriptions were unfortunately lost.

[4] Since Yama is the ruler of the southern direction and called the Lord of the South (*Dakshinasa-pati*), it is not surprising that this relief panel is in the southern gallery of the 3rd enclosure, sculpted facing south.

[5] Of the 36 topics listed below, the first four do not refer to or describe specific Hells.

[6] The *Trai Phum* – one of the most important Thai literary works – lists at the top the four realms of the World Without Form which cannot be imagined or described. Below them is the World of Partial Form where the gods (*called brahmas*) dwell in sixteen heavens or realms. Lower still is the World of Desire with eleven realms. They include the heavens of the lesser gods, the chief of whom is Indra, and the realms of the asura, humans and animals (with *garudas* and *nagas*). Further below is the terrifying realm (the 31st realm) of the 'screaming, crushing and smashing' and fiercely burning Hells (Gosling 1991: 63). Since the humans' realm was ruled by the *Chakravartin* (Universal Monarch), the perfect king who preached at length about just rule and the avoidance of evil, he served as a model for Southeast Asian rulers. Since the *Trai Phum* tells also of the great kings of ancient India, it was considered a treatise on kingship, besides being a fundamental religious work.

[7] In the *Padma Purana*, a text of the VIII century, Yama is perceived in one way by the virtuous people and in another by the sinners. To the former he appears to be like Vishnu, crowned and smiling, with four arms, riding Garuda. To the sinners, he appears as Yama himself, monstrous and terrifying, riding his buffalo (Ugra). This is relevant to the relief of Angkor Wat, because either as a vision of Vishnu or as Yama he would fit into the general symbolism of the narrative cycle.

[8] In the *Mahabharata*, which is earlier than the various *Puranas* and the *Ramayana*, Vishnu merely grants more energy to the *deva* and *asura* while they churn the ocean. He neither intervenes to support the churning pole, nor to keep it stabilised; he does not participate in the actual pulling of the snake's body. Even the tortoise described in the text is simply the King of the tortoises, not necessarily Vishnu's avatar Kurma. The final products, however, are the same and include the all-important amrita.

In the pedimental relief of Preah Vihear (*Gopura* III N), the use of the *Mahabharata* narrative seems to be combined with those of the *Puranas*. In it, the churning pole is fitted inside the jar where the amrita is being collected while the other end terminates with a small capital on which a small figure is crawling or kneeling, most likely Vishnu. Below this, on the churning pole is the traditional figure of Vishnu holding it in balance, and, at both sides, three deities are depicted in niches, probably Indra, Brahma and certainly Shiva (as an ascetic). We know from the text that they watched and approved Vishnu's actions from the sky. The pediment shows also the peculiar presence of Garuda as a spectator, ready to steal the *amrita* (from the *Mahabharata* I, 32-34) and standing close to an emaciated figure, perhaps Kaaraikal-Ammaiyar, Shiva's female devotee. On the right side of the pediment, two small personages ride a large elephant, possibly Indra and his mahout on Airavata. In the lintel below the pediment, the scene of *Vishnu Anantasayin* is illustrated. In it, the lotus stem emanating from the god's navel terminates in a flower on which the four-headed Brahma sits. The sculpting of the myth of Vishnu *Anantasayin* (lintel) in combination with that of the Churning (pediment) may support the theory that the two myths could have been fused into a wider concept of Vaishnava creation.

[9] In Indian mythology Aditi is considered the mother of the gods and therefore the mother of Vishnu as well (hence his name Aditya). Devaki, the mother of Krishna is considered to be a new manifestation of Aditi.

[10] Goloubew V., *Artisans Chinois a Angkor Vat*, BEFEO, 1924: 519; Boisselier J., *Note sur les bas-reliefs tardifs d'Angkor Vat*, JA, 1962: 244; Giteau M., *Iconographie du Cambodge Post-Angkorien*, EFEO, 1975: 93-111.

[11] Mannikka counts 91 *asura* instead of the 92 usually considered by scholars, because she believes that one of the large 'generals' amongst the asura is another form of Vishnu.

[12] See the publication of the Musée Albert Kahn, *A l'ombre d'Angkor. Le Cambodge, années vingt*, edited by M. Mattera-Corneloup & J. Beausoleil, Vilo, Paris, 1992: 40.

Chapter 3

[1] Western pediment of the eastern wing of the Northern Complex (between *Gopura* North III and *Gopura* North II).

[2] At Preah Khan, in the northern temple dedicated to Shiva.

[3] In Khmer iconography, the ascetics are represented within an indented ogival frame, the latter being symbolic of the cave in which they practise penance. In several other instances, the same ogival frame has very pointed, flame-like contours which are here interpreted as the flame generated by the *tapas*, as it is commonly held that asceticism (*tapas*) generates heat, a form of power that can be symbolised by fire.

The name *tapas* comes from the Sanskrit root tap, 'to burn', 'to be hot', 'to suffer'. Subsequently, tapas came to refer also to the generation of magic heat or power by ascetic practices, and hence the performance of any ascetic practices (Doniger 1973: 58).

[4] During a visit to the site in December 1998, I observed that vandals or thieves had chiselled the image of Shiva out. Only the lower part of the relief is preserved, with the crocodile and the small *rishi*.

[5] In the *Brahma Purana* (Part I, chapter 23) it is narrated that one day Shiva assumes the form of a brahmin boy caught by a crocodile when playing in a lake; his intention is to distract Parvati, who, dispirited, is sitting on the shore. On hearing the laments of the boy, she begs the crocodile to let him go in exchange for all the penance she has performed. The crocodile replies 'there won't be any wastage of your penance over a small boy. I shall release him.' The crocodile tells Parvati to take back her penance as well as the boy, and grants her a boon. However, she refuses on the grounds that she meant to give the penance away for the release of the boy, and once this intention is expressed, the penance cannot be taken back; she will therefore go on making new penance. After this, both the boy and the crocodile vanish, and Shiva appears before her and asks her not to perform penance; he grants her one thousand 'credits' in return. She happily agrees and waits for the *svayamvara*. The moral of this story is that one cannot be too proud of his/her *karma* (deeds) and feel to have reached total detachment from earthly things, from illusions. Only through an absolute devotion to the god can one achieve victory over the senses.

[6] Bruno Dagens (1969: 144) made interesting comments on the reptile appearing in reliefs sculpted at the time of Jayavarman VII (or later) when Buddhism was the state religion. He noticed that the reptile depicted above Shiva at Bayon (in the eastern inner gallery and in a pedimental fragment illustrated in his fig. 16) and at Beng Mealea (Southwestern Annex) is a chameleon and is related to the episode narrated in the *Mahaumagga jataka*.

According to this text (*Jataka* No. 546, section 19), there was once a chameleon that had established its abode on top of the arched gateway of the park of the king of Mithila. He had the habit of descending and squatting in front of the king, as if he were paying respect. The king, pleased, ordered his servants to feed him regularly. One day, however, no meat was available and instead a coin was offered to the reptile. This made the creature proud and when the king appeared, the chameleon did not come down from the archway. He thought that if the King was rich, then he also was. A Bodhisattva explained to the astonished king that since the reptile possessed something he never had before (a coin), he despised the Lord of Mithila.

[7] The follow-up to the episode of 'The Sages of the Pine Forest' is narrated in the Shiva Kotirudra (12.6-54), in which Shiva incurs the wrath of the sages for having exposed himself naked to their wives. Because of their wrath, his penis (linga) falls off, and blazing like fire, roams through the Three Worlds. Gods and sages, not having recognised this disembodied terror as Shiva, seek refuge in Brahma who advises them of the remedy. They must worship the mountain-born goddess, and when she assumes the form of a vulva (*yoni*), they must place the linga on top, reciting mantras and casting a spell. With this Shiva is placated and peace and prosperity return to the world.

[8] These flying objects with a tails and a flower sculpted at the centre could actually be the flowers that the gods shower on earth to bless good and heroic actions, as we are told in the *Purana*. In some cases, they may also represent flying flames, symbolic of concentrated energy, or sparks of *tapas*-generated fire. These fire sparks appear in several other reliefs like the one of 'Krishna Killing Kamsa' in the central tower, and of 'Krishna on Garuda' of the northern *gopura* of Enclosure IV(GP4N).

[9] The monkey Hanuman will cause Ravana's death. He arranged for Rama to meet Sugriva, the ex-king of the monkeys, with whom Rama will conquer Lanka and kill Ravana, fulfilling thus the prophecy.

[10] Ravana's boon excluded the possibility of being killed by men. In fact, only Vishnu's human incarnation, Rama, will be able to kill him.

[11] The epithets of Kama are remarkable: *Madana*, 'the one who brings madness'; the one who can not be conquered by gods or demons; the one who is born in the mind, and the one who is impossible to delimit, going here and there like the wind, with his bow and arrow.

[12] In Hindu mythology, Shiva allows women to dominate him more than Vishnu does. Parvati often intercedes and persuades Shiva to be lenient, as she does in the case of Kama. In addition, Shiva misses women more when they go away. Parvati when practising asceticism suffers the agony of desire for the god and Shiva suffers in his turn. These are typical examples of *viraha*, the suffering caused by separation from the beloved. This phenomenon is also mentioned in the *Ramayana* when Sita expressed extreme sadness and longing, although Rama also suffers for his abducted Sita. However, Lakshmi, one of Vishnu's consorts, is subservient to Vishnu, as Radha is to Krishna and Sita to Rama. With Vishnu, the male aspect is firmly in control. Like Radha, Sita misses her lover more than he misses her.

[13] In another version of the *Purana*, Shiva allowed Kama to be born again as Pradyumna, son of Krishna and Rukmini.

[14] His origin is described in the *Linga Purana*: a blind rishi named Sailadi practised penance in the hope of obtaining a son born through divine intervention. Indra noticed the *rishi's* severe austerities, and told him that only Shiva could satisfy his desire and therefore he must address his prayers to that god. As a result, Shiva became so pleased that he appeared to him, promising that he would himself be born as the *rishi's* son. After some time a boy appeared, looking like Shiva, with the *jata-mukuta* on his head, three eyes and four arms, carrying the trident (*trisula*), the chisel (*tanka*), the club (*gada*) and the thunderbolt (*vajra*). Shiva gave the boy the name of Nandi. However, when Sailadi and Nandi retired to the *ashram*, the boy started to look like an ordinary mortal, loosing his divine form. Furthermore, two visiting *rishi* forecast that he would die within one year. Nandi, although perturbed, began to meditate so intensively on Shiva, that the god appeared in front of him. He embraced the boy, changing him into a being with three eyes and ten arms looking exactly like Shiva himself and giving him the gift of immortality.

[15] 'Ellipsis' is a canonical narrative tempo (or speed), occurring when one or more components in a situation that is being recounted, are missing. See Prince G., Dictionary of Narratology, no editor's name or date available.

[16] Perhaps a justification of this behaviour can be found in Rama and Sugriva being dethroned and wife-deprived, a misadventure they share in common and that naturally makes the two initiate a friendship. Rama, imbued with the feeling of loss and separation that permeates all of Book IV, is psychologically ready to feel a strong bond with Sugriva. As Sugriva says that he lives in fear (chapter 5), in the forest without his wife, Rama responds immediately, without knowing the facts, promising vengeance. But there are no excuses why Rama, after having heard Sugriva's story, would not reconsider his solution to the problem, nor for the way he afterwards rebukes the dying Valin (obviously, Rama did not know – and never knew – that, after all, it was Sugriva who took over Valin's domain, including his wife Tara). Sugriva was infatuated with Tara and this is one of the reasons why Rama almost ended his friendship with him. His addiction to Tara had caused him to overlook the passing of the rainy season and delayed putting into action his part of the bargain that sealed (or caused) the friendship, namely the search for Sita (chapter 30).

Rama's moral ambiguities aside, the Epic uses the episode of Rama killing Valin to convey some very important didactic principles through each of its characters (see Masson 1975). In chapter 17 we are told that the dying Valin asks Rama what merit he would hope to earn by striking him from behind, and what would he answer to an assembly of virtuous people for having committed such a reprehensible deed. The regicide – continues Valin – the brahmanicide, the slayer of the cow, the thief and the one who finds pleasure in the destruction of other beings, the unbeliever and the one who weds before the elder brother, all these enter hell. The informer, the miser, the one who slays his friend or defiles his guru's bed, undoubtedly descends to the region of evildoers. In chapter 18, Rama replies that, despite having been addressed in such an inappropriate way by Valin in his 'simian folly', he was filled with good will towards him, but he accuses Valin of having violated justice and acted for lust, ignoring his royal duties. He had married Ruma, Sugriva's wife, who was his sister-in-law, aware that the man who makes his daughter, sister or sister-in-law an object of lust, is punishable by death. Moreover, righteousness demands that a younger brother (Sugriva), a son and a virtuous disciple should be regarded as one's own offspring. Rama calls him a heedless monkey surrounded by irresponsible simian counsellors, a king who has acted in opposition to the law of dharma, and therefore deserving death. Finally Rama reproaches Valin that he did not follow the example of other kings who – after sinning – have practised penance, subduing their passions. Therefore, Rama concludes, his death was decreed in accordance to his dharma, and not the result of Rama's personal impulse.

In this dialogue are thus encapsulated all the most important ethical and social principles of the time, in particular those that governed the relationship between father and daughter, daughter-in-law, sister, brother and son as well as with the guru and the cow. These precepts were presumably equally essential to the Khmer elite. Suryavarman II may have considered very appropriate the condemnation of regicide, the importance for kings to perform penance, and most of all, Rama's concept that 'kings are like gods' on earth.

[17] The water festival today celebrated in Thailand and Cambodia is probably Buddhist in nature, but is thought to have been ultimately derived from the Hindu Dvaravati water festival mentioned in the *Puranas* and *Harivamsa*.

[18] Jewellery of this type is described by Groslier G., *Recherches surles Cambodgiens*, Challamel, Paris, 1921: 82 and fig. 51, who considers them as hand insignia or emblems, and as such related to a hierarchy of power.

[19] According to Indian iconography (Rao 1914: II, 273) there are differences between Shiva's appearance as a teacher of the *Shastras*, *Shiva Vykhayana-Dakshinamurti*, or as a yoga teacher *Yoga-Dakshinamurti*, particularly concerning the

seating positions, the number and the attitude of the arms. One aspect of the *Dakshinamurti* iconography that is shared in all of its manifestations is the god's attendance by numerous *rishi*. The numerous royal personages depicted in the relief are not mentioned. Moreover, in India, Shiva *Dakshinamurti* is depicted facing south (*dakshina*), his right foot resting on the demon of ignorance and his right hand in the *vitarka-mudra* of explanation. Although this Shaivite event is depicted on the southern wall of the eastern arm of the pavilion, the actual image of Shiva is facing north. Furthermore, Shiva's left hand is holding a lotus jewel in his lap while his right one is extended towards the figure to his right, and it is hard to imagine that it could be in the *vitarka-mudra*. Given this, Bhandari's interpretation seems unlikely even though the poor condition of this relief forbids a clear reading of the *mudras*.

[20] Initiating thus the cult of the mountain, so dear to the Khmers.

[21] At the time of this specific episode, not only was Brahma already in existence, but he was the leader of the 30 Immortals who went to Vishnu to ask him to descend on Earth as an *avatar*.

[22] In the *Ramayana* Kalanemi is the *rakshasa* uncle of Ravana. In the *Purana* he is a great *asura*, son of Virochana, the grandson of Hiranyakasipu (killed by Vishnu in his Lion avatar, *Narasimha*). He was killed by Vishnu, but was said to live again in Kamsa and Ravana.

[23] The *rakshasas* and the *yakshas* were originally anti-gods, but become accepted amongst the gods because of their good deeds; their king is Kubera.

[24] The concept of the moving of mountains dates back to the *Vedas* where references are made of mountains constantly moving from place to place and Indra having the task to settle them. Later, in addition to the legend of Mount Maniparvata described here, are the stories in the *Mahabharata* (I, 17-19) in which Indra places Mount Mandara on the back of the King of Tortoises to initiate the Churning of the Ocean of Milk. In the *Ramayana* (Book VI, 74), to get the magic herbs Hanuman uproots Mount Dronariri (part of the Himalayas), and Ravana shakes Mount Kailasa with the intention of uprooting it (Book VII, chapter 6).

[25] It has been assumed that the *Ramayana* masks an account of an Aryan king from the Gangetic basin (Rama) who led a military expedition into Central India (Lanka), where he allied himself with tribal people (monkeys and bears) to defeat a local Dravidian ruler (Ravana) (in W.L. Smith 1988: 15).

[26] The relief's most outstanding feature is that the two prone bodies seem to be floating in water. As such there is another possible source to be found in the *Bhagavata Purana* (Book 10, chapter 28), an episode entitled 'Krishna at the Brahmahrada Pool'. However, as will be shown below, this story has a more pastoral tone than the one of Akrura, where a divine aura of religiosity permeates the scene.

After the kidnapped Nanda (Krishna's foster-father) has been returned by Varuna, the gopas start to believe Krishna himself is a god, and they long to be absorbed into his subtle being, and thereby taken into his eternal regions. Out of mercifulness, Krishna contrives to fulfil their desire by bringing them to the Brahmahrada pool (also called Para-Brahman). Here the cowherds are made to remain immersed in a trance (*samadhi*), and then roused from this state by Krishna revealing to them the transcendent realm of Vaikuntha, Vishnu's paradise.

There is yet another story from the *Bhagavata Purana* (Book 10, chapter 44) that could be conceived as a possible subject of the relief. In Mathura, Krishna and Balarama enter a wrestling competition in the public arena with Kamsa's bodyguards, Chanura and Mushtika. The fight ends when Krishna 'dashed him [Chanura] to the ground, where he lay stretched with ornament and garlands scattered and hair dishevelled', and Mushtika 'fell down dead on the ground, like a tree uprooted by a stormy wind'. In this case the two bodies should be those of Chanura and Mushtika depicted lying on the ground. However, they do not seem to be like other dead in Khmer relief sculpture. Furthermore, the two bodyguards are described as having powerful bodies, almost the opposite of what is shown in the relief. Finally, considering the love the Khmer had for the representation of fights, there seems to be little likelihood that they would instead represent its aftermath.

[27] In the introduction to a new translation of the *Ramayana*, Sheldon Pollock (in Goodman 1991: 71) notices that Valmiki has framed the 3rd book of the epic (*Aranya Kanda*) with two symmetrical episodes in which Rama confronts monsters, first Viradha (chapters 1-3) and later Kabandha (chapters 65-69; see relief N. 12). Both are characterisations of the ugly traits of the *rakshasas*. However, these two demons are not really *rakshasas* because they live permanently in the forest, in isolation, not in groups. They are also marginalised physically, their physical deformity reflecting moral deformity, stressing a symbolic correlation between physical and moral qualities, which is common in the *Ramayana*. A further detail is that both are in reality celestial beings, relatively benign, who have been cursed with a monstrous form as a consequence of moral transgression. Tumburu became Viradha by neglecting his duties towards Kubera, as a result of his indulging in sexual pleasures, and Danu (a *danava*, a sort of good *asura*) became Kabandha by arrogantly attacking Indra. They are creatures of fantasy and are symbolic of the fear of the unknown. They are fallen creatures who can be liberated only by the spiritual sword of the god-king Rama. Since their hatred and violence is directed essentially against the brahmins, they take it out against the brahmins' protector, Rama. However,

there are several 'good' *rakshasas* capable of responsible choices like human mortals, such as Trijata, Vibhishana and others (see reliefs N. 5, N. 8 and N. 9), but their character makes them more frightening.

[28] Ravana had previously stolen the Pushpaka chariot from Kubera, the god of wealth. It had many magic features; besides the capacity of flying, it obeyed vocal commands and could talk (*Ramayana*, Book VII, chapter 75).

[29] The beautiful rendering of the acacia tree, in full adherence to the *Ramayana's* story, can be seen as one of the many examples of the symbolism of the tree which reappears in many other reliefs of Angkor Wat. In Indian art, Buddhist reliefs of the Shunga period (200-100 BC?) are the first known to show deities standing under trees, and in the Kushana period (II and III century AD) many images had a tree carved at the back. The love of Khmer artists for magnificent trees is reflected in the reliefs showing Vishnu and the gopis (N. 11) and Ravana shaking Mount Kailasa (S. 5).

The tree is often depicted as the apex of the triangular composition converging on the divine protagonist of the story, which clearly alludes to some symbolic value. One such value is referred to in the *Bhagavad Gita* (Maxwell 1997: 91), when Krishna uses the allegory of the branches of trees that take root and so create new offshoots, to describe the endless samsara in which the spirit is enmeshed. He says that this tree with its prolific roots must be cut down with the powerful weapon of non-attachment. The weapon of salvation is the axe that cuts down the entire tree of samsara. It is only the maya, the web of illusions that are mistaken for reality, that supports the material world, and through Vishnu's teachings humankind can be freed from infatuation with the world. Vishnu provides the axe with which to sever one's attachment. This explains why, in iconography, the axe is one of the god's major attributes, besides the conch, the discus, and the lotus (or the egg-shaped fruit).

The Pancharatra texts mention also the association of the axis of the world with a branching tree (*visakha*). The trunk is also the column sustaining the world, while the branches are extending to the four directions of the cosmos. The tree is a metaphor for the cosmic nature of Vishnu who personifies both the universal principle, stable and indivisible, and the plurality of creation.

[30] Khmer sculptors usually represent the monkeys with erect tails, waving vertically.

[31] Also in this relief, as in the one depicting Rama killing Valin (S. 8), and Kama shooting an arrow at Shiva (S. 7), the bow is never represented with the offending arrow in it. Instead, the protagonists are shown in the process of arming the bow, or after having released the arrow.

[32] The *svayamvara* is the occasion when a bride is given to a bridegroom who distinguishes himself in a particular tournament.

[33] See Goldman's translation, chapter 66.12.

[34] This type of target has raised several speculations. In the *svayamvara* described in the *Mahabharata* (I: 184-92) for the princess Draupadi, Arjuna is the central contestant. This possible, but ultimately unlikely reading of the relief would then imply that the central archer would be Arjuna and the four figures to his right would be his brothers, the four Pandavas, who were disguised as brahmins. However, according to the text, Arjuna is also meant to be disguised as a brahmin, and in the relief this is certainly not the case, nor is it the case with all except the first of the figures to the right. Moreover there is no evidence, amongst the assembled figures in the relief, of Karna, Dhastadyumna and other witnesses indispensable to the *svayamvara* of Draupadi. However, in support of its identification with the text of the *Mahabharata* is the fact that in the *Ramayana*, Rama simply lifts and bends the bow in a demonstration of strength, whilst in the *Mahabharata*, Arjuna aims it accurately at a target, a sort of 'aerial machine', in a trial of skill.

A possible solution to this dilemma might be found in a local version of Rama's legends. In the Cambodian Ramaker (Martini 1938: 33) Rama bends the bow, shoots the arrow, and later, he makes the bow to turn in his hand like a wheel. Rama thus must not have broken the bow, an action also not illustrated in the relief. Furthermore, according to Martini, the relief depicts two events: Sita's *svayamvara* in the upper register, and – below – the wedding ceremony attended by the two families. The three princes behind Vishvamitra are Rama's three brothers: Lakshmana, Bharata and Satrughna. The two personages in the register below are the two kings and fathers (Janaka and Dasaratha); amongst the courtly women depicted beside princess Sita is possibly the queen mother.

The *Ramaker*, however, gives no indication at what Rama shot, leaving the wheel and the bird an unresolved problem of this relief. One possible clue could be found in the popularity of the concept of *svayamvara* amongst the Khmers. An inscription of Loley (Barth, ISCC: 393-402) contains in the eulogy of Yashovarman, reference to the episode of Arjuna's shooting at the target (55th stanza): 'By hitting the target, though it was not fixed [i.e. moving], through a hole at the centre of a [revolving] wheel, he was not only like Arjuna in his exploits, but also like Bhima in his impetuosity'. No mention is made, however, of the presence of the bird as (or on) the target.

An explanation of the bird may be found at the beginning of the *Ramaker* (Martini, 1978: 2-3) where it is narrated that one day, when Vishvamitra is busy performing the rituals of a sacrifice, the perverse *asura* Kakanasura appears in the shape of a giant crow. He repeatedly strikes the ritual oblations with his beak. To put an end to this, Vishvamitra manufactures some magic arrows and invites Rama and Lakshmana to slay the demon. Rama obliges. He takes the bow, adjusts the lethal arrow and releases it, instantly transfixing the demon bird which falls straight to the ground and then descends to the Patala, one of the regions of the Hells.

This story is the equivalent of that recounted in the *Ramayana* (Book 1, chapter 30), where we are told that Vishvamitra is performing a sacrifice, when the two demons Marica and Sabahu appear in the sky and release showers of blood on the sacrificial altar. With a powerful arrow Rama seriously wounds Marica who is flung into the sea. With other arrows he kills Sabahu and the remaining demons. The only difference between the two stories resides in the fact that in the Ramaker the demon is a single crow, while in the Ramayana, the two demons are rakshasas, since they are not described otherwise. In the *Ramaker*, the killing of the bird is Rama's first archery test, an episode immediately followed by those of King Janaka discovering Sita; offering her hand to the man who would lift his magic bow; and Rama winning that offer by being the only person able to lift the bow and shoot it. Perhaps in this relief the sculptors have conflated all the episodes of Rama slaying the crow Kakanasura as well as the *svayamvara* to demonstrate Rama's great ability in archery.

Other variations are known of the target of the archery competition. In a relief of the Hoysala temples (Southern India, 12th century) the target is a fish (*matsyayantra*) on a platform on top of a pole (Evans 1998: 135), as described in the Pampa telling of the *Mahabharata*. Arjuna transfixes the fish with an arrow by looking at its reflection in the oil bowl below. The target has to be hit through a hole in a revolving wheel below it. Unusually, Arjuna is depicted as a *kshatriya* and not as a *rishi* as he was disguised in the text.

Fragments of a door pillar lying on the ground (photo Baphuon 1) at the side of the Bapuon temple, under restoration by the EFEO, show a bird perched on a pole being the target of a crowned archer. The temple's reliefs which antedates Angkor Wat by 60-80 years, may have been used as models by the builders of Angkor Wat.

[35] The *Rasa krida* is a circular dance during which a number of female dancers dance with their hands interlocked in the company of men who place their arms round the neck of the women; it is also called *Rasa mandala*. In this context it is a circle of dancers with Krishna between two dancing ladies and a lady between two figure of Krishna. The *Rasalila* is, instead, a dance in which a male dancer plays his part with a number of female dancers moving in a circle around him.

[36] In R.P. Goodman, III, 1991.

[37] Stansbury-O'Donnell 1999: 18.

Chapter 4

[1] In Khmer reliefs the *asuras* are depicted to the south, the *devas* to the north.

[2] Several are Kirshna's enemies. With the intent to kill him they took different disguises. The list include Trivinarta (whirl-wind), Vatasura (calf), Bakasura (crane), Aghasura (serpent), Dhenuka (ass), Kaliya (water snake), Pralamba (human giant), Arishta (bull), Kesin (horse), Kavalayapida (elephant), Mustica and Chanura (wrestlers) and Kamsa (human king and step-uncle of Krishna).

[3] For a complete discussion of the symbolism of this image, refer to the entry for N. 1, pp. 133.

[4] In iconography the *asura'* and rakshasas' kings Hiranyakasipu, Kalanemi, Bali, Bana and Ravana are all depicted with multiple heads and arms and monstrous faces.

Chapter 5

[1] A similar representation occurs in the south-facing pediment of the Southern *Gopura* II of Banteay Samré.

[2] The Parijata tree was produced at the Churning of the Ocean of Milk and kept in Indra's heaven until Krishna's wife induced him to take-it away. This lead to a great battle between the two gods in which Indra was defeated.

[3] The costumes and hair ornaments of these devata has been graciously described in detail by Saffo Marchal in 1927.

Chapter 6

[1] In Sanskrit, the name *avatara* means 'descent', and here it applies to Vishnu descending to earth in one of his manifestations, an event of his own free will and not caused by the law of karma. It involves taking the form of human life – including conception, birth and natural death – for the sake of a specific cosmic purpose. Vishnu as a creator creates himself, as a preserver preserves himself, and as a destroyer destroys himself (*Bhagavata Purana*, Book 1, 2.66).

[2] The Shaivite doctrine of the Pashupata emphasises the strict need of asceticism in honour of Shiva, the first of the ascetics. The Pashupata cult first arrived in Southeast Asia towards the end of the VII century and its ascetics soon enjoyed the confidence of Khmer kings, as revealed by several inscriptions.

Chapter 7

[1] Claude Jacques suggested (1997: 157) that the statue now standing in a southern room of the Western *Gopura* is that of Vishnu formerly in the central shrine of the temple. The real nature of this statue, however, remains obscure. If is heavily restored in concrete, most of its 8 arms also have cement hands in which Vishnu's attributes are not recognisable because they simply hold a small cylinder that, when not broken, terminates with a lotus bud. Furthermore, the physical features, the small *sampot* and the carving quality are in the 'Bayon style', as are the other two statues standing in the noethern rooms of the same *gopura*. If they were of the Bayon period, they could be the Bodhisattva Lokeshvara, but they do not display the small icon of *Amitabha* at the front of the chignon (it may have been defaced). Christine Hawixbrock (1997: 70) has gone as far as to think that these statues depict Vishnu and that they were installed at Angkor Wat by Jayavarman VII, because for this Buddhist king Vishnu had remained the *Chakravartin* (Universal Sovereign) through which he could exercise the royal power.

[2] Chapter XLVII, *slokas* 8-18.

[3] Filliozat's hypothesis implied an edition of the *Kurma Purana* much later than its VI century attribution. He believes that description of the Hari sanctuary was an addition to the text from the first half of the XII century, as a result of information reaching India about Angkor Wat. The opposite conclusion, that the monument of Suryavarman II had been built and decorated according to the *Kurma Purana's* description is also plausible, but less believable, as there are no Indian temple even remotely equivalent to it in terms of either architecture or decoration. The mountain-temple – on the contrary – is part of a Khmer architectural tradition, and Angkor Wat is unique amongst these Khmer monuments because it is a mountain/temple dedicated to Vishnu, not Shiva. It is also unusual in its many representations of beautiful women (*devata*) and perennially praying ascetics (*uogini*) surrounding their god. Similarly, the idealised beauty of the Harivarsa continent must surely correspond to the real beauty of the Khmer landscape. Jean Filliozat's theory highlights the possibilty that the cultural exchange between India and the Khmer country may not have always been one way, with India having supremacy.

[4] With reference to the splendour of Khmer temples, about 150 years later than the time of Angkor Wat, we are told by Zhou Daquan that the Bayon temple was covered in gold and the Baphuon sanctuary in bronze. Although he did not describe Angkor Wat in any detail, recently, during repair works on the main tower of Angkor Wat (damaged by a thunderbolt) traces of stones gilded with gold leaf have been discovered.

[5] Bruno Dagens (1995: 28) has reported the peculiar adventure of a Japanese pilgrim who, while travelling to the holy places of India, arrived at Angkor Wat in c. 1623-36, believing he had reached Magadha (Bihar), the cradle of Buddhism, or the Jetavana of the old Chinese texts. In his fervor, he made a plan of the temple – quite accurate for that time. This was copied in 1715 and a key added (in Japanese). Although the key does not mention the names of Angkor or even Cambodia, the general layout of the monument and its western orientation are those of Angkor Wat. This attribution is confirmed by the mentioning of a sculptural relief with 'four gods pulling a rope', which clearly refers to the large figures appearing in 'The Churning of the Ocean of Milk'. In reality in the relief there are four large personages pulling the snake (the rope) and one holding the head and another the tail of the snake.

[6] Several late inscriptions report how people travelled, individually or in groups, to present homage to the old temple of Angkor Wat. The best known is the '1747 inscription' on the pillars in the galleries connecting the 2nd and 3rd enclosures. It narrates the story of an important Cambodian official who was offered a promotion in rank by the king for having subdued a rebellion. He apparently refused, choosing instead to travel to Angkor Wat in pilgrimage, together with his wife and family. According to the inscription, on a Thursday of a specific month of 1747, and 'at an auspicious moment,' the official requested all the ranking members of the sacred order, including lords, teachers, elders and novices, to assemble 'in the right proportions.' Then he and his wife went up the steps to perform a ceremony with which they would earn merit, and invited the monks to recite 'bansukula aunica' at Brah ban. Then the official asked the congregation to recite the great *jataka*; following which he presented offerings to the Law of Buddha and to his parents (up to seven degrees of kinship) to gain further merit. (Chandler 1998: 22).

[7] Equivalent to a modern 20-storey apartment building. Mannikka 1996: 238

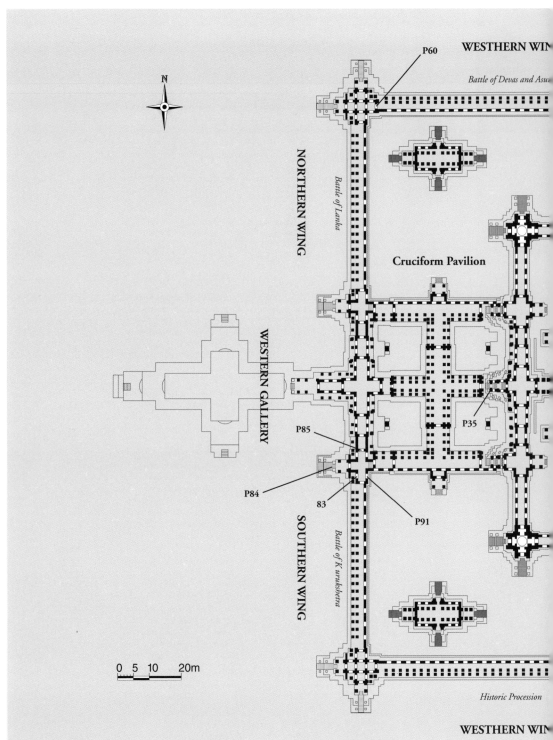

Plan 9 Schematic plan of Angkor Wat showing the locations of the main tapestry relief.

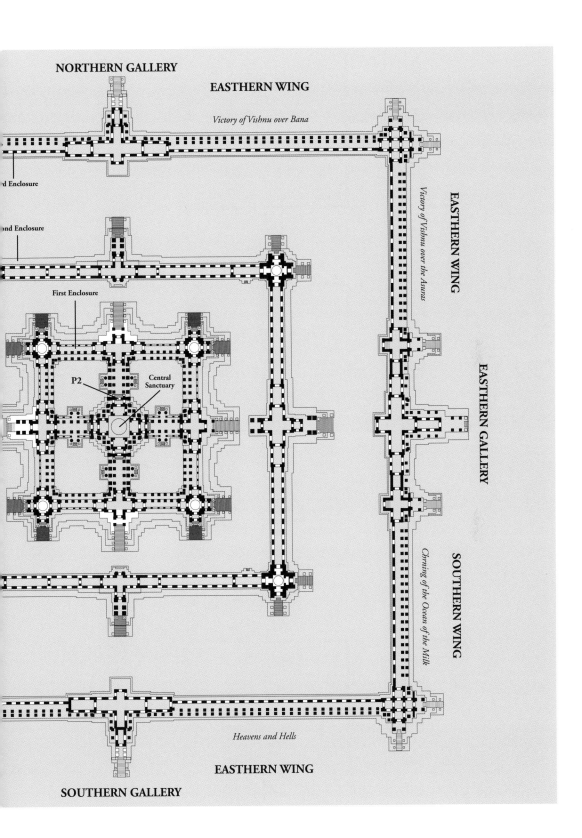

NORTHERN GALLERY

EASTERN WING

Victory of Vishnu over Bana

Victory of Vishnu over the Asuras

EASTERN WING

EASTERN WING

EASTERN GALLERY

SOUTHERN WING

Churning of the Ocean of the Milk

rd Enclosure

nd Enclosure

First Enclosure

P2

Central
Sanctuary

Heavens and Hells

EASTERN WING

SOUTHERN GALLERY

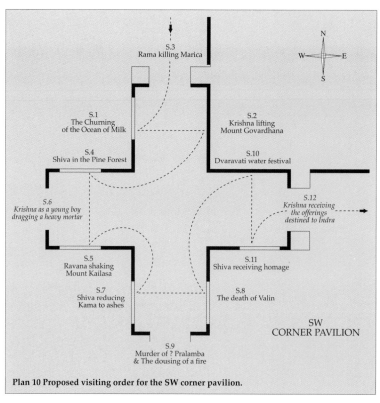

Plan 10 Proposed visiting order for the SW corner pavilion.

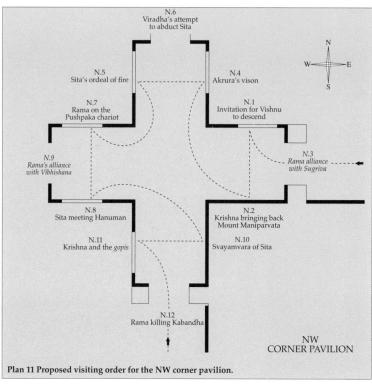

Plan 11 Proposed visiting order for the NW corner pavilion.

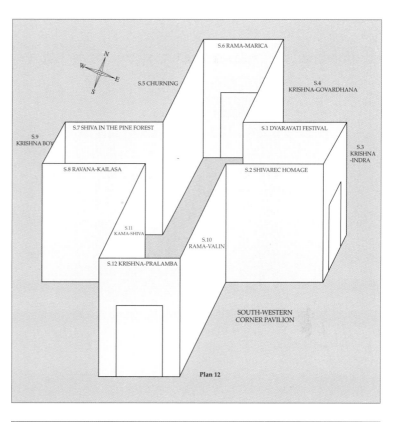

S.6 RAMA-MARICA

S.5 CHURNING

S.4 KRISHNA-GOVARDHANA

S.9 KRISHNA BOY

S.7 SHIVA IN THE PINE FOREST

S.1 DVARAVATI FESTIVAL

S.3 KRISHNA -INDRA

S.8 RAVANA-KAILASA

S.2 SHIVAREC HOMAGE

S.11 KAMA-SHIVA

S.10 RAMA-VALIN

S.12 KRISHNA-PRALAMBA

SOUTH-WESTERN CORNER PAVILION

Plan 12

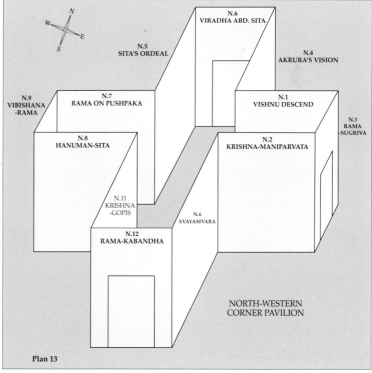

N.6 VIRADHA ABD. SITA

N.5 SITA'S ORDEAL

N.4 AKRURA'S VISION

N.9 VIBISHANA -RAMA

N.7 RAMA ON PUSHPAKA

N.1 VISHNU DESCEND

N.3 RAMA -SUGRIVA

N.8 HANUMAN-SITA

N.2 KRISHNA-MANIPARVATA

N.11 KRISHNA -GOPIS

N.6 SVAYAMVARA

N.12 RAMA-KABANDHA

NORTH-WESTERN CORNER PAVILION

Plan 13

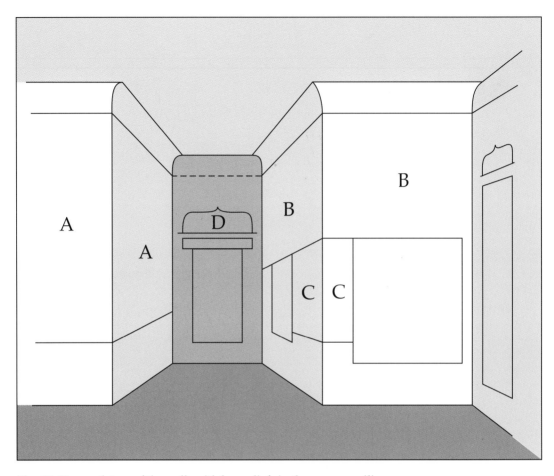

Plan 14 Nomenclature of the walls with low-reliefs in the corner pavilions.

    A = Full wall
    B = Wall over the window
    C = Wall beside the window
    D = Pediment over the lintel

Glossary

Gods and mythological personages

Agni   the fire-god.

Airavata   sacred elephant transporting the god Indra. Also one of the elephants that support the four quarters of the world.

Amaravati   the capital city of Indra.

Ananta   the multi-headed serpent on which Vishnu rests during his withdrawal from the world.

Anantashayin   epithet of Vishnu when resting on Ananta.

Angada   the monkey warrior son of Valin.

Arjuna   the king of the Haihayas, of the Pandava tribe.

Asvins   the twin sons of the Sun, equivalent to the Dioscuri.

Bhakti   fervent devotion.

Bali   a king of the demons.

Balarama   elder brother of Krishna.

Bikshatanamurti   epithet of Shiva appearing as a mendicant in the Pine Forest.

Caturbhuja   Vishnu with four arms.

Dasharata   king of Kosala and father of Rama.

Devi   title given to Parvati, wife of Shiva.

Garuda   king of the birds, vehicle of Vishnu.

Indra   the king of the Gods.

Indrajit   son of Ravana.

Janaka   king of Mithila, father of Sita.

Kalanemi   an *asura* enemy of the gods In the Ramayana he is Ravana's uncle. In the *Puranas* he is the son of Varochana, the grandson of Hiranyakasipu. He was killed by Vishnu, but was said to live again in Kamsa and in Kaliya.

Kama   god of love.

Kshatriya   member of the warrior class.

Kubera   the god of wealth.

Kurma   king of tortoises.

Lakshmana   one of Rama's brothers.

Maruts   the Forty-nine Lords of the Tempests.

Mudra   particular attitude of the hands.

Nandi   the sacred bull of Shiva.

Narasimha   "man-lion", one of Vishnu's *avatara*.

Para-**Vasudeva**   the undifferentiated central reality of Vishnu-Vasudeva from whom emanate the *vyuhas* and the *avatars*.

Parvati   Shiva's consort known also as Devi, Uma etc..

Rahu   mythical demon said to cause eclipses of the sun or moon by assuming the shape of a meteor.

Ravana   the demon king of Lanka.

Sesha   mythical snake of the depths of the Primordial Ocean.

Shiva   (the auspicious), god of ascetics, and of cosmic destruction and creation.

Shri   Vishnu's wife, Lakshmi.

Simhasara   prancing lion.

Sita, (the furrow)   wife of Rama, daughter of Janaka.

Sugriva   monkey king ally of Rama.

Surya   sun god, father of Sugriva.

Sushena   monkey general, father of Tara, Valin wife.

Skanda   the god of war, son of Shiva.

Tara   wife of Valin.

Tilottama   female divine being created by the gods to pacify two fighting *asuras* who were creating havoc on earth.

Trijata   a female *rakshasa* who spoke in favour of Sita.

Trisula   the trident held by Shiva and his followers.

Trivrikrama   epithet of Vishnu when making three steps.

Uma   daughter of the Himalayas, wife of Shiva.

Vahana   the mount of a god.

Valin   king of the monkeys, son of Indra, brother of Sugriva, and husband of Tara.

Valmiki   sage composer of the *Ramayana*.

Varuna   the sovereign of the waters.

Vasudeva   father of Krishna; spelled Väsudeva, it means a formless Vishnu.

Vasuki   great king of the snakes.

Vibishana (terrifying)   *rakshasa* brother of Ravana, who left Lanka to join Rama.

Vishnu (the pervader)   supreme god, the Maintainer of the Universe.

Yama   king of the dead, sovereign over hell.

General terms and names

Abisheka   religious consecration or initiation by sprinkling water (Indrabisheka if with Indra's water).

Adityas   a group of celestial deities including Indra and Vishnu.

Amrita   the nectar of immortality.

Angkor   capital (from nagara).

Anjali mudra   a gesture of respect and salutation in which the two hands are held together near the chest, palms touching.

Antarala   small building interconnecting the mandapa to the shrine.

Apsara   celestial water nymphs, wives of the Gandharvas (celestial musicians); commonly considered to inhabit the sky.

Ascetics   sages who practised austerities (rishis).

Ashokavana   the *ashoka* bush.

Ashtadikpalas   (sentinels of the eight directions).

Ashvameda   horse's sacrifice by royalty.

Asura   devilish monster, anti-god.

Avatara   *avatar,* the 'incarnation' of a deity, especially Vishnu.

Banteay   citadel, temple with enclosure walls.

Bhakti   religious devotion to a supreme god, especially Krishna.

Beng   pond.

Brahmacharin   the ascetic who has renounced everything.

Brahmin   Anglicised form of Brahman (from the Sanskrit Brahmana). A priest member of the highest form of varna (caste).

Chakra   wheel, disk, one of the attributes of Vishnu.

Chakravartin   Indian royal title, Universal Sovereign (that makes the wheel turn).

Chandrahasa   the glittering scimitar, Ravana's sword, which he received from Shiva as a boon.

Clerestory   the upper part of the library with horizontal windos.

Danda   sceptre or the baton of punishment (and, indirectly, of command).

Daityas and *Danavas*   two classes of demons.

Deva   deity.

Devaraja   god who is king', the divinity who rules the Khmer country.

Devata   female deity.

Dharma   order and custom which make life and the universe possible; behaviour necessary for the maintenance of order; rules which govern society; social duty.

Dikpala   the guardians of the eight points of the compass.

Dvarapala   door's guardian divinities.

Ganas   Shiva's attendants.

Gandharvsa   heavenly musicians.

Garbhaghra   inner chamber of the shrine.

Gopa   male cowherd.

Gopi   female cowherd.

Gopura   entrance pavilion of a temple or of an enclosure of the temple.

Hamsa   goose (or swan), vehicle of Brahma.

Howdah   the chair placed on the back of an elephant to carry people.

Indrabisheka   royal consecration by water ritual.

kala   a marine monster with the head of a lion or a dragon.

kalpa   unit of time consisting of 4 ages (s), named after 4 throws of the dice: the first, the Krita Yuga is the best; it is followed by the Tetra Yuga, the Dvapara Yuga, and finally the Kali Yuga, the present age.

Kala   monster's mask seen frontally.

Kautsubba   the famous jewel produced during the Churning of the Ocean of Milk, worn by Vishnu or Krishna.

Kinnari   deity half man- half bird (lower part).

Kiratas   a race of hunters.

Kompong   rural village.

Kumbha   pot, vase.

Lalisana   a seating position with one leg up, the other hanging down or bent under the body.

Linga   phallus.

Lokapala   guardians (4) of the Earth, protector deity of cardinal points.

Mahendras   mythological mountain at the centre of the Ocean.

Makara   marine monster represented by a crocodile or a fish with the head of an elephant.

Mahout   the man who drives the elephant.

Meru   the mountain home of the gods.

Mandala   (circular) geometric figure representing the cosmos.

Mandapa   antechamber, a pavilion in front of the main shrine.

Mandara   mythological mountain of the gods, the king of mountains, used to churn the Ocean of Milk.

Makara   marine monster mixing dolphin, crocodile and elephant features.

Moksha   release from transmigration, from rebirth.

Mukuta   headgear with a combination of diadem, crown, coronet and cloth.

Mudra   symbolic position of the hands and/or fingers.

Muni   holy sage.

Nagas   a class of semi-divine snakes.

Padma   lotus.

Phkak   characteristic Khmer weapon, long handled club with two blades inserted at an angle.

Phnom   hill, mountain.

Prakirti   in Samkhya, the original germinal matter from which the material universe evolves; synonym of Pradhana.

Prasada **or prasat**   sanctuary tower, palace, temple.

counter-clockwise   (*prasavaya* or funerary) direction.

Preah, Prah, Pra   belonging to anything sacred, holy.

Purusa   in Samkhya, the principle of consciousness which interact with Prakirti.

Raikakshyaka   crossband over the chest.

Rajalalisatana   a way of sitting with one knee high, used mainly by princely people.

Rakshasa   demon.

Rakshini   female *rakshasa.*

Rasa lila   a circular dance.

Rishi   a great sage or illuminated being.

Sampot   short skirt around the waist, for men (sarong for women).

Samkhyas   a school of philosophy stressing the dualism of material nature and consciousness.

Samsara   transmigration of the soul; reincarnation.

Sarabhanga   ascetic group visited by Rama, Sita, and Lakshmana.

Shilpin   worker, artist, artisan.

Simhasana   prancing lion often acting as a mount, throne.

Sadhana   path to liberation and power.

Shakti   the creative power.

Shastra   instruction-book, manual.

Skambha   sacrificial Vedic pole, cosmic pillar.

Sloka   the lines of a Sanskrit poem.

Spean   bridge.

Sras   pond, water basin.

Srei   woman.

Stung   river.

Srivatsa   a particular mark, said to be a curl of hair, on Vishnu's of Krishna's chest, in a shape similar to a flower or a *swastika.*

Sudarshana   name of Krishna *chakra* or the discus weapon.

Swayamvara   a ceremony where a bride can choose her consort.

Syncretism, contemporaneous acceptance of different religious beliefs

Tapas   the ascetic self-restraint and self-mortification to which one voluntarily subjects in order to gain uncommon powers. Tapas is considered a form of power, or heat, obtained from asceticism; in practical terms, it means the merits that an ascetic (rishi) can gain from the exercise of penance.

Thom   large, big.

Vajra   symbol of thunderbolt.

Vahana   mount or vehicle of a god.

Varman   protector.

Vat, Wat   temple.

Vedic   pertaining to the Veda, the foundation of the Hindu religion.

Vihara   rectangular building to house a Buddha sculpture.

Vahana   sacred animal, mount of the gods.

Vimana   the temple built according to tradition (*shastra*) by the application of various proportionate measurements; it is the house and body of the god. By temple is understood the main shrine only, in which the garbhagrha, the womb, is contained.

Viradha   *rakshasa* who attempted to abduct Sita.

Vyuha   emanations of God.

Yakshas   semi-divine beings, protectors and owners of wealth, associated with Kubera.

Yogasana   a sitting position with crossed legs, feet touching the ground, and knees slightly drawn-up and supported by a special tape (*yogapatta*).

Yuga   one of the 4 ages of the world (Krita, Treta, Dvapara and Kali).

Yupa   column.

Bibliography

Legend
AA, Arts Asiatiques.
BEFEO, Bulletin de l'Ecole Française d'Extrême Orient.
PEFEO, Publication de l'Ecole Française d'Extrême Orient.
JA, Journal Asiatique.

Aymonier E., *Le Cambodge*, I-III, Leroux, Paris, 1904.

Atherton Packert C., *The Harsat-Mata temple at Abaneri: levels of meaning*, Artibus Asiae, 55, 1985: 201-224.

Bal M., *Narratology*, University of Toronto Press, 1980.

Bastian A., *Die Voelker des Oestasien*, Leipzig, 1866.

Beylie de, general, *Photographie des reliefs de Banteay Chmar*, Musée Guimet, Paris, 1913.

Bénisti M., *Scène nautique*, BEFEO, LI, 1963: 95-98.

Bénisti M., *Une scène d'offrande*, BEFEO, LII, 1965: 547-50.

Bénisti M., *Representations Khmères de Vishnu couché*. AA, XV-1, 1965: 91-117.

Bénisti M., *Rapports entre le premier art khmer et l'art indien*, EFEO, Mémoire Archéologique V, 1970.

Bhandari C. M., *Saving Angkor*, White Orchid Books, Bangkok, 1995.

Bhattacharji S., *The Indian Theogony*, Cambridge University Press, 1970.

Bhattacharya K., *The Pancaratra sect in Ancient Cambodia*, Journal of the Greater India Society, XIV-2, 1955: 11-116.

Bhattacharya K., *La secte des Pasupata dans l'ancien Cambodge*, JA, CCXLIII, 1955: 479-490.

Bhattacharya K., *Etude epigraphique de Banteay Samre*, AA. II-4, 1955: 294-308.

Bhattacharya K., *Note d'iconographie Khmère, I-IV*, AA, III, 1956: 193-194.

Bhattacharya K., *Note d'iconographie Khmère V-VIII*, AA, IV, 1957: 208-216 & 293-298.

Bhattacharya K., *Note d'iconographie Khmère, IX-X,* , AA, V, 1958: 217-220.

Bhattacharya K., *The theme of Churning of the Ocean in Indian and Khmer art*, AA, VI, 1959: 121-134.

Bhattacharya K., *Les Religions Brahmaniques dans l'ancien Cambodge d'après l'épigraphie et l'iconographie*, PEFEO, XLIX, 1961.

Bhattacharya K., *Les religions du Cambodge ancien et l'épigraphie sanskrite*, Réunion des Musées Nationaux, 1997.

Bizot F., *Représentations khmères de Vishnu couché*, AA, XI, 1965: 91-117.

Bizot F., *Les ensembles ornamentaux illimités d'Angkor*, AA, XXI, 1970: 109-132.

Bizot F., *Ramaker*, PEFEO, CLV, Paris, 1989.

Boeles J. J., *A Ramayana relief from Pimai*, Journal Siam Society, 1969: 163-169.

Boisselier J., *Note sur les bas-reliefs tardifs d'Angkor Vat*, JA, 1962, II: 244-48.

Boisselier J., *Asie du Sud-Est, Tome I, Le Cambodge*, Picard, Paris, 1966.

Boisselier J., *Pouvoir royal et symbolisme architectural. Nean Pean et son importance pour la royauté angkorienne*, AA, XXXI, 1970.

Bosch F. D. K., *Le temple d'Angkor*, BEFEO, XXXII, 1932: 7-21.

Boulbet J. & Dagens B., *Les sites archéologiques de la région du Bhnam Gulen*, Arts Asiatiques, 1973: 27.

Brown R. L., *The Dvaravati Wheels of Law and the Indianisation of Southeast Asia*, Brill, Leiden, 1996.

Cannadine D. & Price S., (edit.s), *Rituals of Royalty*, Cambridge University Press, New York & Victoria, 1987.

Chandler D., *Facing the Cambodian Past*, Silkworm Books, Bangkok, 1998.

Chatterji B. R., *Indian cultural influence in Cambodia*, University of Calcutta, 1964.

Coedès G., *Les bas-reliefs d'Angkor-Vat*, Bulletin de la Commission Archéologique de l'Indochine, Paris, 1911: 170-220.

Coedès. G., *Note sur l'iconographie de Ben Mala*, BEFEO, XII, 2, 1912.

Coedès G., *Etudes cambodgiennes, VII, Second étude sur les bas-reliefs d'Angkor Vat*, BEFEO, XIII-6, 1913: 13-36.

Coedès G., *Angkor Vat, temple ou tombeau?*, BEFEO, XXXIII, 1933: 303-309.

Coedès G., *La date d'exécution des deux bas-relief tardif d'Angkor Vat*, JA, II, 1962: 235-243.

Coedès G., *The indianized States of Southeast Asia*, Univ.Press.of Hawaii, Honolulu 1968.

Coedès G., *Articles sur le Pays Khmer*, EFEO, Reprint of 63 papers from BEFEO edited by C. Jacques, 1989/92.

Coedès G., *Angkor*, Oxford University Press, 1990

Coedès G. & Dupont P., *Les stèles de Sdok Kak Thom, Phnom Sandak et Prah Vihar*, BEFEO, XLIII, 1943: 56-154.

Commaille J., & Coedes G., *Le Bayon d'Angkor Thom. Bas reliefs publiés par le soin de la commission*, Paris, Leroux, 1910 & 1914.

Coral (de) Rémusat G., *L'Art Khmer, les grandes étapes de son evolutions*, Van Oest, Paris, 1951.

Conze E., *Buddhist scriptures*, Penguin Books, 1959.

Dagens B., *Etude sur l'iconographie du Bayon (frontons et linteaux)*, AA, XIX, l969: 124-167.

Dagens B., *Mayamatam*, Motilal Banarsidass, Dehli, 1994.

Dagens B., *Angkor, la forêt de pierre*. Gallimard 'Decouvertes' No.64, 1989.

Boisselier J., *Note sur les bas-reliefs tardifs d'Angkor Vat*, Journal Asiatique, 1962, II: 244-48.

Boisselier J., Asie du Sud-Est, Tome I, *Le Cambodge*, Picard, Paris, 1966.

Boisselier J., *Puovoir royal et symbolisme architectural. Nean Pean et son importance pour la royaute angkorienne*, Arts asiatiques XXXI, 1970.

Dange S. A., *Myths from the Mahabbharata, Vol.1*, Aryan Books Internat., New Delhi, 1997.

Dehejia V., (edit.), *The legend of Rama. Artistic visions*, Marg Publications, Bombay, 1994.

Delaporte L., *Voyage au Cambodge*, Delagrave, Paris 1880.

Delvert J., *L'"erosion" des grès des monuments d'Angkor*, BEFEO, LI, 1963: 453-534.

Delvert J., *Le Cambodge*, PUF, 'Que sais-je? 2080, 1983.

Dimmitt C. & van Buitenen J. A. B., *Classical Hindu Mythology*, Temple University Press, Philadelphia, 1978.

Doniger O'Flaherty W., *Siva, The Erotic Ascetic*, Oxford University Press, Oxford, 1973.

Doniger O'Flaherty W., *Hindu Myths*, Penguin Books, 1975.

Doniger O'Flaherty W., *Women, Androgynes, and other Mythical Beasts*, University of Chicago Press, 1982.

Dufour H., *Le Bayon d'Angkor Thom*, Ministère de l'Instruction Publique et des Baux Arts, Leroux, Paris, 1913 (Folio).

Dufour H., & Carpeaux G., *Le Bayon d'Angkor Thom*, Paris 1913 (Folio).

Edwardes A. *The jewel in the lotus*, A. Blond, London, 1961.

Eliade M., *Images and symbols*, Princeton University Press, 1991.

Filliozat J., *Le symbolisme du monument du Phnom Bakhen*, BEFEO, XLIV, 1947-50: 532-64.

Filliozat J., *Le temple de Hari dans le Harivarsa*, Arts Asiatiques, VIII-3, Paris, 196: 195-202.

Filliozat J., *Sur le civaisme et le bouddhisme au Cambodge*, BEFEO, 1981: 59-99.

Filliozat J., *The Ramayana in South-East Asian Sanskrit Epigraphy and Iconography*, New Delhi, 1983.

Finot L., *Sur quelques traditions indochinoises*, Bulletin de la Commission Archéologique de l'Indochine, Paris, 1911: 20-37.

Finot L., *Goloubew V., et Coedès G., Le temple d'Angkor Vat*, PEFEO, Mémoires Archéologiques. II, 1927-32.

Finot L., Parmentier H. et Goloubew V., *Le temple d'Ishvarapura (Banteay Srei)*, EFEO, Mémoires Archéologiques I, Van Oest, Paris, 1926.

Fontein J., *The sculpture of Indonesia*, Harry N. Abrahams, New York, 1990.

Freeman M. & Warner R., *Angkor: The Hidden Glories*, Boston, 1990.

Garnier F., *Voyage d'exploration en Indochine*, Le Tour du Monde, 1869-1873.

Giteau M., *Le Barattement de l'Océan dans l'ancien Cambodge*, Bulletin de la Societé des Etudes Indochinoises, XXVI, 2, 1951: 141-159.

Giteau M., *Une image de Shiva Bikshatanamurti à Angkor Vat*, AA, XI-1, 1964-65: 131-137.

Giteau M., *Iconographie du Cambodge post-angkorien*, PEFEO, Paris 1975.

Glaize M., *Le Guide d'Angkor: les monuments du groupe d'Angkor*, Paris, Maisonneuve, 1963.

Goldman R. P. (edit.), *The Ramayana of Valmiki*, Princeton Library of Asian Translations, Princeton University Press, Princeton, 1984-90.

Goloubew V., *Artisans chinois à Angkor Wat*, BEFEO, XXIV, 1924, 513-519.

Groslier B. P., *Indochine, Carrefour des arts*, Michel, Paris, 1960.

Groslier B. Ph., *Les Siam Kuk des bas-reliefs d'Angkor Vat*, Orients, pour Georges Condominas, Paris Sudestasie/Toulouse Privat, 1981, p.107-126.

Gupta Sanjukta, *Laksmi Tantra. A Pancharata Text*, Brill, Leiden 1972.

Hart G. L. & Heifetz H., *The Forest Book of the Ramayana of Kampan*, University of California Press, Berkeley, 1988.

Hawixbrock C., *Jayavarman VII ou le renouveau d'Angkor, entre tradition et modernité*, BEFEO, 85, 1998, 63-85.

Higham C., *The archaeology of Mainland Southeast Asia*, Cambridge University Press, 1989.

Holliday P. J. (edit.), *Narrative and event in ancient art*, Cambridge University Press, 1993.

Hubert J., Sacred beliefs and beliefs of sacredness, in Carmaichel Edit., *Sacred Sites, Sacred Places*, Routledge, London, 1994: 9-19.

Hutchins F. G, *Young Krishna.* Amarta Press, W.Franklin, 1980.

Jacq-Hergoualc'h M., *L'armament et l'organisation de l'armée khmère aux XII et XIII siècles*, Publ.Mus.Guimet, Tome XII, Paris, 1979.

Jacques C. & Dumont R., *Angkor, Bordas*, Paris, 1990.

Jacques C., *Angkor*, Thames & Hudson, London, 1997.

Kerpelès S., *Reamker, fasc.I-IX & LXXV-LXXX*, Edit. Bibliothèque Royale, Phnom Penh, 1937.

Kramrisch Stella, *The Hindu temple,* Motilal Banarsidas Publishers, Delhi,1976, reprint 1991.

Kramrisch Stella, *Exploring India's sacred art*, selected writings edited by B.S. Miller, University of Pennsylvania Press, Philadelphia, 1983.

Kulke H., *The Devaraja cult*, Cornell University, 1978

Le Bonheur A., *Cambodge. Angkor. Temples en peril*, Paris, Herscher, 1989.

Le Bonheur A., *Of Gods, Kings, and Men,* Serinda, London, 1995.

Lefeber R., & Goldman R.P., *The Ramayana of Valmiki, Vol. IV. Kishkindakanda*, Princeton University Press, 1994.

Lefebvre H., *The production of space*, Blackwell, Oxford, 1974.

Legendre H., *La légende de Rama dans la sculpture des pavillons d'angle du tem ple d'Angkor Vat*, Traveaux du Département de Geographie de l'Université Laval, Quebec, 1986.

Legendre-De Konink H., *Angkor Vat: Quelques éléments d'asymétrie*, Mappemonde, Montpellier, 4/1992: 45-49.

Mabbett I. & Chandler D., *The Khmers, Blackwell*, Oxford, 1995.

Malleret L., *Contribution à l'étude du thème des Neuf Divinités dans la saculpture du Cambodge et du Champa, Arts Asiatiques*, VII-3, 1960: 107-126.

Mannikka E., *Angkor Vat: Meaning through measurement*, Univ. of Michigan dis sertation, 1985.

Mannikka E., *Angkor Wat, Time, Space and Kingship*, Univ. of Hawai'i Press, Honolulu, 1996.

Marchal H., *Le décor et la sculpture khmèrs*, Van Oest, Paris, 1951.

Marchal H., *Les temples d'Angkor*, A.Guillot, Paris, 1955.

Marchal Sappho, *Costumes et parures Khmèrs d'après les devâta d'Angkor Wat*, Vanoest, Paris & Bruxelles, 1927.

Martini F., *En marge au Ramayana Cambodgien*, BEFEO, XXXVIII, Paris, 1938: 285-295.

Martini F., *Note sur l'empreinte du buddhisme dans la version cambodgienne du Ramayana*, JA, 1952: 67-70.

Martini F., *La goire de Rama. Ramakerti*, Les Belles Lettres, Paris, 1978.

Mascaro J., *The Bhagavad Gita*, Penguin Books,1962.

Matsubara M., *Pancaratra Samhitas and early Vaishnava theology*, Motilal, Benares, 1994.

Maxwell T. S., *The gods of Asia,* Oxford University Press, Calcutta, 1997.

Mitchell W. J. T., *Iconology,* University Press, Chicago, 1987.

Moura J., *Le Royaume du Cambodge*, Leroux, Paris, 1883.

Mus P., *Le sourire d'Angkor*, Artibus Asiae, XXIV, 1961: 363-381.

Nafilyan G., *Angkor Vat. Description graphique du temple*, PEFEO, Mémoires Archéologiques, IV, 1969.

Parmentier H., *L'Art Khmer Classique. Monuments du quadrant nord-est*, PEFEO, 1939.

Pottier C., *Restauration du perron nord de la Terrasse des Elephants*, EFEO Annual Report, 1996-1997.

Przyluski J., *La legende de Rama dans les bas-reliefs d'Angkor Wat*, Arts et Archéologie Khmeres, I, 1921-23: 319-330.

Richman P. (edit.), *Many Ramayanas*, University of California Press, 1991.

Rodriguez N., *Arjuna et le Kirata*, European Association of Southeast Asian Archaeologists, 6th International Conference, 1966, Leiden, in press.

Roveda V., *Khmer Mythology*, River Books, Bangkok, 1997.

Roveda V., *The use of drawings for the making of the reliefs from Angkor Wat*, in Southeast Asian Archaeology 1998, Centre for South-East Asian Studies, University of Hull & Ethnologishes Museum, Staatliche Museen zu Berlin, Hull, 2000, 169-175.

Roveda V., *Khmer narrative reliefs and Art historical chronology*, Proceedings of the VIII International Conference of the European Association of Southeast Asian Archaeologists, Sarteano, 2000. In press.

Rukmani T. S., *A critical study of the Bhagavata Purana*, Chowkhamba Publ., Varanasi, 1970.

Singaravelu S. *A comparative study of the Sanskrit, Tamil, Thai and Malay versions of the story or Rama*, Journal Siam Society, LVI-2, 1968: 137-185.

Schrader F. O., *Introduction to the Pancaratra and the Ahirbudhya Samhita*, Adyar Library, Madras, 1916.

Sharan M. K., *Sanskrit Inscriptions of Ancient Cambodia*, Abhinav Publ., New Delhi, 1974.

Smart N., *Dimensions of the Sacred*, Fontana Press, 1997.

Smith W. L., *Ramayana Traditions in Eastern India*, Dept. of Indology, Univ. of Stockholm, 1988.

Smitthi S. & Veraprasert M., *A comparative study of Khmer lintels in Thailand and Cambodia*, Special publ. by the Siam Commercial Bank, Bangkok, 1990.

Stencel R., Gifford F. & Moron E., *Astronomy and cosmology at Angkor Wat*, Science, vol. 193, July 1973.

Stern P., *Les monuments khmers du style du Bayon*, Publ. Musée Guimet, IX, Presses Universitaires de France, Paris, 1965.

Sutterheim W. F., *Rama-Legends and Rama-Reliefs in Indonesia*, Translated by Paliwal & Jain, India Ghandi National Centre for the Arts, New Delhi, New Delhi, 1989.

Van Stein Callenfels P. V., *Le mariage de Draupadi*, BEFEO, XXXIII, Paris, 1933.

Van Nooten B. A., *The Mahabharata*, Twayne Publishing, New York, 1871.

Wolters O. W., Khmer Hinduism in the 7th century, in *Early South East Asia*, ed. R. B. Smith & W. Watson, New York, Oxford University Press, 1979.

Zieseniss A., *The Rama Saga in Malaysia, its Origins and Formation*, Singapore, 1963.

Sanskrit Texts

Agni Purana, translated by N.Gangadharan, edited by J. L. Dhastri, Motital Banardsidass, Dehli, 1984-87.

Bhagavata Purana, translated by Tagare G. V, Motilal Banardsidass, Dehli, 1994 reprint.

Brahma Purana, edited by J. L. Shastri, Motital Banardsidass, Dehli, 1985-87.

Harivamsa, translated in French by M. A. Langlois, 1834-35

Kurma Purana, edited by J.L. Shastri, Motital Banardsidass, Dehli, 1981-85

Linga Purana, edited by J.L. Shastri., Motilal Banardsidass, Dehli, 1973.

Pancaratra Samhitas, translated and edited by M. Matsubara, Motital Banardsidass, Dehli, 1994.

Ramayana, The Ramayana of Valmiki, translated by H. P. Shastri, Shanti Sadan, London, 1992.

Vishnu Purana, translated by H.H.Wilson, Truebner & Co., London 1864-87.

Further Reading

Ang Choulean, *Les etres surnaturels dans la religion populaire khmère*, Paris, 1986.

Banerjee P., *Rama in Indian literature, Art & Thought*, Sundeep Prakashan, Delhi, 1986.

Boisselier J., *Le Cambodge*, Picard & C., Paris 1966.

Boisselier J., *Il Sud-est asiatico*, UTET,Torino, 1986.

Briggs, L. P., *The Ancient Khmer Empire*, Philadeplphia 1951.

Blurton T. R., *Hindu Art*, B.M. Press, London, 1992.

Chou Ta-Kuan, *The Customs of Cambodia*, The Siam Society, Bangkok, 1992.

Chandler D. P., *A Histyory of Cambodia*, Westview Press, Boulder 1992.

Chandler D. P. & Mabbet I., *The Khmers*, Blackwell, Oxford, 1995.

Coomaraswamy A. K., *History of Indian and Indonesian art*, Dover, N. Y, 1927.

Eliade M., *The Sacred & the Profane*, Harvest Book, San Diego, 1987.

Giteau M., *Khmer sculpture and the Angkorean Civilisation*, London, 1965.

Giteau M. & Gueret M., *L'Art khmer*, Asa edit., Paris, 1997.

Groslier B. Ph., & Arthaud J., *Angkor, Hommes et Pierre*, Paris, 1956.

Groslier B. Ph., *Indochina*, Methuen, London, 1960.

Groslier B. Ph., *La cité hydraulique angkorienne*, BEFEO, LXVI, 1979: 161-202.

Huntington S. L., *The art of ancient India*, Weatherhill, N. Y., 1985.

Jessup H., & Zephir T., *Angkor et dix siècles d'art khmer*, Réunion des Musées Nationaux, Paris, 1997.

Joung C. G., *Man and his symbols*, Aldus Books, London, 1972.

Leclere A., *Cambodge: fêtes civiles et religieuses*, Paris, 1917.

Mabbett I., *Varnas in Angkor and the Indian caste system*, Journ. Asian Studies, 36/3, 1977.

Mabbett I., *The symbolism of Mt. Meru*, History of Religions, 23, 1, 1983.

Macdonald M., *Angkor and the Khmers*, Praeger, N. Y., 1959.

Mazzeo D., & Antonini C. S., *Ancient Cambodia, Grosset & Dunlap*, London, 1978.

Mouhot H., *Travels in the Central Parts of Indochina*, London, 1986.

Pelton R. D., *The trickster in West Africa*, Univ. of Calif. Press, Berkeley, 1980.

Pou S., *Ramakerti*, PEFEO, CXXXII, 1988.

Quartrich-Wales H.G., *The Making of Greater India*, Q-W. edit., London, 1951.

Rawson P., *The art of Southeast Asia*, Thames & Hudson, 1967.

Ribaud M., *Angkor, the serenity of Buddhism*, Thames & Hudson, 1993.

Rooney, D., *Angkor, an introduction to the Temples*, Odyssey, Hong Kong, 1994.

Tarling N., *The Cambridge History of Southeast Asia*, 1, Cambridge, 1992.

Thierry S., *Les Khmers*, Kailash, Paris, 1996.

Vickery G. B., *Cambodia after Angkor*, Michigan, 1977.

Walker G. B., *Angkor Empire*, Calcutta, 1955.

Wheatley P., *Nagara and Commandery*, Chicago, 1983.

Zimmer H., *Myths and symbols in Indian Art and Civilization*, Princeton Univ. Press, 1972.

Visual Narrative

Brilliant R., *Visual narrative*, Cornell University Press, Ithaca and London, 1986.

Bryson N., Holly M. A., Moxey K., *Visual theory*, Polity Press, 1996.

Dehejia V., *On modes of visual narration in early Buddhist art*, The Art Bulletin, LXXII/3, 1990.

Dehejia V., India's visual; narrative: the dominance of space over time, in *Paradigms of Indian architecture*, edit. G. H. R. Tillotson, Curzon, 1998: 80-106.

Dehejia V., *Discourse in Early Buddhist Art, Visual narrative of India*, Munshiram Manoharal, New Delhi, 1997.

Elkins J., *On the impossibility of stories: the anti-narrative and non-narrative impulse in modern painting*. Word & image, 7- 4, 1991.

Evans, K., *Epic narratives in the Hoysala temples*, Brill, Leiden, New York, Koeln, 1997.

Gandelman C., *Reading Pictures, Viewing Texts*, Indiana University Press, 1991.

Klokke M. J., *Tantri reliefs on Javanese candi*, KITLV Press, Leiden, 1993.

Lewis S., *Reading Images*, Cambridge University Press, 1995.

Marin L., Towards a theory of reading in the Visual Arts, in N.Bryson *Calligram*, Cambridge Univ. Press, 1988: 63-90.

Saint-Martin F., *Semiotics of visual language*, Indian University Press, 1990.

Stansbury-O'Donnell M. D., *Pictorial narrative in ancient Greek Art*, Cambridge University Press, 1999.

Index